Real life, real answers.

BOOKS BY DANA SHILLING

Fighting Back
Be Your Own Boss
Making Wise Decisions
Redress for Success
William E. Donoghue's
Lifetime Financial Planner (co-author)

Real life, real answers.

Earning,
saving, investing,
enjoying –
a realistic guide
to managing
your money.

Dana Shilling

with the staff of

ARBOR HOUSE · William Morrow · New York

Library of Congress Cataloging in Publication Data

Shilling, Dana.
    Real life, real answers.

    Includes index.
    1. Finance, Personal. 2. Investments. I. John
Hancock Financial Services. II. Title.
HG179.S465   1988   332.024   87-19538
ISBN 1-557-10-004-7

Design by Robert Bull Design

Manufactured in the United States of America

Published in Canada by Fitzhenry & Whiteside Ltd.

10 9 8 7 6 5 4 3 2 1

"Real life, real answers" is a registered service mark of the John Hancock Mutual Life Insurance Company.

*

This publication is designed to provide accurate and authoritative information in regard to the subject matter covered. In publishing this book, neither the author nor the publisher is engaged in rendering legal, accounting, or other professional service. If legal advice or other expert assistance is required, the services of a competent professional should be sought.

CONTENTS

To our customers, present and future

"I love you, Jenny Katherine . . ."

A young father tells his infant daughter he's planning for her future.

"Real life, real answers," John Hancock Financial Services' national advertising campaign, made its debut during the fall 1985 network season. Public reaction was immediate and enthusiastic.

Marked by an almost documentary flavor, the "Real life, real answers" television commercials introduced America to a wide variety of people with real-life needs. And delivered a straightforward message: John Hancock Financial Services offers real answers.

Probably most important, the people in those commercials ring true. John Avery and young Jenny Katherine. Margaret and Tom Fitzgerald. Michael Mark and his older brother, Dave.

Their situations are real. Young adults taking the first tentative steps toward mapping out their future. A middle-aged couple thinking about starting their own business. An established business executive just beginning to consider retirement.

Not all of the situations are easy. A divorcée faces difficult decisions. A brother and sister try to do what's best for an elderly parent.

In short, the situations *are* real. So are the answers John Hancock Financial Services offers in stark black-and-white at the end of each mini-story.

John Hancock created the "Real life, real answers" campaign for many reasons. One was a reaction to the then-current style of advertising. At the time, cartoons and jingles and famous faces ruled the commercial airwaves. In a climate in which every personal financial decision you make has to count, John Hancock couldn't see asking you to plan your future on the advice of a comic-strip character.

Instead, the company—actually a complex of companies offering investment, banking, real estate, and insurance services—turned to its own corporate mission statement. A mission statement is just that, a statement of why we're in business. And, compressed to remove the corporatese, ours just says, "Be profitable by offering our customers products that meet their real financial needs and by backing those products up with the best possible service."

Going from there to "Real life, real answers" didn't take much effort. Because it's hard to say you're meeting your customers' needs if your advertising treats them like children. "Real life, real answers" is advertising for grownups. There's nothing make-believe about your future.

Arbor House and Dana Shilling quickly recognized the appeal of "Real life, real answers." Go to any bookstore and you will find the shelves lined with thick volumes packed with financial facts. What's missing is how those facts fit into real people's lives.

In *Real Life, Real Answers*—the book, not the advertising campaign—you again meet John Avery, the Thompsons, Michael Mark, and all the other people whose concerns seem so like your own in our television and print advertisements. Only here, the sixty-second glimpses into their lives are expanded into full-bodied stories.

Real Life, Real Answers—again, the book—fills a large gap in the personal finance section of your library.

But books alone don't build a lifetime financial plan. Real people—like those who populate our commercials—rarely take time out from raising a family, pursuing a career, and dealing with all the demands of daily life to plan ten, twenty, or thirty years ahead.

That's why John Hancock Financial Services has 7,500 professional marketing representatives in communities throughout the nation. Their assignment isn't just to sell you shares in a mutual fund or a universal life insurance policy. It's to help you plan for a lifetime. To help you to grasp the opportunities of real life through a program of real answers.

INTRODUCTION

In novels, movies, and TV miniseries, we constantly meet people who have it all. They are eternally youthful, with faces and designer wardrobes forever unwrinkled. They have highly glamorous, fulfilling careers that deposit millions of dollars into the appropriate Swiss bank accounts. Their lively, adorable children never mess up the white carpets or the white suede upholstery at the mansion, and are perfectly happy with whatever "quality time" their parents can spare as they run chains of boutiques and multinational corporations.

In real life, *nobody* has it all. Real life involves plans, compromises, and trade-offs; real people are inconsistent sometimes, and sometimes they make mistakes. Real life isn't segmented into tidy crises guaranteed to be relieved by the commercial break—and you can't change the channel if you don't like what's happening to you! What you *can* do is take practical steps to improve your situation. This book explains the financial choices that are open to you, and how to decide which choices are best for you.

In the real world, there is no single perfect investment; in fact, there are no perfect investments at all—only investments that meet your objectives and are likely, but not guaranteed, to increase in value. Nobody can give you a budgeting method that is work-free and painless, but you can learn to spend a little time each week and develop a system for controlling your expenses and managing your cash.

This book won't make you rich, beautiful, or adored, a financial superhero able to take over giant corporations in a single bound. But it will help you confront most of the financial problems most of us have, and the realistic choices you can make. You'll learn which of your goals are within easy reach, which ones will take a little stretching, and which ones are frankly implausible. You'll be able to refer to this book for advice on anything from buying a car to choosing a bank.

Real Life, Real Answers concentrates on four of the most important areas of your financial life:

- *Earning* (planning a career; making the best use of the benefits your employer provides)
- *Saving and Investing* (using a budget to control spending; finding money to save; using investments to build wealth)
- *Enjoying* (choosing a home and car to improve your life; being a wise and selective user of credit)
- *Problem solving* (financial strategies for coping with illness, divorce, a death in the family, and other serious problems; on the more

cheerful side, coping with the problem of finding money for college tuition).

Case histories, based on the *Real Life, Real Answers* advertising campaign, use fictional families to explore how real people confront financial problems. These case histories stress real *answers*—in the plural because there's no single answer that fits every person's and every family's financial needs. But the more information you have, the higher the odds that you will make good decisions.

One thing is certain: You *will* make mistakes sometimes. You *will* make choices that don't pan out. You might invest in a new company that doesn't do as well as you anticipated. You could buy U.S. Savings Bonds—right after the Treasury cuts the interest rates. You could buy a house in a pleasant neighborhood that you like a lot, but where property values are going down instead of up.

However, taking steps to control your personal and family finances pays off. The pilot of an airplane gets a tremendous amount of information from charts, the plane's gauges and radar, and the air-traffic controllers. This information can be difficult to interpret, and sometimes it's contradictory. But you can be sure that the pilot doesn't ignore all the information and trust to luck, or assume that the co-pilot will take care of the plane.

Sometimes you may feel that you have two, equally serious, financial problems: not enough money and too much information! This book will show you some ways to supplement your income, and make the money you have go further. It will also show you how to sort through and evaluate the information available to you.

You'll learn when to go to an expert to get the sort of financial planning analysis that will work for your family (see p. 119.) But now you'll be able to participate and understand what your adviser is recommending. There's also a form (on p. 6) that you can use when you see your adviser. Financial planners can take the information you give them and work out a "capital needs assessment" plan that balances your need for savings, investment, retirement, and estate planning.

There are trade-offs in real life, and especially in real people's financial lives. For example, if you become a parent, you sacrifice nights of unbroken sleep and a spotless house. You know that a lot of your money has to go to the children's needs, and you take the risk that your children will get involved in an automobile accident or come home from school one day with safety-pin earrings and Mohawk haircuts dyed purple. But in return, you get the joy of loving and being loved by the new people whom you raise from infancy to maturity. In your financial life, the trade-offs you'll inevitably encounter include:

• *Risk versus return.* If you put your money in a safe investment (like Treasury bills), you probably won't get a very high return in the form of interest rates and/or profits. If you buy stock in a new high-tech company, you might double or triple your money—or lose most of it.

• *Your money versus your time and effort.* In simplest form, you can usually save money by "doing it yourself"—whether you paint your own living room instead of hiring a painter, or choose your own stocks in which to invest instead of buying shares in a mutual fund that charges a management fee. But in the long run, hiring an expert can save money as well as effort.

•*A big chunk of money right now versus a lot of small payments.* This is a trade-off whether you're paying the money or receiving it. For instance, if you need a car, you could pay cash for the car (a few thousand dollars all at once), or you could arrange a loan and make monthly payments (which means you'd have to pay interest). If you're about to retire, many pension plans let you choose between receiving your pension in a single lump sum (which you must then invest) or getting monthly payments.

This trade-off involves an important economic concept called "the time value of money." Getting money *now* is more valuable than the right to receive the same amount of money later. First of all, if you agree to wait for the money, you take the risk that you won't get the money, or that it will be worth less because of inflation. Second, if you get the money now, you can invest it—and earn more money— which brings us to our next trade-off.

•*Something good you can do with money versus another good thing you can do with money.* Traditional economic language calls this "opportunity cost." Let's say you make a large down payment on your new condo. That's good because it reduces the size of the mortgage you need and, therefore, the size of your monthly mortgage payment. But it's also bad because then you can't invest the down payment money in stocks, bonds, Certificates of Deposit (CDs), or other potential money-makers.

•*Spending more cash to save money.* Let's say you know of a discount store where you can buy the best paper towels in the world for only 10¢ a roll. It's a super bargain, isn't it? Yes—but you have to buy 1,000 rolls at a time, and you have to pay cash. Do you want to tie up $100 this way? Maybe you're short of cash right now (perhaps you've just finished paying the Christmas bills), even though your income for the year as a whole is comfortably higher than your expenses. You're not short of money—just temporarily short of cash. There's yet another trade-off: Your convenience versus saving money. Where would you put all those . . . paper towels?

•*Current income versus long-term appreciation.* Some investments are valuable because they provide income you can spend right away. Some mutual funds mail you a check every month; a savings account or interest-paying checking account yields interest every month or every quarter. Other investments are worthwhile because you hope to sell them later, at a profit. You buy 100 shares of stock at $19 a share, and the stock never pays a nickel in dividends, but eventually you sell for $43 a share. The stock doesn't provide any current income, but it does "appreciate" (increase in value) and give you a handsome profit.

Some investments provide both current income and long-term appreciation. You buy a two-family house for $112,000, live in half of it, collect $500 a month rental income from the other half, and finally sell it for $189,000. Or, you buy a bond that pays interest, and eventually sell the bond at a profit because interest rates have dropped. But in many cases, you must decide whether income or appreciation is more important to you, and choose your investments accordingly.

•*Investment wisdom versus tax wisdom.* Sometimes an investment or financial strategy is successful on one level (because you make money) but a failure on another (because it forces you to pay additional taxes, or is bad for your estate plan). Keep your eye on what happens to any planned transaction after all the taxes have been paid.

In this book, you'll see a lot about the Tax Code of 1986, nicknamed TC '86. This statute makes major changes in the way income and investments are taxed, and in retirement planning. Why so much fuss about a law that's over a year old? Although Congress passes a tax bill just about every year, those bills are usually called "Tax Reform Acts." This one is so revolutionary that it constitutes an entire new Internal Revenue Code—the last time a new code was enacted was in 1954. TC '86 affects almost every part of your financial life—and its provisions will be effective until TC '86 is amended, or another Tax Code is drawn up.

If you've been a sophisticated investor for several years, you have probably developed strategies for building wealth without high tax cost. Well, most of those strategies are now useless or counterproductive. You need new ones in this new tax environment.

•*Enjoyment now versus saving for future enjoyment.* You'll have to decide how much of your income should be put into savings for "a rainy day," how much should go for insurance, how much should be invested—and how much can be spent for a VCR, a better car, dinner at a good restaurant, a skiing vacation. There's more to life than sitting in a cold, dark cellar counting piles of money.

Speaking of counting piles of money, use the checklist on page 6 right now to start your financial plan. Find out what you own, and how your assets and liabilities compare (you may be pleasantly surprised). See if your debts are kept in control, or if they're threatening to swamp your financial well-being.

You'll use this information as you move through the book. For instance, if you're delighted to see how valuable your household goods really are—make sure you have enough homeowners' insurance. Maybe you need a safe deposit box to keep that surprisingly large collection of stock certificates. Maybe you should consult a lawyer about updating your will—the children are grown now, and you'd like to leave each of them some money or property. Perhaps when you get your tax refund, you'll use it to pay off that uncomfortably large credit card bill instead of buying a new living room sofa.

Once you have the knowledge, you can take action. Formulate a career plan, use your income wisely, decide what you want out of the options life offers you, be ready to deal with the common financial problems you can expect. Then go after your goals, knowing that you've made sound plans based on solid information.

"THE BIG CHECKLIST"

Use this checklist to assess your financial position: what you own; what you owe; and what your financial plans should be for the future.

PART ONE: YOUR INCOME

A. Salary: Your salary $_____ Your spouse's: $_____

B. Overtime, bonuses, etc. you have received or expect for this year: Yours

$_____ Your spouse's $_____

C. Interest from bank accounts, bonds, etc.: Yours $_____

Your spouse's: $_____ From joint accounts: $_____

D. Dividends from money market accounts, mutual funds, stock: Yours

$_____ Your spouse's: $_____ From joint accounts: $_____

E. Rental income from property you own: $_____

The property is: ☐Yours ☐Your spouse's ☐Joint

F. Other income: (explain; describe whose it is) $_____

_____

G. **Total Income:** $_____

PART TWO: YOUR ASSETS.

Indicate whether each asset is yours (Y); your spouse's (S); or joint property (J). This information will be needed for estate planning, and in case of divorce. For each asset, also indicate what you paid for it (OP—original price); your estimate of what it's worth now (CV—current value); and your estimate of what it would cost to replace (RC). This information will come in handy for planning your insurance portfolio, and for tax and estate planning.

				OP	CV	RC
A. Your home	☐Y	☐S	☐J	$_____	$_____	$_____
B. Your car	☐Y	☐S	☐J	$_____	$_____	$_____
C. Home electronics: Computer	☐Y	☐S	☐J	$_____	$_____	$_____
TV Set(s)	☐Y	☐S	☐J	$_____	$_____	$_____
VCR(s)	☐Y	☐S	☐J	$_____	$_____	$_____
Stereo equipment:	☐Y	☐S	☐J	$_____	$_____	$_____

Other ☐Y ☐S ☐J $____ $____ $____

Total ☐Y ☐S ☐J $____ $____ $____

D. Furniture in your home:
Especially valuable pieces:

_____ ☐Y ☐S ☐J $____ $____ $____

_____ ☐Y ☐S ☐J $____ $____ $____

_____ ☐Y ☐S ☐J $____ $____ $____

Other furniture:
_____ ☐Y ☐S ☐J $____ $____ $____

Total ☐Y ☐S ☐J $____ $____ $____

E. Art and collections:

_____ ☐Y ☐S ☐J $____ $____ $____

_____ ☐Y ☐S ☐J $____ $____ $____

F. Jewelry, furs, clothing:
☐Y ☐S ☐J $____ $____ $____

G. Silver, china, appliances, housewares:
☐Y ☐S ☐J $____ $____ $____

Total ☐Y ☐S ☐J $____ $____ $____

H. Bank accounts and CDs:

____ Bank ☐Y ☐S ☐J $____ $____ $____

____ Bank ☐Y ☐S ☐J $____ $____ $____

I. Money market funds:

_____ ☐Y ☐S ☐J $____ $____ $____

_____ ☐Y ☐S ☐J $____ $____ $____

J. Asset management accounts:

_____ ☐Y ☐S ☐J $____ $____ $____

K. Mutual funds:

_____ ☐Y ☐S ☐J $____ $____ $____

_____ ☐Y ☐S ☐J $____ $____ $____

_____ ☐Y ☐S ☐J $____ $____ $____

L. Stock:

_____ ☐Y ☐S ☐J $____ $____ $____

_____ ☐Y ☐S ☐J $____ $____ $____

8

_____ ☐Y ☐S ☐J $_____ $_____ $_____

M. Bonds:

_____ ☐Y ☐S ☐J $_____ $_____ $_____

_____ ☐Y ☐S ☐J $_____ $_____ $_____

N. Vested pension benefits including 401K plans, profit sharing:

Yours $_____ Your spouse's $_____

O. IRA/Keogh accounts: Yours: $_____ Your spouse's $_____

P. Real estate investments:

_____ ☐Y ☐S ☐J $_____ $_____ $_____

_____ ☐Y ☐S ☐J $_____ $_____ $_____

Q. Cash value of life insurance ☐Y ☐S $_____

R. Fair market value of business that you own $_____

S. Other Assets (describe):

_____ ☐Y ☐S ☐J $_____ $_____ $_____

_____ ☐Y ☐S ☐J $_____ $_____ $_____

Total: $_____ $_____ $_____

Total of All Assets: $_____ $_____ $_____

PART THREE: YOUR LIABILITIES

A. Home mortgage: ☐Y ☐S ☐J $_____

balance; _____% APR (interest rate); mortgage has _____ more

months to run; monthly payment is $_____

B. Loans, credit purchases (not credit cards—see item C) Auto loan ☐Y ☐S ☐J

$_____ balance; _____% APR; loan has _____ more months to

run; monthly payment is $_____

Home equity loan (list amount borrowed, not line of credit) ☐Y ☐S ☐J

$_____ balance; _____% APR; loan has _____ more months to

run; monthly payment is $_____

Student loan ☐Y ☐S ☐J (whether for your own education, or your children's):

$_____ balance; _____% APR; loan has _____ more months to run; monthly payment is $_____

Personal loan ☐Y ☐S ☐J $_____ balance; _____% APR; loan has

_____ more months to run; monthly payment is $_____

C. Purchases on credit (such as furniture bought on credit from the furniture store) ☐Y ☐S ☐J $_____ balance; _____% APR; purchase agreement has _____ more months to run; monthly payment is $_____

Total loan/credit balance: $_____ Total monthly payments: $_____

D. Charge accounts, credit cards

_____ ☐Y ☐S ☐J APR:_____% Balance: $_____

_____ ☐Y ☐S ☐J APR:_____% Balance: $_____

_____ ☐Y ☐S ☐J APR:_____% Balance: $_____

Total liabilities (mortgage, loans, credit, charge accounts, credit cards, and all other): $_____

Total monthly payment (include the amount you usually pay on your charge accounts and credit cards): $_____

Divide your annual income (see above) by 12: $_____

Monthly income minus monthly debt payments: $_____

Total assets (see above): $_____

Total liabilities $_____

Net worth (assets minus debt): $_____

Part One: EARNING

Earning is the foundation of your financial plan. The career you choose, the company you work for, your salary and benefits give you most or all of the money available to pay bills, start a savings program, invest, and plan for the future. So I'll start this section—and this book—with a short discussion of how to plan the twenty, thirty, or more years you'll spend in the work force.

An important part of choosing a job, or making the most of the job you already have, is to understand your compensation package. "Package" is the operative word here because you earn more than the salary that appears on your paycheck. The employer is probably making pension payments for you and buying health insurance for you and the other employees.

The employer may also offer many other benefits, such as reimbursement for tuition if you study subjects related to your work, low-cost mortgage loans, help with day care for your children. It all depends on your employer and on your level within the company. Some employers specify the benefits you'll get; others have a flexible, "cafeteria plan" that allows workers to decide which benefits they want from a "menu" of available benefits. Workers in these companies need the most information about benefits to make an informed choice.

This section also contains information about Individual Retirement Arrangements (IRAs) so that you can supplement the pension plan your employer provides (or take care of your own needs, if your employer doesn't provide a plan). IRAs are investments as well as ways to get ready for retirement, so be sure to reinforce what you learn here by studying the information about investments later in the book.

Finally, the section concludes with a short discussion of starting your own business—not a career move for everybody, but one that has provided satisfaction (not without risk) for many people.

1. Career Planning

Career planning, like all financial planning, calls for making important decisions about what really matters to you and what are your priorities. It requires research and a leap of faith as you fearlessly predict the future. Also needed is constant attention to what's really happening so that you are prepared to make dramatic adjustments as conditions change.

I think that today's "success" ideology does many people a disservice. People on the "fast track" deserve a certain amount of admiration, but not if admiring them implies despising those in the other "lanes." Everyone should be able to take pride in working hard, meeting his or her obligations at work and at home, and in being productive—whether or not this brings "success" in conventional terms. If everyone's career goal is to head a Fortune 500 corporation, then only 500 people at a time can be satisfied; everyone else is doomed to disappointment.

Setting Career Goals

The first step in setting career goals is to be realistic. Ambition is terrific, as long as you don't find it necessary to hate yourself for failing to meet impossible standards. No matter how many books you read that tell you how you can become fantastically successful by becoming self-confident or ruthless, or whatever kind of snake-oil the author is selling, there are no guarantees.

The second step is to realize that employers (or customers, if you're self-employed) aren't all that interested in your self-development. You may *want* a particular job because it fits into your long-range career plans, or because you can get important skills, or because you want to relocate because your spouse just got a better job. But whether or not you *get* the job depends on whether the employer thinks you have the skills to get the job done efficiently.

Which brings up the third step: developing skills that will be usable over time, throughout the country, and despite changes in technology and in the economy. This is where a crystal ball comes in handy. Another problem is that you can make a completely accurate analysis of the skills employers will need next year, or in three to five years' time, and can make realistic plans for developing these skills, only to find out that plenty of other people have the same idea.

So it pays to concentrate on basic skills. There will probably always be a need for people who can fix things (even if you have most of your experience on a particular kind of obsolete appliance or computer, you can learn how to fix other devices), people who are fluent in languages other than English, people with sales and management skills, and people with "people" skills, whether they're secretaries who anticipate an executive's business needs or psychotherapists who listen to people's problems.

One excellent book about career planning is aptly titled *What Color Is Your Parachute?* because it's often necessary to "bail out" of a job that isn't working out well, or even to change careers completely. If you lose your job, or even if the job could continue forever but you're unhappy, you have to think about what went wrong, and what you can do to improve the "fit" of your next job. If you're starting out (whether you've just finished school or are entering or re-entering the job market after years of full-time child care), you must decide what it is you really want from a job—then decide where such jobs can be found.

Interview Tactics

You must accomplish two things at an interview: get a job offer and decide whether or not you want to take the job! So you'll have to spend the time (anywhere from ten minutes to three days meeting various company personnel) not only stressing your qualifications but also finding out the "real story":

• *What is the job title?* Is the title an accurate reflection of the work involved, or is it used as a cheap way to get someone to do too much work for too little money?
• *What are the possibilities for promotion?*
• *How many people have held the job in the last five years?* Promotions or internal transfers are good signs; it's a bad sign if no one can hold the job for long. Perhaps people get fired after they're expected to do the impossible, or maybe they quit because they're fed up with unreasonably long hours, poor working conditions, and bosses who drive them crazy.
• *To whom will you report? Who will report to you?* It's essential to understand these basics of office politics before you take a job. You may get into trouble because you're caught in a political struggle between two vice presidents or two divisions of the company, or you may find out (too late) that you've been giving information to the wrong person and not to the one who should have it, or you've been taking orders from the wrong person.
• *What is the compensation package?* Consider salary, of course, but also consider bonuses, deferred compensation (pension and salary reduction plan), profit-sharing, and other employee benefits (such as health, disability, and life insurance). See pages 16 to 24 for a discussion of these items and how to analyze them.
• *Will the job give you an opportunity to develop new—and marketable—skills?* For instance, if you're an experienced personnel administrator but have never used a computer, computer skills could be helpful in your next job.
• *How would the job fit into your long-range career plan?* You might want to take a pleasant, well-paid job even if it doesn't fit into your plan, or you might turn down the job because you eventually want to become editor-in-chief of a magazine and need more financial experience, or because you need a higher salary to pay off your college loans or continue your investment program.
• *What are the business's short-term and long-term economic prospects?* A company that's experiencing a series of banner years will be in a better position to offer raises and improved working conditions than one that's teetering on the brink of bankruptcy. Of course, the newest employees tend to be the first ones laid off or fired. If the company is involved in takeovers—on either side—there's a risk of

huge economic loss. Furthermore, if the company is taken over, its assets may be sold off or its staff reduced so that the new owners can substitute their own "team."

• *What is the business's "corporate culture"?* How does the company think of its products or services, and is the company more interested in maintaining an existing position, developing new products, winding down? How much emphasis does it place on marketing, research and development, cost-cutting, productivity? (It's impossible for a business to achieve all these good things at once; choices must be made.)

You can (and should) get much of this information before the interview by doing a little research. The amount of research depends on the job and how important it is to you. If you hope to spend the next twenty-five years working for a company, you must know more about it than if you need a temporary job until your spouse's new job comes through, or if you want to work part-time to pay off some pressing bills.

Similarly, if you're in your last semester of college or graduate school, you'll probably have lots of interviews and must concentrate your research on the most promising one. If you've already got a job but are thinking about switching, you'll probably have comparatively few interviews (but not too much time to do research because you've got your existing job to worry about).

Information about a company comes from its annual reports and other financial data released to the public, from business magazines such as *Forbes* and *Fortune,* and from trade publications such as *Variety* and *Chemical Week.* It sounds very good at an interview if you can say something favorable about the company based on your research—but it's tactless at best to express sympathy about the poor fourth-quarter profits and the total failure of a much-ballyhooed new product.

2. How to Assess a Compensation Package

When you're choosing between job offers or making a long-range career plan, you must consider all the elements of the compensation plan (salary, bonuses, employee benefits, pension plan) as well as opportunities for advancement and the pleasure and interest to be found in the job itself.

Your job also helps finance the time after you stop working: your retirement. So it's important to understand if your employer offers a pension plan, when and how the employer will begin to make pension contributions for you, whether or not you can contribute to the pension fund yourself, and what your options will be after retirement.

Your employer doesn't have to have a pension plan at all; employers sometimes offer pension plans without claiming a tax deduction for the contributions they make to fund the plan. But if the plan is a *qualified* plan (qualified for tax deductions), your employer has to follow a detailed (and often confusing) set of rules imposed by the federal government.

A book this size can't make you an expert on every detail of pension law and practice, and you'll still have to consult with your employee relations department for the finer points of your company's plan, but check pages 25 to 31 for a quick look at the basics of pensions provided by the employer.

This chapter begins with a discussion of "work-time" employer benefits: the health insurance and group life insurance that protects you while you're working. The rest of this chapter deals with the steps that can be taken to save for retirement while you're still working (the pension plan your employer may provide, IRAs, Keogh plans). See Chapter 60, beginning on page 269, for a discussion of your financial options when you plan retirement and after you retire.

Health Insurance

These days hardly anyone can afford to get sick without a good strong health insurance plan provided by the employer. But employers don't get health insurance for free—they have to pay insurance premiums with funds that would otherwise be used to pay employee salaries and bonuses, or the expense of premiums reduces the employer's profits. So employers have an incentive to find ways to reduce medical care costs while making sure employees get quality care.

You must learn how your health insurance works. If your employer doesn't offer this benefit, or if you've changed jobs or been laid off, you must understand how you can get health insurance protection for your family. Because of recent changes in federal laws, your ex-employer may have to continue providing health insurance after you're laid off or after you retire.

Types of Health Insurance Coverage

Five basic types of health insurance coverage are provided by employers. It's up to each individual employer to decide which type or types of coverage will be provided, how much the employer will spend, and which insurance company or companies provide the best plans.

If the employer has a "flexible" or "cafeteria" plan of employee benefits (employees choose which benefits they want from a "menu" devised by the employer), you may have a choice between enhanced medical coverage and other benefits (such as tuition assistance or day-care assistance)—but usually, the employer calls the tune.

The five basic types of benefit are:

• Hospital insurance (hospitalization or hospital benefit plan)
• Regular medical/surgical insurance

- Major medical insurance
- Dental insurance
- Disability insurance

Hospital benefit plans are probably the most common. These plans pay part or all of the hospital bills employees encounter for illnesses and injuries that are *not* work-related. (Workers' compensation programs deal with work-related health problems.) Many plans also cover the employee's spouse and dependent children. Usually, employers who provide this coverage do so by buying insurance from a company such as Blue Cross/Blue Shield; sometimes the employees are enrolled in a Health Maintenance Organization (HMO) which provides hospitalization benefits for its members. See pages 20 to 21 for more about HMOs and PPOs (Preferred Provider Organizations).

Under a hospital benefit plan, you receive cash payments when you're hospitalized, or your employer pays hospital bills directly, up to a set maximum, or you pay the bills, then apply for reimbursement— again, with a maximum set.

Hospitalization insurance pays hospital bills, but people encounter many other medical costs (visits to doctors' offices and doctors' visits to hospitalized patients, for instance). The job of regular medical/surgical plans is to deal with these expenses. Usually, these plans pay for visits to the doctor's office to treat illnesses. Traditionally, these plans did not pay for checkups; today's emphasis on maintaining health (and cutting medical costs) means that some more forward-thinking plans cover checkups, courses for quitting smoking, and other "health preservers." Usually, the plan pays cash to the employee, with a maximum dollar amount set for each visit to the doctor. Again, the employer usually handles this by buying insurance policies: the Blue Shield part of Blue Cross/Blue Shield is the main provider of these policies.

Major medical plans start paying benefits after the regular hospitalization or medical/surgical plan's benefits are exhausted (as they might be after a prolonged bout with cancer or a long stay in a coronary-care unit). Most major medical plans set a maximum on the amount they will pay. For instance, a major medical plan might require you to use up your benefits provided for under other plans, then pay a "corridor" amount after this coverage is exhausted (such as $50 to $150, or 1% to 2% of your annual earnings). Then the major medical plan takes over, paying up to $100,000, or even $200,000.

Usually, major medical plans also make you pay "deductibles," "coinsurance," or both. (These are basic insurance concepts that will be encountered several times in this book.) A deductible is a minimum amount which you must pay before filing an insurance claim. Some policies are written so that the deductible applies once in a lifetime; others require you to pay the deductible every year, or even before filing every claim. Coinsurance is the percentage of the costs that the insured must pay (for instance, 20% to 25%).

To see how this works, let's say your major medical plan has a $100 corridor, $250 deductible, and 25% coinsurance. You encounter $5,000 in bills that are not covered by your hospitalization or regular medical/surgical insurance. First you pay the $100 "corridor" amount; then you pay the $250 deductible; then you pay 25% of the remaining $4,650 in bills. The major medical policy pays the rest.

A very desirable feature in some plans is the "stop loss" provision, which says that you won't have to pay more than a certain amount in medical bills each year (e.g., $1,000 per family member)—the plan will take over the rest. However, many employers are unwilling to pay the high premiums that plans with a stop-loss provision require.

Dental plans pay for dental care. In addition to covering the employee, some of these plans also cover the employee's spouse and dependent children.

Disability Insurance

Disability plans provide benefits to replace the income employees lose when a disability prevents them from working. Employers can offer insurance coverage for both short-term (usually up to six months) and long-term disability. Because insurance for long-term disability is more expensive, fewer employers offer it. Furthermore, some employers limit long-term disability insurance to employees who have been working for them for at least five years.

A typical long-term disability plan replaces about 60% of the employee's salary, but not overtime pay (often, payments are limited to $2,000 to $3,000 a month), starting from six months after the disability is incurred, and finishing when the employee recovers, or when he or she dies or reaches age 65. A few of the plans average in the bonuses an employee would earn over time.

It's good advice for many families to supplement this coverage with private disability insurance. These policies also provide income for those unable to work. The best policies pay if you are unable to work at your usual occupation; more limiting policies won't pay unless you are unable to work at any occupation. The premium for private disability insurance for a 40-year-old tends to run about $20 to $30 a year for every $1,000 in income that will be replaced.

Disability insurance is not the only source of income for the families of disabled people. The state workers' compensation systems provide benefits to people who become disabled in the course of their work. The Social Security system provides benefits to disabled persons and their families as part of the same system that provides retirement benefits to retired persons and benefits to the surviving families of workers. However, it can be very hard to prove entitlement to these benefits, and the benefits will probably be too small for a comfortable lifestyle—so many planners feel private insurance is a necessity.

Furthermore, some employers provide disability benefits as part of their pension plans instead of, or in addition to, the disability insurance plans already described. But these plans tend to include strict age and service requirements (for instance, a worker may not collect disability benefits from the pension plan unless he or she is at least fifty years old, with fifteen years' seniority), and are therefore not available to every disabled worker.

An *HMO (Health Maintenance Organization)* provides "one-stop shopping" for its members' medical care in return for a single insurance premium. Legally, employers who have more than twenty-five employees and who provide health benefits to employees must give employees the option of joining any HMO in the area that meets federal standards as an alternative to conventional hospitalization and medical/surgical policies. (Employees of smaller businesses, or employees without health insurance, may be able to join HMOs as individuals by paying premiums directly to the HMO.)

Some HMOs have their own hospitals, and HMO members are admitted to these hospitals when they need hospital care. Others have affiliation agreements with outside hospitals. (If you belong to an HMO and don't like its hospitals, preferring another hospital, you'll have to go to a doctor with admitting privileges at that hospital and pay the doctor's bill, plus the hospital bill, yourself because you didn't use doctors and hospitals covered by your HMO policy.)

Most HMO personnel, including the doctors, are paid annual salaries instead of fees for each procedure they perform. This can be a powerful cost-cutting measure; so can the fact that HMOs can perform medical tests on the premises and maintain centralized records so that doctors can see a patient's entire medical record at once, without duplicating tests already performed.

Critics of HMOs say that HMO subscribers may be fobbed off with "assembly-line" medicine, with long waits and cursory care by clock-watching personnel who perform the least expensive procedure, not the one most beneficial to the patient. So before you sign up with an HMO, find out if it really does deliver quality care (or, to be more cynical, if the waits are longer and the medical personnel less skillful or more unfeeling than local fee-for-service medical offices).

The *Preferred Provider Organization (PPO)* may be the health care delivery system of the 1990s. A PPO is an organization set up by an employer to cut costs by recommending "preferred providers": efficient doctors and other health care providers. Generally, the PPO offers a discount price to its members for services performed by participating health care providers. The PPO gives you a much wider choice of doctors than the HMO, which assigns physicians to HMO members (who in turn must pay the bills themselves if they want a non-HMO doctor).

Another variation on the theme of cost-cutting is the Negotiated Provider Agreement (NPA). Here, the employer makes a deal and sets up reimbursement schedules with various doctors, medical groups, or hospitals. The employer may be able to set up its own DRG program (see page 282 for a discussion of Medicare and the Diagnosis Related

Group system). For instance, it may arrange with a hospital to pay a flat fee for the whole treatment of an employee's heart attack, rather than paying by the day for the treatment. If an employee's family doctor signs an NPA, the employer saves money and the employee won't have to change doctors, as he or she would by joining an HMO (the HMO itself assigns doctors) or by participating in a PPO (where an employer recommends certain doctors).

How to Understand a Health Plan

The best time to learn about a plan is when you're comparing job offers, or right after you've been hired. If the plan doesn't meet your needs, talk to your insurance agent about supplementing it with private coverage. Here are some factors in deciding whether or not the employer-provided coverage is adequate.

• Which benefits (regular medical/surgical, hospitalization, major medical, dental, disability) are provided? Are mental health benefits included? Are orthodontia and plastic surgery covered or are they excluded as "cosmetic"?

• Are "preexisting conditions" (medical conditions already in existence when coverage begins) excluded? If so, how are they defined? Do you have any chronic illnesses which might be excluded by such a provision? If you do, can you afford private coverage until the employer's package takes over, or can you continue insurance from a previous employer (so that the condition will not rank as preexisting under that policy)? See page 22 for more on continuation coverage.

• How long must you be employed in order to participate in the plan? The plan may provide rapid or even immediate participation, but exclude pre-existing conditions, which is a real problem if you change jobs during pregnancy—you might find yourself without medical insurance for the delivery.

• Does the policy cover your spouse or dependents? Can you pay an extra premium and get coverage for them?

• How does the plan provide its benefits: by paying you cash, paying bills directly, or reimbursing you for part or all of the payments you've already made? How long does it usually take for the plan to process a claim? Must you get advance approval for certain procedures (such as medical tests) to be covered by the plan? Does the plan require you to get a second medical opinion before benefits will be payable for surgery?

• What is the maximum amount the plan's regular medical/surgical coverage will pay? What about major medical coverage? What's the deductible, coinsurance, corridor amount? Are maximum amounts applied per illness (the option most favorable to the employee—no matter how much is paid out for one illness, benefits are still possible for other illnesses), per year, or only once in a lifetime?

Health Insurance and Marriage

When both spouses work, they must "coordinate" the health coverage each employer provides; most policies provided by employers forbid duplicate coverage. Each spouse must look first to his or her own coverage, and can't collect benefits under the spouse's policy until his or her own coverage has been exhausted. However, insurers can't refuse to pay benefits to an employee's spouse just because he or she also has coverage as another employee's dependent.

Continuation Coverage

Stay covered! You could lose your health insurance coverage if you're fired or you quit your job, if you divorce or are widowed. It's a terrible risk for a family to be without health insurance. Fortunately, employers are often required to provide continuation coverage for health insurance; some employers may do this voluntarily. Although you'll probably have to pay for continuation coverage, you'll remain a member of the group plan provided by the employer. That's an advantage because group premiums are usually lower than premiums on individual policies, group policies are usually more comprehensive, and you won't have to worry about waiting periods or pre-existing illnesses if you're still a member of the same group.

A federal law signed in April 1986, effective for plan years starting after July 1, 1986, covers most health benefits plans provided by employers. (The exceptions are plans maintained by churches, government agencies, and employers with fewer than twenty employees.)

Under the law, employers must provide continued health coverage for employees (and, in some cases, spouses and dependents) for eighteen or thirty-six months after a "qualifying event" (something that would otherwise mean the loss of health insurance coverage), such as when

- The employee dies (of course, the employee no longer needs health insurance—but the survivors do)
- The employee no longer works for the employer (but continuation coverage need not be offered if the employee was fired for gross misconduct)
- The employee's work hours have been reduced, and he or she is no longer a full-time employee entitled to plan coverage
- The employee separates or gets a divorce, and the ex-spouse and children need continuation coverage
- The employee reaches the age of Medicare eligibility and is dropped from the plan
- The employee's children reach age 19, or otherwise lose their eligibility for coverage as dependents

Employers are allowed to charge employees (or family members) for continuation coverage—as you can imagine, they usually do. But they can't charge more than 102% of the premium that the health plan charges to cover an employee who has not gone through a qualifying event. (The extra 2% is for administrative costs.)

However, qualifying events tend to cut the family income, thereby making it hard to afford continuation coverage. One option is for employees to protect themselves by buying a "conversion" policy that allows conversion of the group policy to a less expensive (and less comprehensive) individual policy if a qualifying event ever occurs.

Continuation coverage never comes automatically; the employee, spouse, or dependent must ask for it. Employers must allow a period of at least sixty days to make the election—and the period for requesting continuation coverage must last at least sixty days after the qualifying event or after the employee or beneficiary is notified of these rights. Once again, the moral is to read the fine print. What seems to be more routine blah-blah from the employer could be an explanation of valuable rights.

Group Life Insurance

Everyone with financial responsibilities needs life insurance; and sensible life insurance buyers shop for the best deal they can find. Many people actually have life insurance policies they haven't paid for and don't know about because the employer buys group life insurance policies for its employees, as one of their employee benefits.

Group life insurance lets employers provide a very valuable benefit at low cost. Group rates are low. Depending on the plan, either the employer pays for the policies or the employees pay part of the premiums. Health examinations are not required, so employees who would otherwise be uninsurable, or who would have to pay extra-high rates, can be insured at the same rates as their co-workers.

In fact, employers often continue life insurance coverage for retired, laid-off, or disabled employees throughout their lifetimes. And state insurance laws usually require employers to provide "conversion" privileges; employees whose group life insurance coverage is about to be terminated can convert the policy to an individual whole-life policy (and pay the premiums from then on), without taking a medical exam.

Most group life insurance plans qualify for favorable tax treatment. Employees do not have taxable income if the employer provides $50,000 or less worth of insurance coverage. If the group policies are larger, the employee does have taxable income, but only a small amount because the taxable income is limited to the employer's cost for providing the extra insurance.

Therefore, group life insurance is a good deal for everyone. It's a good deal for the employer, who motivates employees by providing valuable benefits inexpensively; it's a good deal for insurance companies because it costs them less to sell large group policies than it does to sell single policies; and it's certainly a good deal for the employee, who gets all the financial and income protection advantages of life insurance at no direct cost while paying little or no tax on the benefit.

But don't rest on your laurels. Find out whether or not your employer provides group life insurance (and if so, how much). Turn to page 62 to see if the group insurance, plus the life insurance you already own, is enough; if it isn't, find out the best combination of life insurance protection and investment for filling the gap.

Other Employee Benefits

All the states require the employer to provide at least *some* benefits, such as paid vacations. Depending on the state, employers may be required to offer anywhere from two to fourteen benefits to all employees. For instance, thirty-eight states require employers with health plans to provide maternity coverage (the health plan must cover the expenses of prenatal medical care and childbirth). Federal law says that maternity benefits for female employees and for the spouses of male employees must be equal. Thirty-seven states require health plans to cover alcoholism treatment; twenty-nine states mandate mental health care coverage for all plans.

Depending on state law, the employer's decision, and the employee's seniority and value to the company, any or all of these benefits may be available.

- Bonuses, keyed either to the employer's smashing success for the year or the employee's exceptional achievement
- Vacations, frequently keyed to seniority: the longer the employee has worked, the more vacation time is available each year
- Paid sick leave or personal days that can be used to care for a sick child, wait around for the washing machine repairperson, or attend a child's piano recital or soccer game
- Use of a company car (see page 43 for more about the tax deduction you may be able to take if you use your own car in business)
- Partial or total tuition reimbursement for work-related studies
- Dependent care assistance, which could include advice or reimbursement for part or all of the cost of caring for children or dependent elderly parents
- Stock options
- Prepaid legal services, which allow an employee to telephone a group of selected lawyers for advice, drafting of simple wills, reviewing of mortgages, and the like
- Severance pay and/or outplacement assistance (that is, career counseling, help with lining up interviews, etc.) when an employee is laid off or fired

3. Retirement Benefits from Your Company

When many employees retire, they get a pension from their employers in addition to Social Security benefits. But this is not true for everybody. Not every worker participates in a pension plan—not every employer maintains a plan. Even if there is a plan, temporary and part-time workers don't qualify for participation. There are even many pension plan participants who will never collect a pension because they don't work for any one employer long enough to "vest" (become entitled to the amount in their pension accounts).

To protect yourself and make intelligent plans for retirement, you must learn about your employer's plan (if there is one), whether you can make your own contributions to the plan, how to do so (the times at which you can sign up for the plan may be restricted), and whether this is a smart financial move. Finally, if your employer's plan won't meet your retirement needs, you must be prepared to supplement it with your own investments.

This section deals with contributions to your retirement fund made during your working life. Turn to page 269 for a discussion of planning steps to take when you're about to retire, and financial planning for the postretirement years.

Learning about Pension Plans

You can learn about pension rights from your company's employee benefits coordinator or from your shop steward (if you're a union member). Either person can help you decipher the three pension documents that federal law requires the employer to give you.

- The Summary Plan Description (SPD), which is a description of the terms of the pension plan.
- The Summary Annual Report (SAR), which is an outline of the pension plan's investments and how those investments have done over the past year.
- The Statement of Accrued Benefits (SAB)—unlike the SPD and SAR, which are uniform for all plan participants—sums up the size of your own pension account and the benefits you can expect based on assumptions about your salary at the time you retire. Most employers give out SABs routinely, but theoretically employers can insist on a request before giving one out. Employees are entitled to one SAB per year.

In addition to these documents, which are required by federal law, many employers prepare their own handbooks and brochures about the pension plan; unions prepare explanatory material about the pension plans they negotiate as part of the union contract.

Qualified Plans

From the employee's point of view, if a plan is qualified (that is, if the employer is entitled to a tax deduction for its contributions), it means certain rights for the employee are guaranteed because federal labor and tax laws impose strict requirements on the plan. Such laws deal with determining which employees can participate, how much the employer must contribute, and when employees become fully vested. These laws are supposed to make sure that plans do not discriminate in favor of a company's top management and against the rank-and-file employees. However, there are many loopholes, and pension plans usually do favor top management.

A qualified plan has to be a permanent plan, set out in writing, under which the employer sets up a trust and deposits money in the trust (or buys insurance policies to accomplish the same result), set up for the exclusive benefit of the employees. That is, the employer can't take back the money, or even borrow it back, when times get tough. (See page 30 for a discussion of what happens when a plan is terminated, and how employees' rights are protected.)

The two basic types of qualified plans are defined-contribution plans and defined-benefit plans; each one has many variations. Think of going to the gas station. If you ask for $10 worth of gas, that's a defined-contribution plan; if you ask to have the tank filled and then pay whatever that costs, that's a defined-benefit plan.

Each participant in a defined-contribution plan has a separate account. The employer makes contributions every year (or every year where there's a profit, if the plan is set up as a profit-sharing plan and does not require contributions unless the employer earns a profit). Usually, the contribution is set as a percentage of the employee's salary. At retirement, the size of the account determines the size of the employee's pension.

In a sense, then, the defined-contribution plan puts the "investment risk" on the plan participant—he or she takes the risk that the economy will be down, or that the pension administrators will make bad investment choices.

A defined-benefit plan is a little harder to explain. Instead of the employer knowing how much to contribute, with the employee's final pension determined by the amount in the account and the plan's success in investing it, the employer decides the retirement benefit to which each employee will be entitled. Once the benefit level is set, the employer hires an actuary (a kind of statistician) to decide how much must be contributed for each employee in order for that benefit level to be available at retirement. There's a risk for the employee here too: The employee could get stuck with a fixed income that seemed adequate, or even generous, when the plan was set up, but that fails to keep pace with inflation.

Defined-benefit plans are more popular than defined-contribution plans. The Department of Labor's 1985 survey of large and medium-sized companies showed that 80% of the employees in these companies were covered by a defined-benefit plan. About 40% of employees participated in defined-contribution plans (not all of them pension plans; some were plans for distributing profits in the form of bonuses). Obviously, there's some overlap; employers can have more than one pension plan, and there's a special, unusually complicated, set of rules these employers must follow.

Participation and Vesting

The fact that you work for a company that maintains a qualified plan doesn't guarantee that you are a plan participant. Employers are allowed to impose age and length-of-employment requirements before allowing an employee to participate in the pension plan. However, federal laws governing participation requirements have been getting steadily more generous to employees. Now, if you work full-time, you must be allowed to participate in a qualified plan if you are over 21 and have worked for the employer for at least a year.

"Participation" means that the employer makes contributions to the plan for the employee. Some plans are written allowing you to make voluntary contributions to the plan. Usually this is done through payroll deductions; whether it's a good idea depends both on the pension plan's success in investing and on your own savings patterns. If you find it hard to save, payroll deductions could make it easier to accumulate retirement funds. Other plans require you to make contributions in order to participate, or specify that the employer will "match" your contribution.

To collect a pension, you must work for the same company long enough to be "vested." Once you're vested, part or all of your pension account or pension benefits must be paid to you at retirement age—even if you've taken a different job in the meantime. What if you quit or are fired before you vest? What if part of your account or benefits are unvested? In those cases, the money goes back to the pension plan, and can reduce the amount of contributions the employer must make to fund other employees' pensions—but the employer is not allowed to take these "forfeitures" out of the pension plan and spend them, or use them to increase pension benefits to other vested employees.

Every qualified plan must choose one of the vesting schedules allowed by law, showing the percentage of vesting achieved each year. Qualified plans are allowed to use "cliff vesting"—that is, to say that there will be no vesting until a certain number of years (usually, five) has passed—when, suddenly, the entire account vests.

To oversimplify a little, all qualified plans must provide for 100% vesting after seven years or less. Furthermore, you're always 100% vested in your own contributions to the plan. If you quit or get fired, you're entitled to have your own contributions returned—some plans pay interest on them; some don't. Top-heavy plans (plans that provide most of their benefits to highly paid executives) must vest even faster: three-year cliff vesting, or 100% vesting after six years.

Plan Integration

Plan integration is one of the loopholes that allow companies to save most of the pension goodies for highly paid executives without breaking the law. Integrated plans are "integrated" with Social Security. An employer that chooses to integrate its defined-contribution plan is allowed to reduce the contribution it makes to the plan in order to compensate for the Social Security tax it pays.

If a defined-benefit plan is integrated, the pension benefits retirees receive are reduced by a certain percentage of their Social Security benefits. (The employer chooses the percentage, but can't exceed the maximum percentage set by law.) Again, this is permitted because part of the employee's Social Security benefits comes from the Social Security taxes paid by the employer.

This is bad news for lower-paid workers because the Social Security tax is a regressive tax. Social Security tax is due on the first dollar of earnings—but is not required above a maximum level (for 1987, that level is reached when a person earns $43,800). Employer and employee each pay Social Security taxes equal to 7.15% of the employee's income up to $43,800 and 0% of income over this amount. (In 1988, the tax rate rises to 7.51% for both employer and employee.)

If the employer's pension contribution is set at 7% of the employee's income, integrated with Social Security, the employer will contribute a lot for a vice president earning $100,000 (because $56,200 of his or her salary is not subject to Social Security tax) and very little for a payroll clerk earning $18,000 (because all of his or her salary is subject to Social Security tax).

Similarly, if the pension plan theoretically provides a $400 monthly pension for the accounting clerk, but also requires the pension to be reduced by 75% of his or her Social Security benefits, the clerk won't collect much from the employer. But if the vice president's $3,000 monthly pension is reduced by an amount equal to three-quarters of *his* or *her* Social Security benefits, he or she won't suffer much because Social Security benefits are a comparatively small portion of the retirement income.

The pension plan can even be based *only* on salary above a certain integration level set by the plan. If the integration level is $20,000, then employees who earn less than $20,000 won't get any pension benefits at all.

In short, if you are a participant in an integrated plan, unless you earn a comparatively high salary, you won't have much of a pension to look forward to. The answer is to protect yourself by setting up a program of retirement investment. Maybe the right solution for you is an IRA; maybe annuities are good investment choices for you. Maybe the best thing to do is to build overall financial security so that you'll have adequate investment income for a comfortable retirement.

Salary-Reduction Plans: CODAs and 401(k) Plans

There are several kinds of salary-reduction plans—plans under which you can cut your tax bill by having part of your salary paid into a retirement account. The most popular kind of salary-reduction plan goes by two names: CODA (for Cash or Deferred Arrangement) or 401(k) plan (named for the section of the Internal Revenue Code permitting the plan).

Usually, you're taxed on your income as soon as you have a right to receive it—you can't put off taxes by refusing to take income to which you're entitled.

But if your company adopts a salary-reduction plan that follows the tax code's rules, you can choose between receiving part of your salary in cash (taxable, but also spendable) or having a percentage of your income (usually 6% to 10%) placed in the plan. Neither the contributions themselves nor their increase in value will be taxed until you retire and begin to draw on the account (although amounts placed in a 401(k) plan *are* subject to Social Security tax).

The maximum permitted salary deferral is $7,000 a year. (This amount will be increased if the cost of living increases.) However, some companies agree to match up to 50% of the employee's contributions. You could end up saving more than 10% of your income—tax-free—until you retire.

This is a terrific benefit, but there are some limitations placed on it. These plans are definitely retirement plans, not savings accounts; you're not allowed to take money out of the plan until you retire, become disabled, or stop working for the employer.

Pensions and Divorce

For many couples, vested pension rights are one of the largest family assets. There wouldn't be much to divide in the case of a divorce if these pension benefits were considered the exclusive property of the spouse who earned them. You'll find much more about divorce starting on page 232, but the pension aspects of divorce will be considered here because understanding them depends on understanding the way pension plans work.

Pension plans are allowed to pay lump sums or make regular payments to the ex-spouses of pension participants—as long as the ex-spouse has what the tax code defines as a Qualified Domestic Relations Order from the right court. Therefore, couples in the process of divorce must understand the availability of pensions, divide their value fairly, and make sure the court hearing the divorce issues an order in proper form.

The Summary Plan Description (SPD) gives information that is useful to both spouses; however, since federal law only requires that plan participants get this information, plan administrators may refuse to give copies to the nonparticipant spouse (or his or her lawyer). In that case, it'll be necessary to request the information from the participant spouse as part of the pretrial process of exchanging information about assets and income.

Dividing pensions, like dividing other assets, is a matter of negotiation. The approach that is finally taken depends on each spouse's bargaining power, financial situation, other assets, and ages. Ages are important because most plans are written so that benefits can't be distributed (whether to a participant or his or her spouse) before the plan's early retirement age—usually either 55 or 62. So the ex-spouse may have to wait until the participant spouse reaches this age before payments can begin. The ex-spouse, however, doesn't have to wait until the participant spouse actually retires. The non-participant spouse can get a lump sum at the time of the divorce, as a replacement for any rights he or she might have in the participant spouse's pension.

Pension Plan Termination

Employers are not allowed to use pension funds as a kind of cookie jar to be dipped into if and when funds run low. Qualified plans must be maintained for the exclusive benefit of the participants and their beneficiaries—not the employer's benefit.

Furthermore, qualified plans are supposed to be permanent plans. If an employer stops making contributions, there's a good chance the employer will lose its tax deduction for all the past years when the plan was in operation and will have to give the IRS a large sum in back taxes (large enough to discourage the employer from stopping plan contributions). The trustees or insurers who run the plan have an obligation to invest pension funds prudently and minimize losses.

But various unpleasant things do happen in the real world. A business can be taken over by another corporation—but then, the new owner will probably take over the pension plan too, and employees who are retained under the new regime will also retain their pension rights. Employers can go out of business. It is possible, but unlikely, that the pension plan's investments will be so disastrous that the fund will be too small to meet its obligations.

The Employee Retirement Income Security Act (ERISA) is a major federal pension law that demands all qualified plans provide for immediate vesting of certain benefits whenever the plan is terminated or partially terminated. "Terminated" means what it sounds like; "partially terminated" means that the employer either fires some employees in order to avoid paying them pension benefits or amends the plan to exclude certain employees from coverage. Sometimes a reduction in the employer's contributions, or tightening of participation or vesting standards, also counts as a partial termination.

When a defined-contribution plan is terminated, the amounts in each participant's account vest right away. Things are a little more complicated for defined-benefit plans. These plans are insured by a federal government agency, the Pension Benefit Guaranty Corporation (PBGC); the employers pay regular insurance premiums. When a defined-benefit plan terminates, the PBGC supervises the collection and distribution of the plan's assets; plan participants are guaranteed that the PBGC will pay their vested benefits, up to a maximum amount set by federal law, if the plan runs out of assets before all the vested benefits are paid.

However, the PBGC has been hard-hit by the collapse of some large pension plans. If it has to make many more large payments, it may collapse itself unless it gets bailed out by more funds from Congress.

Summing Up Employer Plans

This has been a quick introduction to the health, pension, and other benefits provided by employers. As you can see, the benefits make up a major part of employer's labor costs—and of your compensation, even though these amounts don't appear in your paycheck. It's been estimated that employers must spend an additional amount equal to one-third of the employee's salary to pay Social Security taxes and provide pensions and benefits.

Employer plans have a lot of impact on your career decisions. For instance, you may choose a large employer, that offers more security and a better pension package over a smaller or start-up company that offers a larger starting salary but less assurance that the company will be around for the rest of your working lifetime. Or, you may decide not to accept an offer of a new job, even if it has a higher salary and more prestigious title, because leaving your old job would mean leaving before pension benefits have vested, thus forfeiting the amounts contributed by the employer on your behalf.

However, many employees find that benefits from the employer are insufficient for their needs. They can protect themselves by maintaining Individual Retirement Arrangements (IRAs), to accumulate funds for retirement. If they are self-employed (whether full-time or part-time or intermittently), they can also maintain Keogh retirement plans (also called HR-10 plans).

4. REAL LIFE: JOHN AVERY

What is this, a field trip from kindergarten? Look at all those shiny faces. I bet none of them have to shave . . . no, take that back. That guy over there who thinks he looks like Don Johnson is trying to prove that he has to shave by not shaving for a couple of days. Unless he paints on that stubble.

That's what John Avery thought as he settled down in the last empty seat on the commuter train and opened his briefcase. He'd review the third-quarter figures again. Sure, he looked them over last night and made a few notes, but he wanted to be prepared for the regional sales meeting.

Further back in the car, four guys were playing bridge. They always played bridge on every commute. John didn't think he was quite ready for that yet. He thought of them as guys winding down, getting ready to be put out to pasture, just clocking in the last few years before retirement. That's not me, Avery thought. I'm still in there punching. Still showing the young guys what a grizzled old warrior can do. Even though I keep getting more grizzled and they keep getting younger.

The Numbers

Avery supplemented the $65,000 he earned as sales manager of a sportswear firm with $5,000 in interest income and $5,000 in rental income from a summer cottage. It wasn't much of a place—in fact, it was too run-down and beat-up for the Averys themselves to enjoy going there. But they always managed to find a group of tenants to take the place each summer. Seventy-five thousand a year. A nice, comfortable figure—has a nice ring to it.

Jeanine Avery also had a nice ring to her—or several, and a few brooches and a mink coat and a fox coat. John Avery had a coin collection, and some bars of gold bullion that never made it to being coins. Altogether, the furnishing and valuables in the Avery home were worth almost $25,000, and their equity in the fully paid-off home was another $100,000. Their equity in the summer cottage was $20,000, so the "assets" side of the balance sheet added up to $220,000.

However, the Avery family had a hefty tax bill each year: $20,000. They put $13,000 a year into investments, and $3,000 a year went toward insurance premiums. The next largest expenditure was $9,500 for food and clothing. Martin Avery, their eldest child, was a stockbroker in Pasadena, and Nina Stockton, the middle child, was a speech therapist in Detroit, leaving only Pauline Avery in college.

John Avery figured that Pauline would be a millionaire before she was 30. She always had some entrepreneurial angle going. She served as dorm counselor, so she lived rent-free; she started a successful résumé-typing service, then sold it to another student. She was now considering franchising her dormitory pizza-delivery service to three students in other dorms. However, her parents still paid $8,000 a year toward her tuition.

Although there was no mortgage on the house, property tax ran to $1,500 a year. The inevitable miscellaneous expenses totalled $5,000 or so. So John and Jeanine Avery had a very healthy financial situation: $75,000 a year going in, only $60,000 going out, with $13,000 a year invested routinely. That leaves $15,000 a year toward the goal of planning retirement.

The Answers

The Averys discussed their problems with a financial representative, and pinned down their needs. They enjoy the convenience of a centralized asset-management account. Instead of constantly worrying about which bank account, CD, or money market fund pays the best rate, they can put spare cash into the centralized account, knowing that it will be "swept" regularly and reinvested safely and productively.

Neither of them really enjoys investing, so they want a more or less "hands-off" approach that will combine safety with appreciation over a moderately long term. John Avery does not plan to retire early, so he's looking at at least a ten-year investment horizon (he's 54 now).

Both John and Jeanine want a diverse portfolio, but they prefer investing in mutual funds and closed-end investment trusts to buying individual securities. Therefore, they maintain investments in three mutual funds: a stock fund that is oriented toward growth, a high-quality government bond fund, and, because they're in a high bracket, a tax-exempt bond fund.

Unlike younger couples, the Averys don't have a pressing anxiety about how the college tuition problem will be solved. After all, two of the children have graduated, the third is about to. But they still need insurance for financial and income protection purposes. Their choice is variable-life coverage. Although they don't want to spend a lot of time planning investments, they do want to make productive use of their money. They think of their variable-life policies as additions to their investment portfolio and review the results regularly—but they don't make frequent switches, figuring that it isn't worth the time and trouble just to get a few extra dollars of return.

Because their primary financial objective is funding retirement, they complete their portfolio with annuity investments. The Averys don't have to pay taxes on the increase in value of their annuity account—they won't have to, until they begin to collect annuity payments after retirement. Then they can assess their financial situation and choose between annuity payments for a certain number of years, annuity payments continuing over John's lifetime, or annuity payments continuing throughout the lifetime of whichever of them lives longer.

5. Do You Need an IRA?

Not every company maintains a pension plan; even if there is one, you may not qualify. In fact, not everyone works for someone else. Self-employed people can maintain Keogh plans (see page 57), but can also maintain Individual Retirement Arrangements.

An Individual Retirement Arrangement (IRA) is a system of retirement saving under which taxpayers put aside part of their earned income—up to $2,000 a year per person; up to $2,250 for a couple with one working spouse and one homemaker spouse; up to $4,000 for a couple with two working spouses. The great advantage of IRAs is that the increase in value as the IRA builds up over time is not taxed until the IRA owner retires and starts collecting funds from the IRA. Some IRA contributions are tax-deductible in the year they're made. There are two kinds of IRAs—both, coincidentally, with the same initials: Individual Retirement Accounts and Individual Retirement Annuities.

IRAs can be used in two ways: either as your only source of retirement saving (if you're self-employed or are not a plan participant) or as a supplement to a Keogh plan or a qualified plan offered by your employer. IRAs are unbeatable if you qualify for a tax deduction for your contribution; they're still a good idea if you don't because you can defer taxation on investment growth (such as the growth in value of stocks you buy for your IRA).

And don't count too much on the Social Security system; it may not be solvent by the time you're ready to retire. Even if it is, your Social Security benefits probably won't be enough for comfortable retirement. As already explained, your pension benefits may be much, much smaller than you'll need. The answer is to provide investment income, either from your investment portfolio or from an IRA.

Yes, I'm enthusiastic about IRAs. It's all too easy to waste small amounts of money, it's all too hard to save, and retirement time comes before you know it. A comparatively small IRA contribution each year will yield a healthy five- or six-figure retirement fund.

Except for two groups, I'd recommend an IRA to everyone who earns income from employment. The first group includes those who are just getting by and who would not be able to save any money if they opened IRAs. The second group, at the other end of the economic spectrum, are sophisticated, high-bracket taxpayers who do expect cushy pension checks, who don't qualify for an IRA deduction, and who would be better off using the investment dollars either more aggressively (to earn more) or putting them in a tax-exempt investment (such as certain municipal bonds). Although even this group can benefit from skillful IRA investing, they just might be able to do better through other investment choices.

Table 1 shows how much will be built up in your IRA account after one year, five years, and ten, fifteen, twenty, twenty-five, and thirty years—based on making the same contribution each year at the beginning of the year. The table shows how much you'll earn at the rate of 6%, 8%, or 10% a year.

So you see, even a $500 yearly contribution adds up to a sizable account over time. IRA millionaires are not a myth—it just takes patience and investment savvy ($2,000 a year at 10% for forty-one years, or $4,000 a year at 10% for thirty-three years).

IRAs entered the tax law in 1974, as a way for self-employed people to fund retirement. In 1981, the tax code was changed to permit anyone with earned income to maintain an IRA and deduct IRA contributions up to the statutory maximum—even if he or she was an employee, and even if he or she was a participant in a qualified pension plan. The rules changed again in 1986, and now anyone with earned income can have an IRA, and can use the IRA to defer tax on the interest earned or the appreciation in value of IRA assets. However, not everyone is entitled to deduct IRA contributions.

The IRA Deduction

If you're single and are not a participant in a qualified plan, or if you're married and neither you nor your spouse is a plan participant, then you can deduct your IRA contribution, up to the maximum permitted contribution. (To recap, that's $2,000 for a single person, $2,250 for a single-earner married couple, $4,000 for a two-earner married couple.)

If you're a plan participant, the deduction depends on your income. (What matters is being a plan participant, it doesn't matter whether or not you're vested.)

• If you're single, you can deduct up to $2,000 if your adjusted gross income is under $25,000. You can't take any IRA deduction if your

TABLE 1.   IRA GROWTH

		1	5	10	15	20	25	30
6%	$ 500	$ 530	$ 2988	$ 6986	$ 12,336	$ 19,496	$ 29,078	$ 41,540
	$1000	1060	5975	13,971	24,672	38,992	58,156	83,801
	$2000	2120	11,950	27,942	49,344	77,984	116,312	167,602
	$2250	2385	13,444	31,435	55,512	87,732	130,851	188,522
	$4000	4240	23,900	55,884	98,688	155,968	232,634	335,204
8%	$ 500	$ 540	$ 3168	$ 7823	$ 14,662	$ 24,711	$ 39,477	$ 61,172
	$1000	1080	6355	15,645	29,324	49,422	78,954	122,345
	$2000	2160	12,670	31,290	58,648	98,844	157,908	244,690
	$2250	2430	14,254	35,201	66,015	111,200	177,647	275,276
	$4000	4320	25,340	62,580	117,296	197,688	315,816	489,380
10%	$ 500	$ 550	$ 3358	$ 8766	$ 17,475	$ 31,501	$ 54,091	$ 90,215
	$1000	1100	6715	17,531	34,979	63,002	108,181	180,943
	$2000	2200	13,430	35,062	69,898	126,004	216,362	361,886
	$2250	2475	15,109	39,445	78,635	141,755	243,407	407,122
	$4000	4400	26,860	70,124	139,796	252,008	432,724	723,772

adjusted gross income is over $35,000. In between these two figures, the IRA deduction is phased out. Every $5 in income over $25,000 eliminates $1 of the deduction. If you're single, earn $30,000, and contribute $1,000 to an IRA, only $1,000 is deductible.

• If you're married, file a joint return, and are a plan participant—or if your spouse is a plan participant—the deduction is phased out the same way. A full deduction is available if your adjusted gross income is $40,000 or less; no deduction is available if it's over $50,000.

• Married people who file separate returns are not entitled to claim an IRA deduction under any circumstances (tax policy calls for a crack-down on the use of separate returns to cut tax bills).

These new provisions create the need for a new, potentially difficult calculation. When you retire and start withdrawing funds from your IRA, you'll have to determine which part of the withdrawal comes from funds that qualified for a deduction (and, therefore, must be taxed when you withdraw them), and which part of the withdrawal is tax-exempt because you were taxed on the funds in the year you added them to your IRA. If you had an IRA before the Tax Code of 1986 was passed, and add to it afterwards, ask your trustee about setting up separate accounts for deductible and nondeductible amounts.

What Should You Do with Your IRA?

If you already have an IRA, I'd recommend that you continue contributing, even if you no longer qualify for the deduction. I'd recommend starting one if you don't have one. You could either start a mutual fund IRA that lets you switch between funds with different levels of risk, or maybe the best choice is to start several IRAs to stay on top of changing economic conditions. Let's say you start your first IRA in 1987, with a bond fund; in 1988, you open an IRA with a conservative growth-and-income stock fund; and in 1989, you invest in an aggressive, growth-oriented stock fund. (If these terms are confusing, turn to the section on investment, which begins on page 101.) In later years, when you're ready to make a contribution, decide which fund seems like the best place to invest—given current market conditions. Or divide your contribution among the accounts. It's not only the market that will determine how and where you'll invest, but your personality. If you're fiscally conservative, don't fight your nature! You may come out ahead of your more intrepid friends, and you'll certainly sleep easier. Remember, the tax law sets the maximum amount you can contribute to all your IRAs; the investment organizations managing the accounts set minimum contributions they're willing to accept—usually $250 to $500.

IRA Investments

An Individual Retirement Account is defined, for legal purposes, as either a trust or a custodial account maintained under a written agreement with a financial institution (e.g., a bank, brokerage firm, or insurance company). You must name an institution as a trustee, but the account can be self-directed: You can make the investment decisions.

Tax law forbids IRA investments in "collectibles" such as art, Oriental rugs, or wine. Gold and silver coins from the United States mint are considered money, not collectibles; so they're OK.

Outside of these limitations, the choice is wide. You can invest in stocks, bonds, real estate, Certificates of Deposit (CDs). You can have several accounts. You don't have to deposit the maximum amount each year; you can even skip years when you're short of money.

If your goals are convenience and safety of principal, you might prefer a bank as your trustee. Then invest in CDs and direct the bank to roll over the CDs as they come due. However, interest rates aren't very high right now, and this low-risk strategy is also low-return.

Today, with stock prices high, many people are interested in investing in stocks—inside and outside their IRAs. The easiest way to do this is to choose one or more good mutual funds as trustees ("good" meaning that the fund has been around for a while, has plenty of assets, and has compiled a good track record in both hot and tepid stock markets).

If you want more control over IRA investment, choose a brokerage firm as your trustee; instruct your broker which stocks to buy and sell. Similar strategies can be followed to invest in bonds.

Real estate is another possible IRA investment. Of course, since your maximum IRA investment is $2,000 a year ($4,000 for a two-income couple), you can't exactly buy a shopping center every year. But you can buy an interest in a shopping center, apartment building, business complex, or other form of real estate; you can participate in a limited partnership, real estate syndication, or real estate investment trust. In addition to the "normal" risks (that your investment may go down, not up, in value) there's another risk: When you're ready to retire and withdraw funds from your IRA, it may take a long time to convert your real estate investment into cash.

If you want a "one-decision" approach, consider a fixed Individual Retirement Annuity. Once you commit to buying the annuity, you have no further investment choices to make. (Of course, if the investment climate changes so that other investments are much more productive, you may regret this.) You could also pick a variable annuity that gives you a number of underlying choices. Turn to pages 270 and 274 to learn more about annuities.

Managing IRA Investments

IRA investing, like all investing, depends on matching your investment choices to your risk tolerance and the amount of time you're willing to spend analyzing investments. Most experts counsel prudence in IRA investing, saying that it's inappropriate to take big risks because the funds will mean so much to your retirement security.

But another school of thought says that IRA investors—especially young investors—should invest for aggressive growth (which, of course, means higher risks). Because IRA funds are being held for a long time, what you want is growth, not current income—and the longer you have until retirement, the more chance you have to make up for a few bad calls, and the longer you can wait for promising young companies to become successful.

The pundits also have a difference of opinion about using tax-exempt investments such as municipal bonds in an IRA. One side says that it's silly; IRAs already qualify for favorable tax treatment. The tax-exempt investments should be used to shelter non-IRA funds that would otherwise be taxed. The other side? Especially with the limits on the IRA deduction, investors must consider every prudent invest-ment—and municipal bonds are a good, safe choice for investors who don't want to take risks.

It's also important to consider transaction costs. The trustee usually charges an annual fee for its services (often in the $10 to $50 range, but it can go higher), so comparing fees is an important part of shopping for a good "home" for your IRA. Mutual funds always have a management fee; many funds have a "load," or sales charge, in addition. (More about load and no-load funds can be found on page 110.) If you buy and sell individual stocks and bonds, you'll also have brokerage commissions to pay.

It's usually a good idea to pay your IRA fees separately from your IRA contribution. Trustees' fees for setting up and managing an IRA may qualify for a deduction as investment expenses. But brokerage commissions don't fit into this category.

The worst thing you can do is write a single check for $2,000 plus the commission—you may be subject to the 6% penalty tax on excess contributions (that is, contributions made to an IRA that exceed the legal limits). The better strategy: Pay the broker directly. However, if the total of commissions plus your IRA contribution is less than $2,000, you can deduct the total, not just the IRA contribution.

IRA Timing

Nothing in the tax law compels you to make your entire IRA contribu-tion for the year all at once. Theoretically, you could contribute $40 a week—but your trustee probably imposes a minimum contribution re-quirement, such as $250. One way to handle the contribution is to add to your IRA whenever you've accumulated spare funds to equal the trustee's minimum contribution. Another way is to use a lump sum such as a bonus or tax refund. You won't even miss the money if it goes straight to your IRA.

Another timing tip: The law allows you to make a contribution for one tax year up until the due date of your tax return for that year (for virtually all taxpayers, that means April 15 of the following year). But the earlier in the year you contribute, the longer your contributions can be appreciating in value. Over ten, twenty, or thirty years, this can make a difference of thousands of dollars.

IRAs, in essence, are a kind of pension plan. So they must be maintained for the exclusive benefit of participants and their beneficiaries. That's one reason why there's a 10% penalty on premature withdrawals (withdrawals made at any time before the account holder reaches age 59½ and is not disabled). Remember, IRA funds will be available in an emergency, if the tax penalties are paid. But you should not place funds in an IRA unless you're comfortable with having the money tied up for a long time. (See page 271 for a discussion of the taxation of IRA amounts withdrawn after retirement.)

IRA funds are not completely immobile. The "rollover" rules allow you to delay taxation on certain transfers of funds into, or out of, IRAs.

IRA Rollovers

Sometimes employees get a distribution from a pension plan before retirement age. This could happen if the company goes out of business and closes down its pension plan. Sometimes IRA owners want to change their investment strategy, and move funds from one IRA to another. Without special tax provisions, they'd have to pay income tax on a huge sum of money in the year of the changeover.

Luckily for them, special tax provisions allow IRA rollovers. If you follow the rollover rules, you can move money into an IRA and leave it there until retirement age, deferring income tax on the money until you start to make withdrawals. The key is that the money must be "insulated"—kept in a special retirement account at all times—never available for everyday spending.

Rollovers from Qualified Plans

In general, if your entire interest in a pension plan is distributed to you (such as when the plan terminates), you can take the full distribution and place it into an IRA you already have or open a new one. You won't have to pay income tax until you start withdrawing from the IRA.

If you get a partial distribution from a qualified plan—that is, you get at least 50% of your pension account for reasons other than the termination of the plan (for instance, you become disabled or you stop working for the employer)—and if the distribution does not come from your own voluntary contributions to the plan for which you have already taken a tax deduction, you can roll over the partial distribution into an IRA.

Rollover treatment is not automatic, you have to write to the IRA trustee when you make the contribution, indicating that it's a rollover. And once you make a rollover, you can't change your mind and pull the money out of the IRA account until you reach retirement age.

What if you want to spend some of the money from the qualified plan? You can, but you have to pay income tax (without using the special lump-sum averaging rules discussed on page 271) on the part of the plan distribution you don't roll over.

As we'll see on pages 271 and 273, you must start taking money out of an IRA no later than age 70½. Similarly, if you get a plan distribution after age 70½, it's okay to roll the money into an IRA—but you must start withdrawals in the year of the rollover.

Don't let grass grow under your feet. To qualify for rollover treatment, you must get the plan distribution into an IRA within sixty days of the time you got the distribution. (If the distribution is made in installments, you have 60 days from receiving each installment to make the rollover.) What counts is the date you receive the distribution, not the date on the check.

If you follow complicated technical rules, you may be able to roll over pension money from one qualified plan to another qualified plan (such as from your ex-employer's plan to your new employer's plan), but get guidance first from your accountant, union representative, or the employee benefits coordinator at either company.

Rollovers from an IRA

If you get a distribution from an IRA, and if you're not subject to the requirements for minimum distributions (see page 272) and don't want to pay tax, then you can delay taxation by rolling the distribution over into another IRA.

You can roll over the entire distribution, or only part of it—but tax is due that year on whatever you don't roll over. Once again, you're allowed only sixty days to make the rollover. Theoretically, you can use the money in the meantime and put it back before the sixty days elapse, but that's a very chancy business. Somehow the money tends not to be there in time to replace it.

You're only allowed one IRA-to-IRA rollover, where the money is available for spending for sixty days, in every year. That is, a year must pass since your last distribution that was rolled over to an IRA. But if you just transfer IRA funds directly from one trustee to another (say, from a brokerage house to a bank CD), and never have the money in spendable form, you can make as many transfers as you like without tax consequences. There may be transfer fees or premature withdrawal penalties charged by the trustee, but you're in good shape with the IRS.

An IRA can also be used as a "conduit": You can transfer money from a qualified plan to an IRA, then to another qualified plan, a Keogh plan, or tax-sheltered annuity plan. Professional advice is a must here, too.

You can use IRAs to accumulate retirement funds and to supplement your pension from your employer. But if you don't *have* an employer, much less a pension plan (because you're self-employed), or if you're in a high tax bracket and can trade current spendable income for high retirement income and lots of deductions, consider a Keogh plan.

6. Tax Planning for Employees

Some people say that you should be glad to pay lots of income tax each year because it means you're successful. They're distinctly in the minority. Most people want to deduct every single cent they're entitled to, use every single credit, and pay tax at the lowest permissible rate so they can keep as much as possible of their hard-earned cash.

So, on the assumption that you're one of the majority, here are some tips about tax planning for employees. Turn to page 250 for a longer discussion about wrestling with the problems of keeping general tax records, filing your tax return, and dealing with the IRS.

Tax Withholding

The basis of our tax system is "self-assessment": Every taxpayer has to file an annual tax return. However, our government is sensible enough to know that if it had to wait all year—and get paid only if citizens had enough cash to pay their tax bills—the deficit would be many, many times its current level. So most full-time employees are subject to "tax withholding"; the employer subtracts an amount from each paycheck designed to approximate the employee's income and Social Security taxes. The goal is to withhold just about the right amount. If too little is withheld, the taxpayer-employee has to find a lot of cash to pay the unpaid amount, and may have to file IRS Form 2210 to compute and pay a penalty tax. If too much is withheld, the taxpayer loses the use of the money for months at a time, until the overpayment is refunded.

The employer decides how much to withhold based on the Form W-4, Employee's Withholding Allowance Certificate, completed by the employee, and on official withholding tables. (There's also a short Form W-4A.) Table 2 shows the amount withheld for various salary levels and for various numbers of "withholding exemptions."

Withholding exemptions exist because taxpayers are entitled to deductions, personal exemptions, and deductions for their dependents. For instance, a married taxpayer with two children would be entitled to four exemptions: one for himself or herself, one for the spouse, one for each of the children. You can claim extra withholding exemptions if you have a lot of deductions (such as an IRA, heavy medical expenses, employee business expenses). If you claim too many, and are "underwithheld," you'll have to pay the unpaid tax when you file your tax return the following year. If you've underpaid substantially, you'll have to pay penalty taxes.

Your W-4 can indicate that your income should be free of tax withholding—usually because your income is too low to be subject to income tax. But watch out for a new rule: Because of the Tax Code of 1986, taxpayers who can be claimed as dependents on another taxpayer's

TABLE 2. WITHHOLDING TABLE

This table shows the amount that is withheld for income and Social Security taxes. The first column gives weekly salaries; the figures 0,1,2,3, and 4 refer to the number of withholding exemptions claimed. "S" figures are for single people; "M" figures are for married people filing joint returns. (If you are paid by the month, every two weeks, or twice a month, withholding figures will be different.)

	0		1		2		3		4	
	S	M	S	M	S	M	S	M	S	M
$ 300	$ 43	$ 38	37	33	32	27	26	22	22	16
$ 350	$ 53	$ 46	45	40	39	35	34	29	28	24
$ 400	$ 67	$ 53	56	48	47	42	41	37	36	31
$ 450	$ 81	$ 61	70	55	60	50	50	44	43	39
$ 500	$ 95	$ 68	84	63	74	57	64	52	54	46
$ 550	$ 110	$ 76	98	70	88	65	78	59	68	54
$ 600	$ 128	$ 87	115	78	102	72	92	67	82	61
$ 650	$ 145	$ 101	132	91	120	81	107	74	96	69
$ 700	$ 163	$ 115	150	105	137	95	124	84	112	76
$ 750	$ 180	$ 129	167	119	155	109	142	98	129	88
$ 800	$ 198	$ 143	185	133	172	123	159	112	147	102
$ 850	$ 215	$ 157	202	147	190	137	177	126	164	116
$ 900	$ 233	$ 171	220	161	207	151	194	140	182	130
$ 950	$ 250	$ 189	237	136	225	165	212	154	199	144

return are not entitled to escape withholding if they have $500 or more in investment income. This would be true of a high school or college student who works part-time or summers, is dependent on his or her parents, and has a bank account or owns some stock.

Why would anybody claim zero withholding allowances? Some tax-payers have a lot of income that is not subject to withholding, such as self-employment income from moonlighting, interest on bank accounts, or stock dividends. By reducing their withholding allowances, they avoid or reduce underwithholding. If you're in this situation, and have enough extra income, you may have to make quarterly payments of estimated tax to avoid underpayment and tax penalties.

Employee Business Expenses

Whether you're a travelling salesperson or an educator, a mechanic or a computer designer, you're likely to spend some money each year on "employee business expenses"—the costs of doing your job. Some of these expenses (like daily commuting to work, buying and maintaining a business wardrobe) are not deductible because they're considered ordinary expenses of daily life.

Other expenses are not deductible because your employer has reimbursed you for whatever you spent. In fact, check with your tax adviser, if you're reimbursed more than you spent, you may have to include excess reimbursement in your taxable income, or report the reimbursements in income, and then deduct the amount you spent.

Employee business deductions for which you may qualify include:

- Expenses of moving yourself, family, and possessions to take up your first job, or a new job that would add 35 or more miles to your present commute.
- Expenses of using your car in business. Two ways of figuring the deduction are permitted: actual cost (such as gas, oil, parking, tolls, and depreciation on the car) and a standard mileage allowance. If you qualify for both, work out the numbers to decide which yields a larger tax deduction.
- Expenses of business trips away from home and expenses from feeding and entertaining business contacts and clients. The 1986 tax bill tightened up the rules here (limiting the deduction to 80% of the amount spent; denying a deduction in some previously deductible situations), so be sure you understand the new rules before claiming a deduction.
- Expenses of buying and maintaining a home computer for business use. This can be a very tough deduction to nail down; you must be able to prove that your employer made you get the computer, not just that it was useful for career advancement. You'll have to reduce the deduction (perhaps eliminate it altogether) if the computer gets personal as well as business use.
- Union dues and dues for professional associations.

Many of these deductions (but not moving expenses) are considered miscellaneous itemized deductions. That is, you can't take the deduction at all unless you itemize your deductions and your itemized deductions are larger than the standard deduction.

That's the first hoop you have to jump through. The second hoop is the "2% floor" requirement. You can only deduct those miscellaneous itemized deductions (employee business deductions plus other miscellaneous deductions) that are greater than 2% of your adjusted gross income.

Keeping Records

You'll have to satisfy your boss—and the IRS. You'll have to maintain whatever records your employer requires to get cash advances or reimbursement. Then, if (heaven forbid!) you ever get audited on a return for which you claim employee business expenses, you must be able to prove both that you were entitled to take a deduction in the first place and that the numbers you used were accurate. The records you should keep (for personal budgeting as well as tax purposes) are pretty much a matter of common sense.

- If you're moving, record (and save back-up receipts) the cost of the move itself: payments to a moving company; rental fees for a truck;

expenses of looking for a new house; expenses of home sale and purchase; temporary living expenses for a motel room and restaurant meals. Be prepared to prove that you took the most direct route to your new home (your vacation is not tax-deductible!).

•For automobile use, you must show how much of the car's use was business in nature, how much was personal; you must keep records of your business mileage (including where you started out, and where you went on each trip). If you're deducting actual costs, you must keep track of gas and oil costs, repairs, auto insurance, and depreciation.

•For business trips away from home, you must be able to give departure and return dates for each trip, your destination and business purpose, and the costs (for instance, plane fare and hotel bills).

•For business meals, you must be able to prove whom it was you entertained, the nature of your business relationship with this person, where you went, and how much you spent.

Any stationery store will have an assortment of business diaries, calendars, and special notebooks for keeping these records. Check with your tax adviser, or read free IRS publications and tax form instructions, to choose the ones that best fit your needs.

7. Coping with Career Change

If you're making a major job change, you deserve either congratulations or commiseration. Maybe you've put in many nights burning the midnight oil to get a degree that qualifies you for a totally new job. Maybe you have a new idea and will be launching your own business; maybe you're taking a chance on a smashing opportunity.

That's the positive side of career change. The negative side is that your employer is reducing force because of a business slowdown. Maybe you got caught in a political war, and you've been fired. Maybe you've been laid off and don't know if the plant will ever reopen; maybe your job has been transferred from Schenectady to Atlanta and you don't want to move—or you haven't been asked.

The key to making a career change (good or bad) is to find a way to land on your feet in a better job—and to make sure your family is protected in the meantime.

What to Do until the Pink Slip Comes

Sometimes an employee is surprised and shocked to be fired or given notice. But usually the employee knows ahead of time that the storm clouds are gathering overhead. An employee may also suspect that he or she is a victim of discrimination.

If you're in this unenviable position, you must start looking for another job (in case your suspicions are proved correct)—demonstrating the importance of keeping your résumé up to date. Use all your connections—networking and belonging to professional organizations can be invaluable here.

If you think that you were fired as a result of discrimination, not a legitimate business decision by your employer, you must also make sure you don't accidentally do something that will make your position more difficult if you want to file a claim of discrimination. This is the time to (tactfully) start looking for evidence to prove your discrimination claim.

For instance, you might find out that a pattern exists: maybe black managers are always fired a few rungs up the ladder; maybe every woman who has ever held a particular job has been denied promotions because of an unspoken assumption that women are unwilling to undertake extensive business travel. Other employees might also have been subjected to sexual harassment.

If there's any chance you *might* have a legally enforceable claim of "wrongful discharge" (firing for discriminatory or other illegal reasons), run, don't walk to an experienced labor or civil rights lawyer. (Your union or a civil rights organization may know good lawyers in your area; maybe law school professors who teach related courses handle such cases or can refer you to someone who will.)

No, I'm not just drumming up business for my colleagues. There are many technicalities involved in bringing a discrimination case. It may be necessary to go to state administrative agencies, the federal Equal Employment Opportunities Commission, state court, federal court, or all of them. You may have a case against the company that employed you, your immediate supervisor, his or her supervisor, or all of them.

Most important of all, you may lose all your legal rights if you miss certain deadlines (some of them quite short). Or, you might make a decision without knowing how or why that decision prevents you from exercising other remedies. So take the time and spend the money to find out what your legal rights are, how to enforce them, and what evidence you must produce to prove your case.

If your employer has a formal program of performance appraisals, the appraisals can be very useful in proving your case. Supervisors hate to disappoint anyone or make anyone angry, and they like to think of themselves as great leaders, so they tend to rate everyone as "satisfactory," "outstanding," or "excellent." This helps you if you are fired for alleged incompetence after a series of appraisals lauding you as a terrific worker.

After the Ax

Even if there's nothing illegal about your layoff or discharge, and even after you've been told to clear out your desk, you still have negotiating power. For one thing, companies are very aware of the possibility of lawsuits (and even winning a lawsuit takes a long time and costs a lot of money). Negotiate for the best deal possible on:

• How long you can stay on the payroll; whether you can get a lump-sum payment instead of severance pay. It may be an advantage to stay around, if you can use your desk and telephone, plus secretarial assistance, as a base for hunting for another job.

• Whether you can "cash out" holiday, vacation, and sick days you haven't used.

• How long medical insurance will be continued for you and your family.

• Whether other benefits will continue during the severance period. Disability coverage, for instance, probably stops as soon as you cease to be actively employed.

• Whether the company has adopted "golden parachutes" to scare off potential corporate raiders. Usually these very generous benefits to ex-employees are limited to top executives, but sometimes they're available to everybody.

• Whether the company will invest in outplacement services. You may be entitled to anything from a lecture about résumé preparation and dressing for success to months of all-out efforts by an employment agency to land you another job.

• How the employer will describe your tenure there and the circumstances under which you left. You may be able to negotiate a neutral, or even a favorable, recommendation or get a promise that nothing will be stated other than your dates of employment and salary history. Employers are very afraid of being sued for defamation!

The more savvy your soon-to-be ex-employer is, the more likely it is that you will be asked to sign a "release" before you leave, giving up the right to sue the employer because of your discharge. Don't sign *anything* until a lawyer with relevant experience has reviewed it! Otherwise, you could discover that you've given up valuable rights in exchange for almost nothing.

One difficult question is whether it's better, in the practical sense, to quit a job that hasn't worked out, or wait to be fired. Many people feel that quitting looks better, and is less of an impediment when you apply for future jobs. However, if you quit your job, you will not be entitled to unemployment compensation, and it will be much more difficult to prove a case of discrimination or sexual harassment. Difficult, although not impossible to prove is "constructive discharge." Constructive discharge is a legal doctrine which says that an employee has *really* been fired if he or she quits a job after treatment so intolerable that no reasonable person would be able to stand it.

Once you land a new job, think seriously about asking for a written employment contract, which guarantees that you will not be fired except for good cause, and which provides "golden handcuffs" (incentives in money, benefits, and stock options to induce you to keep your job). The best time to negotiate is right after you've landed the job, when your new employer is still enthusiastic. Later on, unless your performance has been not just stellar but "super-nova-ish," you're more likely to be taken for granted.

If You're Fired, Can You Win a Lawsuit?

Employees who have employment contracts (usually either union members or top executives who have unusual bargaining power because they've been wooed by the company) can't be fired except under the terms of the contract. That usually means that the business must have good cause and must give the employee some kind of hearing before firing him or her.

Employees without employment contracts (the majority of workers) are called "at-will" employees because the theory is that they keep or lose their jobs at the will of the employer. As a result of gradual changes in the law, it's still true that an employer can fire an at-will employee for no reason whatsoever. But an employer can't fire an employee for a *bad* reason, a reason which violates law or public policy. Bad reasons include:

- The employee's race, sex, nationality, or religion (such discrimination violates a federal law called Title VII, and most states have similar laws). Discrimination against pregnant women is illegal under federal and many state laws, and many states forbid discrimination based on any person's marital status (single, married, divorced, or widowed).
- Sexual harassment. It's illegal to fire an employee (or take any other negative job action) because he or she refuses to submit to sexual advances from a supervisor (or stops submitting to such sexual advances). Some employees have won sexual harassment cases based on the actions of co-workers or customers of the business where they work. Illegal sexual harassment also includes the creation of a hostile or offensive work environment.
- The employee's age, as long as he or she is still capable of working efficiently without endangering his or her own, or anyone else's, safety.
- A physical or mental handicap that does not prevent the employee from doing his or her job, once reasonable modifications have been made in the work environment. (Federal antidiscrimination law about handicaps only applies to federal contractors, but many states have laws of this type.)
- The employee's refusal to do something illegal; for example, employees may refuse to dump toxic waste illegally.
- The employee's insistence on performing a legal obligation— serving on a jury or answering questions about the employer under a subpoena, for instance.
- "Whistle blowing," which is informing government agencies or the press about the employer's wrongful acts. This is a controversial area,

and whistle blowers are not always protected. So check your remedies before you speak.

• Violation of an implied contract. The employer may issue an employee manual that says no one will be fired without good cause and without being placed on probation first. Some courts hold that this statement is equivalent to a written contract and, therefore, employees have a legal right to rely on it. Other courts disagree, and employers are increasingly likely to protect themselves, either by refusing to make statements at all or by asking newly hired employees to sign a statement whereby they understand they can be fired without cause or notice.

• Violation of "promissory estoppel." Some courts will find that a contract has been created if the employee takes some risk or gives something up based on the employer's promise. For instance, an employee who relocates based on an offer of a permanent job may be able to sue if he or she is fired without good cause. Again, it depends on the court.

Maintaining Benefits

Okay, you're on the bricks—for whatever reason—or you're about to start a new job, and you haven't worked there long enough to join the health plan. What can you do to preserve health insurance and other benefits to protect your family?

As discussed on page 22, you may be entitled to buy continuation coverage from your employer's health plan, for up to eighteen months. The cost is equal to, or slightly more than, the premium the employer pays for the policy. However, that could add up to $1,500 a year (or even more).

If you can't afford that, you should be able to buy a conversion policy from the insurer that handles your employer's health plan. For somewhere between $500 and $700 a year, you should be able to buy an individual health insurance policy covering yourself and your family, without taking a health examination. The catch is that conversion policies usually cover fewer procedures and provide less reimbursement than group policies. Most group life insurance policies provided by the employer can also be converted inexpensively to individual insurance.

There's yet another alternative: You may be able to buy a group health insurance policy because you belong to a group that is not employment-related. For instance, if you belong to a professional association (a bar association, an association of filmmakers, a trade association), you will probably get dozens of offers in the mail suggesting that you buy these policies. This could be the time to take them up on the offer.

Your spouse's employer may also offer adequate coverage for the family—or it may be possible to buy coverage for a spouse and dependents at a reasonable price.

Adapting Your Career Plan

For whatever reason, the job you're leaving didn't work out. Analyze why it didn't. Was it a matter of personalities? A pleasant place to work that didn't offer enough challenges, learning experiences—or money? Were you using your job skills in an industry that's "fading into the sunset" rather than one that's prospering and growing? Can you learn new skills that are in continuing demand? You *will* find a new job; make sure it fits your long-range plan.

8. Financial Strategies for One-Career and Two-Career Couples

Some things about family life are constant. Whether both spouses work, or only one works, the family is going to need to keep a roof over its head, have meals cooked, laundry done, checks made out to pay the phone bill.

However, there are some dramatic variations in the way one- and two-career couples handle these necessities. All the members of the family tend to assume a role in taking care of these needs. Or, if everyone's too tired from school and work, the family ends up spending a lot more money on take-out food, going to restaurants, having the laundry done at the laundromat, and hiring someone to clean the house.

So which family is better off? Usually, two-income families end up ahead, even after the expenses of two spouses at work (business suits, commuter tickets, or an extra car) and the extra household expenses are considered. Even if the financial gain is small, it may be worthwhile for both spouses to keep current with developments in their career field.

However, other families hold values that call for one spouse to stay at home and raise the children. For these families, the financial problem is to make one income stretch to meet all the family's needs. It may be possible to maintain a stricter budget because the homemaker can handle many tasks that would be expensive if an outsider were hired. The major saving is that the family does not have to pay for child care during the working hours.

Dealing with Day-Care Costs

There are many legal and practical issues affecting parents who have paid jobs:

- Whether women can get paid or unpaid medical leave for complications of pregnancy, delivery of the baby, and the period of recovery after the baby is born. It's clearly illegal to fire an employee who can do her job just because she's pregnant. The problems start when a woman wants to leave her job, or is medically unable to keep working. The Retirement Equity Act of 1984 also protects women's pension credits earned before they take time off to have a baby.

• Whether an employer has to reinstate an employee who left work to have a baby.

• Whether either or both parents can get "parenting leave" (paid or unpaid) to take care of a newly born or adopted child.

• Whether parents of older children can get help with day-care— perhaps referrals to good day-care centers or flexible working hours so that children can be dropped off and picked up at school or the day-care center. Maybe the employer will pick up part of the cost of day-care under its employee benefits program. Maybe—although this is rare—the employer will even provide a day-care center on the premises. (In 1986, there were only 50 to 150 on-site day-care centers in the United States, depending on which survey you read. Approximately 2,500 companies, most of them large, provided day-care assistance of some kind.)

Employers can provide child-care assistance as part of an employee benefits plan. Child-care assistance from a qualified benefits plan does not generate taxable income for the employee—as long as the assistance does not exceed $5,000 for a married taxpayer, filing a joint return, or $2,500 for a married taxpayer, filing a separate return. What if the employer sets up a child-care center on the premises and lets the employees use it instead of giving the employees cash to use for day care? The general rule is that what matters is the value of the services provided to the employees—the same dollar limitations apply.

A growing need is assistance for parents whose children are sick. Companies recognize that parents who must take care of a child with the sniffles or chicken pox must either take time off from work or become less productive because they're worrying, calling home to check, or leaving early. Many companies are meeting this need for assistance by subsidizing special day-care centers for sick children, contributing to units in local hospitals for children's minor illnesses, or rebating part of what parents spend for special day-care in this situation.

Rights of Pregnant Employees

The Pregnancy Discrimination Amendment (PDA) (part of Title VII, the general federal law forbidding discrimination in employment) makes it illegal to discriminate against a woman *because* she is pregnant. If the woman can do her job, she must be treated just like all other healthy employees. And if she suffers a disability caused by pregnancy— a complication that makes her unable to continue her normal work— the employer must treat disability caused by pregnancy the same way as any disability that is not occupationally related. So, if paid medical leave is available for employees who suffer a bout with cancer or heart disease, it must be available for employees disabled by pregnancy—on equally favorable terms.

However, employers don't have to start a special program giving favorable treatment to pregnancy. (A common misunderstanding is that the PDA "makes pregnancy a disability"; many people object to this because pregnancy is a healthy function of the female body. But, as we've seen, the PDA deals with *disability* caused by pregnancy; it doesn't treat the fact of pregnancy itself as a disability. Indeed, it makes employers look at the individual abilities of each pregnant employee, instead of stereotyping her because she's pregnant.)

In early 1987, the U.S. Supreme Court ruled that states could (but are not obliged to) pass laws requiring employers to reinstate workers after childbirth—even if the employer doesn't do this for workers returning after other kinds of medical leave. At the time of the ruling, California, Connecticut, Massachusetts, and Montana had state laws of that type; Hawaii, Illinois, Kansas, New Hampshire, Ohio, and Washington State had similar regulations. The High Court's decision could inspire more states to add similar laws.

In another January 1987 ruling, the Supreme Court said that states do *not* have to provide unemployment benefits for employees who are not reinstated after childbirth, if unemployment benefits are not provided to workers who are denied reinstatement after other kinds of absences. Are these two rules contradictory? The Supreme Court says that its aim is to keep employers from imposing extra disadvantages on pregnant employees—but not to require special, favorable treatment for pregnant employees.

Parenting Leave

Legislators, executives, and union officials are taking a closer look at the question of parental leave. The question comes up because maternity leave covers only the medical aspects of childbirth and recovery. After the physical stress of childbirth has been recovered from, many women want to spend time with their newly born children. (Some men also want the option of time off from work for parenting.)

An employee in this situation who quits the job outright will lose salary and employer-provided benefits. Maybe the worker will lose pension credits already earned before the birth of the baby. If and when he or she wants to go back to work, the employee will have no guarantee of being re-employed by the old employer (unless the state has a law of the type upheld by the Supreme Court, and unless the employee fits into the rules set by the law).

From the employee's point of view, it's simple: The employee prefers to take a leave of absence, with seniority intact, and with the job held open until the employee is ready to return to the office or factory. But for the employer, it's not so simple. For one thing, who's minding the store while the parent-employee is minding the baby? For another thing, isn't it unfair to the substitute employee, who takes over during the parental leave, to be pushed aside when the original job-holder returns?

A 1986 survey by Catalyst (an organization concerned with careers and employee benefits) shows that employers were receptive to granting a short paid disability leave for childbirth, followed by three to six months' unpaid leave for mothers, two weeks' unpaid leave for fathers, and were also receptive to part-time work or flexible hours for new parents.

9. REAL LIFE: JOHN AND SANDY WILDER

Sandy hung up the phone, fuming. It was Craig's teacher, asking her to help shepherd twenty-nine kids around the science museum for a class trip. "After all, you don't work." As if it wasn't work, taking care of a house and two kids; as if it wasn't work, mending and sewing all her own clothes just to save a few dollars. As if it wasn't work, cooking a slow-simmered old-fashioned beef stew because chuck was on special this week and home cooking is cheaper than frozen food or something from the gourmet shop.

And as if it didn't take as much skill to manage all that as John showed in his job as personnel manager for a pharmaceutical company. Well, Sandy figured that there'd always be fools in the world. She looked at the kitchen clock: Almost time for the first wave of the invasion. Scotty first, tired and muddy from football. Then Mitchell, coming home from band practice, dragging his cornet case as well as a battered leather briefcase full of homework, computer magazines, and band scores.

John wouldn't be home until much later—tonight was one of the two nights a week he spent in graduate school, working toward an MBA. The company paid for part of that, but the Wilders still had to pay $1,000 a year. They considered it an investment in his career. And then there was Scotty's tuition at St. Anne's. He hadn't done well in public school, and it was (ouch!) worth the $3,000 a year that parochial school cost.

The Numbers

John's salary isn't bad at all: $43,000. In fact, it's so far from being bad that the Wilders pay $9,500 a year in income tax, although they're far from thinking of themselves as the idle rich.

However, they do have some investments—about $10,000 worth—that yield about $1,000 a year. And they have $52,000 of equity in their house—so much that they can keep mortgage, property tax, and homeowner's insurance down to less than $500 a month ($5,300 annually). So they're pretty well off even after they make payments on the car loan and the credit cards (say, $2,000 a year), put food on the table, clothes on their backs (and a cornet in Mitchell's mouth) for about $13,000 a year, and spend a couple of hundred dollars a month on sundries. Their expenses add up to $38,200 a year, and there's $44,000 coming in. What can be done with about $10,000 a year to beef up income, make sure that tuition checks will continue to be paid, and provide security for the family? Quite a bit.

The Answers

John has already shown some flair for investments. He very much enjoys reading the financial press and exploring trends in the economy, and he's a fairly active trader even though he doesn't have the world's largest stock portfolio. So he finds it important to cut down on the commission rates he must pay when he buys and sells stock. Sometimes he likes to "sit out" a market that he thinks is unstable.

Therefore, a cash management account is an important priority for John Wilder. The account allows him to get discount brokerage rates; it also gives him access to safe ways to "park" his cash if he doesn't want to invest. Furthermore, the account takes care of record-keeping. He doesn't have to monkey around with lots of confirmation slips and records of dividends: The account gives him a single monthly statement with everything in comprehensible form. The monthly statements come in very handy every April (John always prepares the family's tax form).

Well, that's the fun and glamorous part. John and Sandy know that a financial plan for a one-income family requires plenty of life insurance. They've decided to get whole-life (rather than term) insurance because of the possibility of policy loans to pay for financial emergencies that might arise. However, they prefer a "conventional" whole-life policy because, as an active investor, John thinks he can get better returns from his other investments than he could get from a universal-life, variable-life, or single-premium whole-life policy.

They also think that an IRA is *still* a good deal, even though their deduction is so small. (They maintain a spousal IRA, making the permitted contribution of $250 a year for Sandy.) So they fund it to the maximum each year, early in the year, so there'll be more time for appreciation.

Sandy takes a more conservative approach to investment. She doesn't see what John finds so fascinating about a lot of little blips on a chart; she's also distrustful about how long the bull market can continue.

She's certain it won't continue long enough to see the kids through school and the senior Wilders through retirement. So her suggestion is that they diversify, and that they supplement investments in individual stocks with a bond fund. That way, they have some additional income (and that always comes in handy)—they'll be somewhat protected if interest rates charge up again, because the yield on their fund will tend to go up, and stock prices dive down. They'll also have the benefit of the professional expertise of the portfolio managers who select the bonds. Both Wilders agree that junk bonds are in for a calamitous fall, so they've invested in a bond fund that invests only in investment-grade corporate bonds.

10. REAL LIFE: RALPH AND WENDY MOXCEY

Sometimes Ralph and Wendy Moxcey feel like they would willingly die for their children. Sometimes it feels more like they'd like to kill them. Like tonight: Ralph spent an extra twenty minutes because Exit 42 was blocked by a jackknifed tractor-trailer. But that's okay, because the meatloaf wasn't burnt when he arrived—it was still a little frozen in the middle. Looks like the microwave's on the blink. Now the french fries—*they* were burnt. Indigestion city.

Ralph and Wendy didn't have time to talk about finances this morning. Ralph, Jr. (he says his name is Rambo, but that doesn't get him too far) couldn't find his gym sneakers. Todd got out the door, came back saying he needed $3.50 as his share of the videocassette for the class project, and missed the school bus. And tonight, when Ralph is trying to have a civilized conversation with Wendy about important financial topics, the kids are giggling up a storm. Isn't it amazing that kids are still into knock-knock jokes? And isn't it amazing how hard it is to talk—or think—or do anything—with wheezing, snorting, and yucking in the background?

The Numbers

Ralph earns $28,000 a year as a drafter for a firm that does architectural blueprints; Wendy's $21,000 salary comes from the local board of education, where she works as an assistant manager of facilities. If there's a broken window in your school, call Wendy Moxcey. If it's possible to get it fixed within the confines of the bureaucracy, she'll get it done for you.

That adds up to almost $50,000 a year, but it goes fast. Their house—fondly referred to as the "elephant" (as in white elephant) is huge, classic, and drafty. Paying the mortgage, insuring it, and paying property tax drains off the first $16,500—in other words, almost as much as all their other living expenses put together. *Those* add up to $17,000, and it's only possible to keep them down that low because Wendy is a fanatical shopper who can get everything at a discount—and because Ralph will happily spend three hours tuning the car to improve gas mileage, and happily spend three minutes prowling the house in search of lights left burning. And let's not forget income tax—almost $10,000 worth of that ($9,800).

At that rate, they probably won't get kicked out of the elephant and into the poorhouse anytime soon. They have about $6,600 left over every year. That money has to be enough to build up a cushion for emergencies (funny, the mechanic didn't take American Express—or VISA—or MasterCard—or a check—or anything except good American cash when the car broke down in that picturesque town on the way back from Thanksgiving dinner at Grandma Rogan's). It also has to be enough to build a college fund. And the Moxceys are no spring chickens—in fifteen years, they'll be able to retire and start drawing on IRA funds, assuming, of course, that there are some IRA funds available.

Speaking of Thanksgiving, of course they're grateful for everything they have. But they'd also like more income. It would be great to say an automatic "Yes" instead of an automatic "No" (infrequently upgraded to "Maybe") when the boys eagerly describe something else "really neat-o" (isn't it amazing that kids still talk that way?) that they can get at the Mall for *only* $50.95—plus tax.

The Answers

Because both parents are working breadwinners, both need life insurance protection and disability insurance to replace their income. The Moxcey's choice was universal-life insurance. Unlike term insurance, universal-life provides cash value and investment appreciation. But it's far from wild speculation: They know that insurance funds will be available in case anything happens to one of them. They particularly like universal-life because they can tailor it to particular needs. They can cut back on premium payments if their policy is doing particularly well, or if there's been an unusually cataclysmic utility bill. They can also expand their coverage—as they plan to do when the kids reach college age.

This year, they're taking a first cautious step into the stock market. No, they're not buying shares of individual stocks. They don't have the temperament for that, and they don't think they can earn enough with the amount they can afford to invest to make the extra risk worthwhile. Instead, they've done some research and selected a growth-and-income mutual fund that has compiled an excellent track record in the eight years it's been doing business. Now, they're having dividends paid to them in cash—a little extra money that can buy some little luxuries. Maybe later on they'll switch and have the dividends paid in the form of extra shares of stock in the mutual fund.

Or, maybe they'll add another mutual fund to their portfolio, or switch from a growth-and-income fund to a more aggressive growth fund, or an even safer fund that invests only in government securities. One thing is certain: With two demanding jobs and two demanding youngsters, the Moxceys aren't willing to spend hours every day monitoring (and then worrying about) investments. They've picked a safe choice that they can hold onto for awhile, and that doesn't take a constant stream of new decisions.

11. How to Secede in Business

People who start businesses often cluster at two extremes: those who are glorious successes in the conventional working world and those who are abject failures. Sometimes people want their own businesses because they already have a directory full of prospective clients and a network of helping hands; sometimes, because they can't get along with anybody and have been fired so often they're gun-shy about working for anybody else.

Most new businesses fail; the conventional estimate is that 80% to 90% go under within five years. You've read about some of the exceptions, the success stories who have created brilliant new products or found a startlingly profitable way to handle an old idea.

But there are many other success stories: People who never make much money, but who manage to scrape by doing something they love and feeling a real sense of accomplishment. I'd be surprised if anyone reading this book will ever become a multimillionaire by starting a business—but I'm sure that many of you readers can earn a decent living doing something you enjoy. I'm also sure that sooner or later some of you will take the first step toward starting your own business.

Get Your Feet Wet

Probably the worst way to start a business is to quit your job, borrow up to your ears, and exhaust your savings in a thrilling burst of enthusiasm. Unless the business takes off like a rocket, you'll be left with no job, no money, a bushel of bills, and a ruined credit rating.

One of the best ways to start a business is to start out as a moonlighter. If you'd like to open your own design studio, see if you can get a few clients for whom you can work on evenings and weekends. (If you work for an established studio, there can be tricky issues of client-stealing, unless it's clear that there's no overlap.) If you want to go into the antique business, spend a few weekends selling attic treasures at a flea market. Even if the business you want calls for a full-time commitment, it might be worth finding a low-capital mail-order business you can operate from your home.

In any of these cases, the purpose is risk a small amount of money (and, with luck, to make some) and find out if you really *like* owning a business and if you're good at budgeting, bookkeeping, accounting, paying bills, and making sure you get paid for your goods and services. Some people are creative, brilliant, hard-working, and *terrible* at running businesses. Others are just as brilliant at business as at creative tasks, but find that they resent the time spent away from the drawing board or the laboratory.

Basic Business Questions

To have any hope at all of surviving, you must understand every detail about running the kind of business you want: its business cycle (the seasons at which money comes in—and goes out), the best suppliers, the best ways to find customers and meet their needs, ways to cut costs without sacrificing quality. But there are some fundamental questions that apply to all businesses (arranged in order of importance, not in chronological order).

- What is the maximum feasible level of business you think you can achieve? If you achieve it, will your salary and profits be enough to support yourself/your family and also give you a reasonable return on the money you invest in the business?
- How much will it cost to run the business when it's in full operation (rent, staff salaries, phone and electric bill, merchandise you order for resale or use in your business)?
- How long will it take for the business to become profitable? How will you support yourself/your family during the time between the business start-up and the time profits start to come in (savings; spouse's salary; part-time work)?
- How much will it cost to get the business started—from the legal and accounting advice you'll need to buying your initial stock to advertising or otherwise attracting customers?
- Where will you raise the funds—start-up funds, funds for continuing operations (savings; borrowing from banks, relatives, investors; forming a corporation and selling stock)? How will you divide the eventual profits?
- What kind of marketing plan do you have? What are the immediate costs of publicizing your business? How much will those newspaper ads or flyers cost you every month?

Legal and Tax Factors

That brings us neatly to the question of how your business should be organized.

• A sole proprietorship means that you are the sole owner. You take all the risks, but you can keep all the profits. If you want a retirement plan, you can have a Keogh and/or IRA.

• A partnership means that you join forces with other partners. You all share the risks and divide profits—but watch out: Your personal assets can be dragooned to pay partnership debts. Again, the retirement possibilities are IRA and Keogh.

• A corporation means that the stockholders own the corporation. The major advantage of the corporation is "limited liability"—stockholders, including the management of the corporation, can't lose more than their investment in the corporation's stock. Their personal assets can't be seized no matter how deep the corporation is in debt.

The tax code lets you set up a special kind of corporation called a Subchapter S corporation. As long as you meet the Sub S requirements (for instance, you can't have more than thirty-five stockholders, although a married couple counts as a single stockholder), you get the benefits of limited liability plus certain tax benefits.

If the corporation is losing money, you get tax deductions on your personal tax return. The flip side is that you must also pay personal income tax on your share of the corporation's profits—even if you haven't received the profits in the form of dividends. Many businesses deal with this problem by starting out as Sub S corporations, then converting to regular (Subchapter C) corporations when the profits start to roll in.

Of course, you can have an IRA if you're a corporate stockholder/employee, but you can't have a Keogh plan; you'll have to set up a qualified pension plan if you want to save for retirement.

Another great advantage of corporations is that you can sell stock to investors, but make sure you follow the maze of state and federal securities laws before you get the first stock certificate printed, much less accept the first dollar from a would-be stockholder.

Tax Advice

It pays to consult a lawyer and an accountant before you start your business. Find out what your obligations are about sales tax, whether you'll have to pay an unincorporated business tax (for proprietorships and partnerships), franchise and/or corporate income tax (for corporations) on the local or state level, and how to handle your personal income taxes and any federal corporate income tax. Also find out how to set up your records.

If you have employees, you'll have to collect W-4 forms from them to find out if you must withhold tax from their earnings; if so, you'll have to handle the withholding, pay some Social Security tax for the employees, and file employment tax returns and make deposits of taxes on a complicated schedule.

Owning a business gives you a lot of control over your income (you can decide how much should be received at once, how much should be deferred; you can decide how much of your compensation should be in the form of salary, how much in profits). You can also make a lot of decisions about tax planning and estate planning, but you'll probably make better decisions with professional help.

Business Insurance

Your business location (office, home office, store), like a home, needs basic insurance protection (fire insurance, insurance on the contents against water damage, theft, etc.). There are also special kinds of insurance tailored to businesses.

- Plate-glass insurance.
- Business interruption insurance that provides substitute income if your business is closed down—say, by a flood that damages your store, if you sell concert T-shirts and the concert is cancelled, or similar situations.
- Key-man insurance is life or disability insurance payable to the business if the business founder or other key executive dies or becomes disabled.

An insurance agent who specializes in business coverage can advise you; your regular agent can probably recommend a colleague with this expertise.

Learning More about Business

Many people (including me, as it happens) have written books about starting a business. Just be sure that the books you read are appropriate for your level of funding (if the book starts out, "First borrow $10 million," you know it's not for you) and your level of sophistication and business knowledge (it won't help to read an explanation of simple bookkeeping, in two-syllable words, if you've been handling a major corporation's financial analysis for 10 years).

Don't forget business magazines (from general-interest magazines such as *Business Week* to specialized publications for startup businesses such as *Inc.* and *Venture*) and articles about business startups in financial and personal-finance magazines (like *Money* and *Sylvia Porter's Personal Finance Magazine*). Think about taking adult education courses at local colleges, informal "learning exchanges," or courses offered by the federal Small Business Administration, local government, or organizations for woman and minority business owners. Even if you have the time (and money) to get an MBA, most MBA programs are aimed at training specialists for huge corporations, so you probably won't learn much that'll help you start a business from the ground up.

However, a few college- or graduate-level courses in accounting, finance, and management can help a lot.

A successful business needs a team of experts: lawyer, accountant, insurance agent, perhaps a business or marketing consultant. One purpose of a partnership or incorporating a new business is to raise money for the business—another purpose is to find co-workers whose skills complement your own.

For many people, starting a business of their own is only a distant dream. A few try it and find it turns into a nightmare. But many people find that owning a business enhances both bank balance and the quality of life.

12. REAL LIFE: KEVIN AND KATHLEEN DRISCOLL

It's a university town, full of cultivated people—anyway, people who think they're cultivated. Most of the movie theaters in town show the usual kiss, kiss–bang, bang Hollywood trash. There's a small "cinema" that shows more artistic films, many of them made in other countries. They've managed to keep the doors open, barely.

There are five videocassette rental stores in town. Half the tapes you can rent are porno, the other half are car-chase and kung fu movies. Kevin thinks that there's a market for better movies on videocassette—the Hollywood classics, of course; French, Italian, even Russian films; and the exciting work that today's filmmakers are doing directly on videotape. Now, if Kevin could open a rental store that specializes in these hard-to-find, exciting films. . . and if he's right that there are enough people willing to pay to rent great films instead of *Halloween Part 119,* then he'll have a successful business.

If he's wrong, he'll have spent a year or two without earning a salary, spending most of the family's savings in the process. Then he'll have to go out and find another job, and work hard to replace the lost money. Well, they won't starve—Kathleen is a well-respected copywriter in an ad agency—but if it's a miscalculation, then it'll take many years to make up for it.

The Numbers

Together, when they're both working, Kevin and Kathleen Driscoll earn $65,000 a year—a bountiful harvest that subjects them to $16,000 a year in income taxes. That's their second biggest expense—living costs for the family of three (Kevin, Jr., is 9) are $23,000 a year. Bringing up the rear are mortgage payments, property taxes, and homeowner's insurance at $12,000 a year. So right now, they're spending $51,000 of their $65,000 income. That gives them $14,000 a year to save, provide insurance coverage, make long-range plans for the family, and get ready for their own retirement.

That money, plus their existing assets ($48,000 in home equity; $15,000 saved) must be the source of the start-up capital for Kevin's business. Although he'll try to get bank loans or attract the interest of other investors, he knows that most of the capital must come from the Driscoll family.

The Answers

Kathleen and Kevin are going to need some expert advice; neither is sophisticated enough to juggle with all the tax ramifications, insurance needs, and investment decisions they have to make. They choose a financial representative (see p. 119), and he works out a capital needs analysis.

The first priority is to make sure that, whether the business is a success or a failure, the family will have a continuing source of income and protection. The fact that theirs is a two-income family gives the Driscolls a "cushion." If they work hard on cutting back expenses, they can live on Kathleen's income, perhaps drawing a little on savings.

Neither Kevin nor Kathleen is a participant in a qualified plan, so both are entitled to the full IRA deduction. Because they don't have a company pension on which to depend, they're careful to make the maximum IRA contribution each year, and to spend a few hours considering the best way to invest the IRA funds.

Both Kevin and Kathleen have life insurance policies, with a face value of seven years' income. They chose variable-life insurance because they think it offers the best balance between safe investment return and insurance protection. Again, they're willing to spend the time it takes to compare the risks and returns of the various options offered under the variable policies, and they do switch from option to option if economic conditions change.

They are also mutual fund investors, with shares in two different stock funds (diversified, in case one portfolio manager has insights much better than another) and in a high-income, "junk bond" fund.

Kevin isn't ready, yet, to burn his bridges and open the cassette rental store. First, he has to do a lot more research: market research, on how high a rental he can charge, and what volume of business he can expect; research into ways of publicizing the business, what he can expect to spend for rent, how much stock he'll need to begin business, and how often he'll have to buy new cassettes to restock the store. He'll need tax and accounting advice. But the home equity is an important resource and can be tapped quickly for a loan. The Driscolls can use some of their savings (it would be imprudent to use up all of them). Kevin isn't an impulsive man; he won't make a move until he has a good reason to believe that the new business will be a success.

13. Financial Strategies for the Surviving Family

A complete financial plan must be flexible, and must be able to cope with the possibility that death can come at any age—when the children are still young, and the family short of assets, or after many years of asset-building, when the children have grown and founded families of their own.

This section focuses on one of the major strategies for the surviving family: using life insurance to provide funds for the survivors.

Life Insurance

There are two reasons to include life insurance in your financial plan: protection and investment. The second is optional; the first is not. As long as you have adequate protection for your family, or enough to settle your obligations if you have no dependents, you can do without investment-oriented insurance if other investments are better for your strategy. But you wouldn't build a house without door locks just because you couldn't find—or couldn't afford—the particularly beautiful bits of brass that took your fancy. You'd make sure that the door locked tight and protected your home.

How Much Insurance?

The purpose of insurance is to replace a person's income after his or her untimely death. Therefore, one of the ways to determine your insurance needs is to figure out how much insurance you'd need to replace the amount you earn now—and what you expect to earn in the future. Of course, it's only an estimate. Be aware that even your best estimate may be too low, because inflation is likely to continue and to affect your family's buying power.

The other important factor is your family's financial needs. However, if you're always short of money, it isn't wise—or even realistic—to expect insurance to magically transport your family from just scraping by to luxury. (Apart from anything else, they'd rather have you around—a check is a poor substitute.)

The worksheet that follows gives you a way to estimate the amount of insurance to maintain. Make a copy for each spouse, and work through the calculations based on two different assumptions: that your death occurs soon, at your current level of income and expenses, and that it occurs when you're 75 and drawing on retirement income, not current salary. The purpose of life insurance is to fill the "gap" between family needs and the income available from other sources (such as Social Security survivor's benefits, investment income, pension benefits payable to the surviving spouse).

LIFE INSURANCE WORKSHEET

	Now	At Age 75
1. "Last illness" expenses: hospital bills, doctors' bills, etc., associated with the process of dying. List only the amount *not* covered by insurance.	$_____	$_____
2. Funeral expenses:	$_____	$_____
Total:	$_____	$_____

(Your survivors must have this much cash, shortly after your death, to cope with the expenses of your death. They'll also need a continuing source of income to replace your salary or pension. This income can come from receiving a lump sum from the insurance company and investing it, or from "settlement options": ways of receiving continuing income from the insurance company.)

	Now	At Age 75
3. Monthly family budget (use figures from the budgeting worksheet on page 87)—reduced slightly because there will be one fewer family member	$_____	$_____
Total income required:	$_____	$_____
4. Monthly income that is available from your spouse's assets, or assets you will leave to him or her (e.g., savings accounts, stock, investment real estate)	$_____	$_____
5. Monthly Social Security survivor's benefits available to your family:	$_____	$_____
6. Monthly survivors' benefits payable from your pension plan:	$_____	$_____
7. Your spouse's salary or pension:	$_____	$_____
8. Your children's contributions to the surviving family's finances:	$_____	$_____
Total income available without life insurance:	$_____	$_____
9. Subtract available income from income required:	$_____	$_____
10. Number of years income is required (spouse's life expectancy):	_____	_____
11. Multiply required income by 12 (to convert monthly to annual income), and by the number of years in the spouse's life expectancy:	$_____	$_____
12. Subtract amount of insurance you already have (including group-term life provided by your employer):	$_____	$_____
13. Add last illness and funeral expenses (from above):	$_____	$_____

* * *

This is approximately the amount of life insurance you should maintain. The amount is only approximate because the amount your family needs depends on the amount of interest they can earn on your insurance money. The amount of insurance required changes a lot over time: as your family's expenses get higher (a bigger house, a new baby) or lower (the mortgage gets paid off, the "baby" gets her first job), and as your resources change (if your spouse will inherit half a million dollars' worth of stocks and bonds, the need for life insurance is less crucial).

The worksheet's calculations deal only with the basic expenses of living. If you want to provide for your children's college tuition, add more coverage to provide the cost of four years' tuition. Your parents or in-laws might also become financial dependents of your family, so take their needs into account as well.

How Insurance Needs Change

The purpose of life insurance is to bridge the gap between the surviving family's income and its needs. It's hard to make the calculations because both "sides" of the gap change over time. Single people with no dependents need little if any life insurance—just enough to meet funeral expenses and pay off any debts that can't be covered by their other resources. Newly married couples need insurance to replace each other's income—especially if they own their home together.

But the real need for extensive life insurance coverage begins when a couple has children. There'll be a long time when the children must be taken care of—and many young couples find it difficult to save or accumulate assets while the children are young. If one spouse dies unexpectedly, the family is often left with limited savings and a pile of bills. Then the surviving spouse has to be the sole breadwinner as well as the sole parent.

Once the children are grown up and on their own, the need for insurance diminishes considerably. However, by that time, it's likely that the surviving spouse will be retired or close to retirement age. His or her continuing need for income must be met. In some families, the surviving spouse's own pension, plus joint-and-survivor pension benefits from the deceased spouse, IRA payouts, plus Social Security benefits and the investment income from the assets in the deceased spouse's estate provide a comfortable retirement. But in other families, the surviving spouse's comfort—or even economic survival—will depend on life insurance.

Some Insurance Vocabulary

The "death benefit" (sort of a contradiction in terms) of an insurance policy is the amount that the insurance company will pay if the insured person dies while the policy is in force (and if there are no circumstances that invalidate the policy or relieve the insurer of the obligation to pay). The death benefit is the face amount of the policy: if it's a $50,000 policy, the death benefit is $50,000.

The beneficiary is the person named by the owner of the policy to receive the death benefit. It's a good idea to name a "contingent beneficiary" who will become the beneficiary if the original beneficiary dies before the insured person.

The insured person is the one whose life is insured. Usually—but not always—the insured person owns the policy. People can also buy and own insurance on the lives of other people, but only if they have an "insurable interest" (a close personal or business relationship) in the other person. Without this requirement, it would be much too tempting for unscrupulous insurance buyers to pay a couple of premiums, then knock off the unsuspecting insured person.

On a less melodramatic note, it's also possible to buy an insurance policy on your own life, then give the policy to someone else (your spouse or child, for instance). That way, the other person can take policy loans against the policy's cash value (see page 66), use the policy as collateral for loans, or otherwise exercise the rights belonging to the owner of the policy. If you're in a high tax bracket, this can be a good tax- and estate-planning strategy; discuss it with your financial advisers.

Transferring insurance policies can also make sense in the context of a divorce. Let's say that one spouse wants the other to make sure the children will be provided for—but doesn't trust the richer spouse to do this. One solution would be for the richer spouse to buy insurance on his or her own life, then transfer the policy to the poorer spouse, who'll make sure that the policy is kept up.

Term Versus Whole-Life Insurance

Once you decide how much insurance you need, you'll have to decide what kind(s) to buy, then compare price and service to pick the insurer that offers the best choice for the coverage you need. There are two basic varieties of life insurance—term and whole life—and each is available in several variations.

Term insurance is nothing but life insurance coverage. It's similar to fire or auto insurance. Your premium pays for a year's protection. If nothing happens during that year to trigger a claim, the insurance company keeps your premium and you start all over again next year. Whole-life insurance combines "forced savings" and an investment element with life insurance coverage. That is, part of every premium you pay for whole-life insurance is invested for you by the insurance company.

This discussion starts by describing the major types of term policies that are available, then goes on to cover whole-life insurance and its newer, more investment-oriented "offspring."

Term Insurance. If you buy a term insurance policy the insurance policy will pay the specified "death benefit" if you die during the term (such as one year or five years) that the policy is in force. At the end of the term, if you want insurance, you must buy another policy—which will certainly be more expensive (because you're older and, therefore, the risk of your dying is greater), and may be unavailable, if you no longer meet the insurance company's criteria for insurability. For instance, you might have taken up a dangerous occupation or developed a chronic illness.

However, if you buy a "renewable term" policy, the insurance company agrees at the outset that you will have the right to renew the policy (whatever your health status) until you reach a certain age—usually age 65 or 70. If you buy a "five-year renewable term" policy, the premium will be the same throughout the five years (unlike other kinds of term policy, whose premiums increase each year). If you renew at the end of the five years, the premium will jump, then remain level for the next five years.

Some term policies have a "convertible" feature. That is, the company that issues the policy agrees that you can convert the policy into a whole-life policy at any time by paying the premium for the whole-life policy. If you decide to buy term insurance, try to get a convertible policy. That way, if whole-life insurance ever becomes a better deal than term, or if your health deteriorates so that term insurance would be too expensive or unavailable, you can convert the policy—without taking a medical exam.

Most term insurance policies are "level term" policies; that is, the amount of insurance remains constant throughout the term of the policy. However, you can also buy "increasing term" policies that increase by specified amounts at specified times (say, $2,000 a year for five years), or "decreasing term" policies that shrink by specified amounts. These policies can be helpful if you know your financial needs will change, if you know you'll need more insurance as your children grow or when they enter college, or if you know you'll be paying off a debt (such as a house mortgage) steadily but want to have insurance money available if you die before repayment is completed.

Whole-Life Insurance. Now we're ready to analyze whole-life insurance in conventional policies and also in newer products (universal life, variable life, single-premium whole life) that permit the policy-holder to make more investment decisions and seek higher investment return from the policy.

Except for single-premium policies (see page 68), the premiums for a whole-life insurance policy remain level as long as the policy is maintained. Once you qualify for the policy, and keep up the premiums, you will be insured throughout your life. You know how much the premium will be, and what the face value of the policy will be. The policy also develops "cash value"—a kind of savings account that increases the longer you hold the policy.

This happens *because* the premiums stay the same throughout the policy. To see how this works, imagine a group of 100 19-year-olds, a group of 100 44-year-olds, and a group of 100 85-year-olds, each of whom owns a $100,000 whole-life policy on his or her own life. Before their next birthday, some of the 19-year-olds will die; so will some (probably, a larger number) of the 44-year-olds; and so will some (probably, a whole bunch) of the 85-year-olds.

The insurance company will pay the same $100,000 to the beneficiaries of each of the policyholders who dies—no matter what age they were when they departed from this life. But the company will have to budget a lot more to make payments for 85-year-olds as a group than for 19-year-olds as a group. The company sets its premium level accordingly. The premium the younger people pay is more than it costs the insurance company to provide insurance for a person that age. The "extra" money goes into the policy's cash value.

It's equally true that the premium the older people pay is less than it costs the insurance company to provide insurance for someone of that age—but the insurance company hasn't gone into the philanthropy business. It gets to invest the premiums until it's time to pay up.

Cash Value

Two things can happen to a whole-life insurance policy: The policyholder can keep paying premiums until he or she dies or stop paying premiums. If the policyholder dies with the policy in force, the insurance company pays the face value of the policy (not the cash value) to the beneficiary chosen by the policyholder.

The cash value is important as an element in the policyholder's financial planning. He or she is entitled to get "policy loans": to borrow the cash value at low interest rates, with no application fee and few formalities. If the insured person dies when policy loans or unpaid interest are outstanding, the amount due will be subtracted from the death benefit paid to the beneficiary. Make sure you don't borrow so much that your family could be left without the life insurance protection it needs.

What if the flow of premiums stops? Whole-life policies are written so that they can be converted into smaller "paid-up" policies—the amount of insurance that could be purchased with the premiums already paid. Or, the policyholder can "surrender" the policy—give it back to the insurance company, receiving the cash value. There are two disadvantages to this: Some of the money received from the insurance company may be taxable income; also, there's no more insurance coverage under that policy, so the policyholder needs other ways to provide financial security.

Types of Whole-Life Insurance

At first there was only one type of whole-life insurance: the "plain vanilla" kind already described. However, legal and economic changes led to the development of new kinds of products. Critics charged that whole-life insurance was an uninspiring—or even downright bad—investment. More people gained the income and sophistication to take more interest in investments. New statutes, and tax-law changes, permitted some new policies to be offered, and also changed the after-tax returns that taxpayers could expect on various investments.

In this new environment, three main types of investment-oriented life insurance products have emerged: single-premium whole life, variable life, and universal life. There's also a hybrid, variable universal life, that combines features of the last two.

Variable-Life Policies.   In a variable-life policy, your premiums stay the same as long as you own the policy—but both the death benefit and the cash value vary, depending on the insurance company's success in managing its investments. The death benefit is guaranteed never to fall below the original face value of the policy. It could be much higher, depending on the state of the stock market and the insurer's and insured's investment choices.

Investment choice (and also investment risk) for the policyholder is the basic theme of variable-life insurance. First, the insurer puts together several investment funds, similar to mutual funds. A typical assortment might include a high-risk stock fund, a low-risk stock fund, one that invests in government securities, and bond funds with different risk levels. The policyholder decides how part of the premium will be allocated among the various funds.

The cash value of a variable-life policy is not guaranteed. It can go up and down, or even disappear in a bear market. If the cash value goes below zero, the investment results will have to "repay" the default before the policy regains cash value.

Because variable-life insurance is so intimately linked to investment, these policies are considered "securities" under federal law. So you can only buy them from insurance people who are licensed to sell securities or from brokers who are licensed to sell insurance. You're entitled to get a prospectus before you buy the policy. The prospectus will give you a lot of information about the policy—but not necessarily in easy-to-understand form. The policy may also carry a "load" or sales charge, just like the load imposed on some mutual funds. (More about that on page 107.)

Universal-Life Policies.   Universal-life policies work a little differently. The death benefit is *not* guaranteed; it fluctuates, based on the investment success of your account. What *is* guaranteed is a minimum rate of return on your account.

Watch out: Not all insurance companies use the same assumptions about the insurer's own costs to compute the rate of return. So if you compare two universal-life policies from different insurers, one policy might claim a higher guaranteed rate of return than the other. But under real world conditions, the policies might be equivalent; the supposedly inferior policy might offer a higher real return. About all you can do is develop lightning-fast fingers at the computer keyboard, to bring the figures into line—or rely on objective mathematical comparisons prepared by consumer protection groups or state insurance regulators.

Universal-life policies are also called flexible-premium adjustable life—that is, you can either pay the same premium all the time (in which case, the amount of insurance you have fluctuates, based on market conditions) or adjust the premium to control the amount of insurance. Some policies give you a say in the way your premiums are invested by the insurer; others leave all the investment decisions to the insurance company.

Most universal-life policies give you a choice about how the cash value should be handled. It could be used to add to the death benefit, to compensate for times when your premium payments are too low to maintain the amount of insurance you want, or treated like cash value in a conventional whole-life policy.

As already mentioned, some insurers also offer a combination, "variable-universal-life" policy, with changeable premium and face value levels, and the ability to control investments of the cash value portion of your premium.

Single-Premium Whole-Life Policies. Single-premium whole-life insurance became a hot product after the Tax Code of 1986. "Single-premium" is really a way of investing, with just enough life insurance protection to qualify for the favorable treatment the tax code gives to insurance. Usually, these policies are written so that the policyholder pays only one, large premium. However, some policies do allow later premium payments.

Because the entire premium is paid at once, there's a lot of cash value as soon as the policy is purchased. Conventional whole-life policies don't have much cash value in the first few years of the policy because there hasn't been much time for investment returns to accrue. The advantage of having a lot of cash value is that it can be borrowed at very, very low rates—for instance, if you need to pay private-school or college tuition. Many single-premium policies are set up so that there is no net interest (interest after appreciation is taken into account) if you borrow the policy's cash value; there's only 2% to 4% interest if you borrow the original premium. But watch out: If you need your money back, and surrender the policy, the insurer probably imposes a heavy surrender charge—*and* you must pay taxes on the money you receive that represents appreciation over the premium you paid for your policy.

Single-premium policies can be purchased as either "fixed" or "variable" policies. If you choose the fixed policy, the insurer invests for you and guarantees a particular interest rate for the first few years of the policy. After that, rates fluctuate based on current economic conditions, or are set by the insurer. If you choose the variable policy, you allocate investments among the insurer's investment funds. However, if you want to change your investments frequently, you may be disappointed; the policy could be written so that you can change investments only a limited number of times per year.

Some single-premium policies are considered "securities," so you buy them from a broker or an insurance agent licensed to sell securities. Others are not and can be bought from anyone licensed to sell life insurance. Make sure that anyone you deal with is really knowledgeable about the ins and outs of the product—not someone who's reluctantly taken these policies on as a sideline.

Before you buy, you must make two decisions about these plans: Are they good insurance and are they good investments, once you take all the risks and all the fees charged by the insurer into account? Remember that policy loans that are not repaid at the time of your death reduce your family's insurance protection. So if you favor single-premium policies because of the opportunity for large policy loans, keep reviewing current performance, and make sure you have enough basic insurance for your needs even if you die with policy loans outstanding.

How to Read an Insurance Policy

A basic insurance policy contains these following provisions. (Note that term insurance policies don't have provisions about cash value or policy loans; only whole-life policies do.)

- A clause specifying that the document really is a life insurance policy with a certain face value.
- Provisions for paying the premium—how much it is and whether it is to be paid monthly, quarterly, or annually. You may be able to save a little by paying the premium annually, in advance—but this means that you lose the investment return on the money you prepay.
- The name(s) of the beneficiary(ies).
- Conditions under which you can change the beneficiary.
- The "grace period"—usually 31 days—during which the policy will remain in force even if the premium payment is late.
- Conditions for reinstating a policy that has lapsed past the grace period.
- The outcome of a policy that lapses and is not reinstated. Usually, you get the cash value back, or get a smaller amount of "paid-up" insurance (the amount of insurance that can be purchased with only the amount of premiums you've already paid).
- If it's a participating policy (one which pays dividends to the policyholders), the conditions to your right to receive dividends and how those dividends will be paid.
- How and when you get policy loans and the interest rate you must pay on these loans.
- Conditions on your right to assign the policy to someone else. Usually, the insurer will not be bound by the assignment unless you follow the policy's procedure for notifying the insurer.
- An "incontestability" clause. Usually, once you maintain a policy for two years, the insurer can't refuse to pay—even if you die of a condition you had when you bought the policy—even if you commit suicide (unless your application for the policy contained fraudulent statements). Most life insurance policies say that if you commit suicide within two years of buying a policy, the insurer will give back the premiums you paid—but will not have to pay the face value of the policy.

• Your beneficiary's right to "settlement options"—the choice to receive a steady income from the insurer, instead of getting a single lump sum when the insured dies.

• "Riders," which are additional, "minicontracts" that are made part of the policy. The most common riders are "waiver of premium" (which allows you to maintain coverage after you become disabled, without paying further premiums); "guaranteed insurability"; allowing you to buy more insurance at standard rates without a physical exam; "double (or triple) indemnity," which pays double or triple the face value if your death is accidental (but your family's needs won't be any greater if you die in an accident than if you die after an illness—in fact, the illness will probably deplete the bank accounts); and "cost of living" (which lets you buy more insurance, without a physical, to compensate for increases in the cost of living your surviving family will face). Riders are good for temporary coverage of an income-protection need (for instance, if your child goes to college).

If you read an investment-oriented policy, it will contain additional provisions about the degree to which you can control investments; your investment choices; and how the premiums, face value, and cash value of your policy will be determined. If you buy a variable-life or single-premium policy, which are considered "securities," federal law entitles you to a prospectus before you buy. (Universal-life policies aren't considered securities, so no prospectus is required.) If you get a prospectus, use its information to find out how the policy performed as compared to the S&P 500, Consumer Price Index, or other measure of the stock market or the economy as a whole.

Which Policy Is Best?

Well, honesty is the best policy—but once that's been said, the question of choosing the best insurance policy is a difficult one. The answer depends on:

• Family conditions (an affluent single with no dependents really doesn't need any life insurance; a young couple with a houseful of children and a handful of bills need plenty)
• What you can afford
• Interest rates and stock market conditions (in a booming bull market, a variable-life or universal-life policy can be an excellent investment; but if stock prices are down and dropping even further, you wouldn't buy one of these policies, or keep your variable-life policies invested in stocks, if you had both oars in the water)
• Your own financial profile

That is, you have to be honest about your own attitude to money and investing. For many people, a whole-life policy is valuable because it forces them to save and accumulate cash value. They will pay the premium promptly, as soon as the bill arrives—and they won't tap the cash value unless they really need the money.

Other people want to take more control over their financial planning. They might prefer to follow the traditional advice from consumer advocates: "Buy term, and invest the difference." Or, they might want to buy an investment-oriented policy and combine financial control with conventional insurance. If you're in one of these groups, make sure you really will invest the money saved by buying term, instead of letting it burn a hole in your pocket. Make sure you'll take the time needed to understand the provisions of an investment-oriented policy, and make the required decisions (such as those about allocation of the premium) intelligently.

Let's say you've done the calculations, or talked to a financial planner you trust. You decide you need $150,000 worth of insurance for yourself, $100,000 for your spouse. If you can't afford that much in whole-life or investment-oriented products, think hard about whether you should get the insurance you need in the form of term insurance, or get less coverage with a cash-value feature. For many families, it makes sense to get the full amount of coverage needed at the lowest possible price—which usually means term insurance. Later on, you can add cash-value policies if they fit into your financial strategy. Life insurance can fit into a financial plan in ways you probably never anticipated.

Creative Planning with Life Insurance

Today, the best life insurance agents are trained to do far more than market the same standard whole-life policy to everyone. The new role for the insurance agent is as financial planner and creator of sophisticated strategies. Although it's still important to use life insurance to protect the family's financial security, there are additional ways to use life insurance.

• As already explained, an investment-oriented policy may simply be a good investment—better than other, equally safe investments open to you.

• If you own a business, life insurance can fund a "buy-sell" agreement under which your business partners or fellow stockholders agree to buy out your heirs after your death. That way, they stay in control of the company, and your family has spendable cash, not hard-to-sell shares in a business they may not want to, or be able to, run.

• Consider cash-value insurance on the lives of your children. Premiums will be very low because their life expectancy is so long. They'll be guaranteed insurance as long as the premium payments are kept up (whether you make them or they do)—even if they become uninsurable. The policy's cash value will be ready for borrowing for tuition, computer camp, a wedding reception, or whatever appeals to your family.

Life Insurance and Taxes

Whatever your income or your tax bracket, life insurance can play an important part in your financial planning. If you have major responsibilities and few assets, life insurance makes sure that your family's needs can be met even if you're not around to meet them. If you're more affluent, with enough investments to take care of the heirs for generations, then you need tax relief. Insurance gets especially favorable treatment under the Internal Revenue Code.

• Life insurance benefits can be payable either to a "named beneficiary" (a specific person, such as your spouse or child), or to your estate. If you own a life insurance policy on your own life, and the benefits are payable to your spouse, the proceeds (no matter how large) will not be part of your taxable estate, because of the unlimited marital deduction. However, if the proceeds are payable to another named beneficiary (such as your brother or daughter), the proceeds will be part of your taxable estate. To avoid this treatment, you can transfer ownership of the policy to someone else. You could, for instance, name your son and daughter as equal co-beneficiaries of a policy on your life, then give the policy to your son. To get the policy proceeds out of your taxable estate, you must give up all "incidents of ownership" in the policy—you must not be able to change the beneficiary, or otherwise act as the owner. Furthermore, you must make the transfer at least three years before your death: transfers of insurance policies made within the three years before your death will be added back into your taxable estate. Before you transfer an insurance policy (or other valuable asset), get professional advice about the tax and estate planning consequences of the transfer.

• You can also make life insurance payable to your estate, not to a named person. You don't do this because you plan to take it with you!—but because your will, or a trust under your will, contains a plan for distributing estate assets, and you want your insurance proceeds to be included in this plan. Don't adopt this strategy unless you're sure your estate will be too small to be taxable, or unless you have other estate planning purposes suggested by your professional advisers.

• Life insurance proceeds paid in a lump sum are not considered taxable income to the person who receives them. However, it's up to the beneficiary to decide whether to take a lump sum or a "settlement option."

If a settlement option is taken, the insurance company invests the proceeds and pays out an income either for a certain number of years (such as ten years) or for the beneficiary's lifetime. Part of every payment under a settlement option is taxable income—the part that represents investment income, not the original lump sum.

Before the Tax Code of 1986, a surviving spouse was entitled to treat up to $1,000 per year of investment income from settlement options as nontaxable. However, the tax reform act eliminated this tax benefit, so settlement options may be less desirable. They still have a valuable place in financial planning: If the beneficiary is financially inexperienced, or is afraid that he or she will invest unwisely, the settlement option provides steady income and professional management.

• Don't forget the function of life insurance in providing "liquidity" in an estate plan. Instead of your family having to wait for your estate to be probated, they will have money available very soon after your death. A bird in hand is proverbially worth more than one in the bush, and immediate cash is especially useful in the sorrowful (and confused) time after a death in the family.

Thus, there are many reasons why life insurance is an important part of a comprehensive estate plan. The next section shows what the other components are, and how to use and adapt them over time to changed conditions.

Part Two:
SAVING AND INVESTING

According to Hollywood, financial planning is the domain of plump plutocrats and slender, sinister financial advisers who slink through dark-panelled offices. The usual scene in the real world features the cold cup of coffee, the calculator, and the attempt to figure out which bills can be paid before the checks bounce.

The essential step toward financial independence is gaining control over spending. You'll always be broke before payday and short at the end of the month *unless* you can keep track of the money you spend, cut back on expenditures until they match your financial standing and goals, and make realistic budget plans.

Realistic budget plans leave room for some enjoyment, even some outright frivolity—strict austerity budgets never last. There's a natural human tendency to swear that you'll never spend another cent except for the direst necessities, and you'll invest every saved penny wisely. Sure. I've given up junk food for good—oh, at least twenty-five times, and I know people who've given up smoking even more often.

There are two kinds of saving that fit into your financial plan. The first is mandatory: You've got to have enough money in your checking account to pay your bills without bouncing any checks! Next, you must accumulate three to six months' salary in a bank account, money market fund, or other safe place where you can reach it easily. This is your emergency fund—the money you'll need if it's April 13 and you owe the IRS, if the car is thoughtless enough to break down a week before payday, the money for medical expenses that are not covered by your health insurance plan (or that you must pay first, and then be reimbursed, if your health insurance plan is set up that way).

This savings cushion works together with your insurance protection. You get insurance so that you won't have to bear the full burden of extraordinary expenses.

You will also need cash for unexpected financial needs. Not all of them are tragic. You'll need to be able to buy birthday presents and take unplanned vacation trips too.

The second kind of saving is an alternative to investing. Once you've established your budget, paid your bills and your taxes, gotten insurance protection, and built up your savings cushion, you may find that you have $1,000, $5,000, even $10,000 a year left over. Now you have the luxury of deciding how to invest this money.

There's no one "right" strategy for combining savings and investments. It all depends on:

•Your needs (a family of six has different priorities than a single person; a couple with one child approaching college age and one preteenager has different priorities from a couple with a toddler and a baby on the way).

•Your personality and tolerance for risk (some people can't cope with the risk of losing any money, *ever*, so they are willing to accept lower yields from a super-safe investment like treasury bills, instead of worrying about what the stock market is doing).

•The amount of work you're willing to do (some people will cheerfully dump everything into a savings account; others will spend hours a day researching the pros and cons of different investments, the qualifications of various advisers, and predicting economic trends).

•Those economic trends just mentioned. When interest rates are high, bank Certificates of Deposit (CDs), money market accounts, bank accounts that pay interest rates pegged to the prime rate, and even NOW accounts (accounts similar to checking accounts that pay interest) can give you a rate of return higher than stocks, or almost as high as the rate of return of stock, with far less risk and with far less work for you.

But when interest rates are low, especially when there's a bull market in stocks, you'll probably be losing a lot of "oomph"—accepting much lower returns—if you save your money instead of investing in stocks, real estate, or tangible property such as art or even gold and silver coins.

Alas, the financial world is never stable; if you work out a strategy that performs brilliantly in June, it could send you to the doghouse in July. The answer here is to diversify. Although some people have scored brilliant coups by "putting all their eggs in one basket," for nearly everyone it makes sense to have several places to "park" your money.

One good combination is a savings or NOW account that pays the best rate you can find, plus an IRA, plus a mutual fund (either a stock or bond fund) that has a good record and specializes in high income, and another top-rated mutual fund that specializes in high growth. That way you have most of the financial bases covered.

You may think that this strategy isn't relevant for you because you're never far enough ahead of the bills to even think about investing. Well, maybe drawing up a realistic budget—and sticking to it—will give you the financial power to save and invest.

14. How to Find Money to Invest

"How to find money to invest" sounds a lot more exciting than "household budgeting," doesn't it? Anyway, the reason to budget is to analyze the way you spend your money and find more effective ways to meet your short-term goals (such as replacing the living room sofa) and long-term goals (such as retiring with a comfortable monthly income). A single person, or a family, has to carry out the same processes as the chief financial officer of a major corporation—just on a smaller scale.

Whether you're piloting a Fortune 500 corporation or a family of five, you must:

- Understand when and how much money comes in and how it's spent (cash flow)
- Plan for an intelligent integration of spending, saving, and investing

And whether you're an MBA or just plain Mr., Ms., or Mrs., you need more than money to do financial planning—you need information. You must set up (and keep up with) a system that gives you the information you need to balance a checkbook, compare investments, do your tax returns (or give a tax preparer enough information to do them), and make tax and estate plans.

Keeping Budget Records

There are many ways to keep good records: in notebooks; in 9" × 12" envelopes or file folders, one for each category of income or expense (file bills and receipts inside; use the outside to keep a running total); or in your computer's memory. The elements of a financial records system include:

- Your check register.
- Your bank statements—and make sure you file your cancelled checks, either by month or by classification of expense (utilities, mortgage, credit card payments, etc.).
- Bankbooks and other records for savings accounts. Don't forget to enter electronic "cash machine" transactions in your records—and save the receipts the machine gives you.
- Statements from your broker and/or mutual funds.
- Credit card receipts.
- Contracts, bills, receipts, and other records of money spent on home improvement.
- A list of items ordered from mail-order houses ("Blue sweater, size 12, $29.98, ordered 3/18 from Julie's Knitwear Shop; check #1244 enclosed"). When the item arrives, cross it off the list—and if it never

arrives, you can trace the lost package or make sure the company
sends the item to you.

• Business diaries, mileage logs, receipts, and other documents proving any work-related expenses that you pay. Be sure to keep track of
reimbursement from your employer.

• Receipts and cancelled checks for charitable contributions—don't
forget, contributions of property (such as furniture and clothing you
don't want any more) can be tax-deductible.

• Records of medical expenses, claims filed against your health insurance, and amounts reimbursed by health insurance.

Turn to page 256 for a discussion of record keeping for tax purposes.
One of the biggest benefits of an efficient record-keeping and budgeting system is that it makes it much easier to do your tax return every
year (or get your records ready for the accountant or tax preparer).

Ways to Make Bill Paying Easier

I was brought up to pay bills immediately, the day they come in. That's
one approach. Other families prefer to save up the bills for a monthly
session, so that they can integrate bill paying with reviewing the family
finances. Either way can work. Here are some tips to make it easier.

• Get a calendar with an envelope attached for each month. (Your
utility company or oil company probably sends you one each Christmas.) File all the bills in the envelope for the appropriate month,
standing up and sticking out of the pocket as a reminder to pay them;
once you pay the bill, file the stub in the compartment for that
month.

• Mark each stub with the date you paid, and your check number. If
it's a partial payment, mark the amount you paid. If you know that
you paid $59.07, but next month's bill credits you with only $12.18,
you know there's a mistake to be corrected; ditto, if you get billed
a second time for something for which you've already paid. (See page
194 for the procedure for challenging incorrect bills.)

When your bank statement arrives, don't just put it in a heap of
papers to be forgotten. Banks make mistakes too, you know—and
sometimes the statements remind you of things you've forgotten. So
check the statement carefully. If you have a NOW or money-market
bank account, enter your interest in the check register for the account. Sort through the checks. If the bank hasn't done this for you,
put them in numerical order.

Budgeting and Home Computers

If you have a home computer, you can get programs that will balance
your checkbook—and even carry out sophisticated tracking and budgeting operations. Depending on your computer and the program you
pick, you might be able to make charts comparing this year's budget to
last year's—and, more soberingly, actual spending to your budget plans.

There are only two problems with using home computers for budgeting. First, it takes time to learn how to use the computer and all its capacities to the fullest. Second, unless you have the computer on every day, and it's easy to switch from whatever you're doing to the personal finance program, you may be tempted to let things slide until you have a stack of ratty little crumpled-up papers slopping over your computer keyboard.

Paying Credit Card Bills

Banks sometimes make mistakes; merchants and credit card companies sometimes make mistakes. So check your credit card bills against your own records (the running tally you keep of credit card spending) and the receipts you've saved. Have you been billed more than the charge, or billed for items you didn't buy?

Don't get nervous if you *know* you charged something that didn't appear on the bill. It takes a lot longer for some merchants to report transactions than for others. (In fact, you might prefer a store that takes a long, long time—the longer it takes to bill you, the more time you have to pay.)

Balancing Your Checkbook

"Balancing a checkbook," or "reconciling a bank statement" is the process of making sure that your interpretation of the balance in the account isn't too different from the bank's interpretation. The worst problem occurs when the bank thinks you have a lot less money than you think you do and, therefore, bounces your check. (It's of academic interest if the bank thinks you have a lot more money than you think you do—but it won't create problems for you as long as you're not trying to close the account.)

Checkbooks have to be balanced (while savings accounts don't) because money flows in and out of the account constantly, and checks take time to clear. (See page 96 for a discussion of what it means to "clear" a check.) So you have to reconcile your records and the bank's by comparing deposits you made to those credited to your account. Then compare the checks you've written to those that have cleared. (Draw a line in the check register, or put an "X" mark in the register, for every check that has cleared. That way, the ones that haven't stand out.) Use the following worksheet when balancing your checkbook.

WORKSHEET

1. The bank's figure for the opening balance for the month: $_____

2. Deposits that the bank has already credited: $_____

3. Any interest credited to your account: $_____

4. Total (add amounts in Steps 1, 2, and 3) $_____
5. Add up all the checks that have cleared and have been returned to you by the bank and enter here: $_____
6. Subtract the figure in Step 5 from the figure in Step 4 and enter here: $_____
7. Enter the total of all cash machine withdrawals that appear in your statement: $_____
8. Enter the total of all bank charges on your account (monthly fee, per-check charges, charges for using the cash machine): $_____
9. Total (Add the amounts in Steps 6, 7 and 8 and subtract from the figure in Step 5 (This is your tentative balance. It should agree with the balance given in your bank statement. If it doesn't, it's probably because there are some transactions that the bank hasn't included.): $_____
10. Add up all the checks that you wrote during the period covered by the statement, but which have not yet cleared, and all cash machine withdrawals during the period covered by the statement that do not appear on the statement. $_____
11. Add this amount to the balance that appears on your bank statement. Yes, add and not subtract—the purpose of this step is to rule out the transactions that you know about but the bank doesn't so that your records will agree with the bank's. $_____
12. Add up all the deposits you made during the period covered by the statement, but do not appear on the statement. $_____
13. Subtract the figure from Step 12 from the balance given on the bank statement. Again, the purpose of this step is to bring your records into line with the bank's by making sure that you're comparing the same transactions. $_____

* * *

After this, your balance *should* agree with the one in the statement. If not, review each check and deposit. Has the bank credited or debited the right amount? (Look at the computer-coded amount printed at the bottom of the check all the way on the right, too—it should agree with the amount of the check.) Did you make a mistake in arithmetic, or add the amount of a check to your balance, instead of subtracting it (or did you make the opposite mistake for a deposit)? Did the bank do any of these things?

If, after all that, you still can't make the checkbook balance, and the gap is wide, then gather up your records and have a chat with somebody at the bank.

Controlling Cash

Okay, now you have a good system for keeping records (and finding them when you need them), and you know what happens to your savings and checking accounts each month. But for many people, the toughest financial problem of all is figuring out what happens to the cash that appears in the wallet every payday, and then mysteriously disappears. The cash-control problem is made harder by the tempting presence of automatic teller machines that make it all too easy to "fill 'er up" when the wallet empties out.

To control cash, you must figure out where the money goes, then give each member of the family a cash "allowance"—a ration that can't be exceeded unless there's a real emergency.

Sometimes all it takes is a small effort of memory to figure out where the cash goes. Start by thinking of a typical day. Maybe you drive to the station, park your car (and either put money in a parking meter or pay for a lot), buy a newspaper and a pack of cigarettes or gum, catch the commuter train (do you pay each day, or have a monthly commutation ticket which you pay for by check, and which comes out of your checking account, not your cash?).

Then you get to the office. At eleven, the coffee cart comes around, and you get a cup of coffee and a doughnut. At one, you go out to lunch (smoked turkey on sourdough roll, iced tea, and an ice cream cone), then pick up a birthday card for your sister. On the way home, you get the evening paper, then stop off at the dry cleaner's and laundry to pick up a week's worth of clean clothes. The last stop is a convenience store for the butter and milk that ran out at breakfast time.

Once you add up these minor expenditures, multiply them by five for a typical work week, and add in the special expenses of the weekend (anything from a couple of Sunday papers to a movie and hamburgers for six), you'll see where most of the money goes!

If there are major gaps—if you have a kind of money amnesia—then follow the "dieting" approach to cash control. For a week, carry a small notebook that'll fit in pocket or purse. Write down *everything* you spend, from a pack of gum to auto repairs. Then go over the figures. Can you justify every expense? Did each one give you either use or at least a dollar's worth of pleasure for every dollar you spent? Could you have handled any expense differently (by buying tires during the annual tire sale, not waiting until the tires are going bald, by inviting friends over for dinner instead of meeting them at a restaurant, using coupons and switching to less expensive brands at the supermarket, or cutting down on convenience foods)? Would you miss any of the things you bought if you didn't spend that money?

Speaking of dieting, maybe this is the time to go on that diet or quit smoking—and save hundreds of dollars on snacks and cigarettes. Maybe you can save money by planning ahead.

• Subscribe to your favorite magazine—it's cheaper than buying it on the newsstand. If you don't want it *that* much, then go to the library and read it there.

• Buy in bulk—not the two-pound box of detergent, but the twenty-pounder; two dozen pairs of socks at the annual linen sale, not one pair when your toe pokes out for air. To save money by using this strategy, you must have storage space for your economical purchases—and you must have enough cash to buy the larger size which costs more overall, even though it costs less per item, per pound, or per quart.

• Plan menus using economical ingredients (chicken, fresh seasonal vegetables, products you like and for which you have "cents off" coupons), and make a detailed shopping list for a weekly or twice-a-month supermarket jaunt. Preplanning cuts down on waste, decreases the number of (usually expensive) impulse purchases, and cuts down or eliminates those endless trips to the higher-priced corner store to pick up forgotten items.

How to Cut Credit Card Expenses

First, figure out where the money went. Save all your charge slips; keep a tally of what you buy with each card and how your balance fluctuates. At the beginning of each year, when you get your tax information, the credit card companies tell you how much interest you paid in the previous year. If the figure comes as a shock, sit down and make a New Year's resolution to cut down in the future.

Trim the flab from your spending pattern. Everyone needs an occasional night out, but how about balcony seats instead of orchestra tickets? It's great to be generous, but could you find less expensive presents that would be just as welcome to your family and friends? Do you feel great and garner compliments each time you put on one of your newest outfits, or are they crumpled up at the bottom of the closet, forgotten (except by the credit card company, which is still billing you every month for them)?

For some families, eliminating waste is all they need to bring credit card spending into line. Other families need to develop a formal system, or they'll run up too much debt. For instance, set goals in advance for credit card use. You could decide that you can't charge more than $250 in any month, and that you won't let your balance get over $1,000 or your interest get over $50 in any month. Be sure to pay at least the minimum balance every month, to keep your credit rating in good shape.

If you have a sturdy checking-account balance and a lot of self-discipline, you can even use credit cards to *save* money. To follow this strategy, never use your credit card unless you find a great deal on something for which you've already budgeted and know you can afford. For instance, if you know your younger son needs a new winter coat, buy him one at the spring coat sale, when it's half-price. If you've decided to splurge on a VCR (but it's not really a splurge; you know you can afford it), buy it at the Columbus Day sale.

But don't pay cash or check—put the purchase on your credit card, and pay the balance in full when the bill arrives. Most credit cards won't charge interest if you pay the full bill within the grace period, so you get free credit for several weeks. (See page 190 for more about credit cards.)

In contrast, some people go wild with a charge plate in their hands. If you're in this group, promise yourself you'll only use each credit card once a month, or only spend $50 a month on each card. It may help to keep them in a bank safe deposit box so that you can't reach them without a lot of trouble. If even that doesn't get your head above water, cancel all your charge accounts and credit cards (well, maybe keeping one for emergencies), and devote as much of your budget as you can manage to paying off the balance.

What Kind of Budget Is Right for You?

It's amazing what people can do when they really have to—as no doubt you've found out by pulling an all-nighter to finish a term paper, or running a department with six employees instead of the eleven you need. You may think that you're already a paragon of economy, or that it takes too much time to prepare and analyze a budget. But you *can* learn to draw up a workable budget—and stick to it.

Weekly or monthly budgets can be done "from the top down" or "from the bottom up"—either approach is valid.

To budget from the top down, start with your total income (salary plus savings and investment income). Now decide which categories belong in your household budget (such as rent or mortgage payment, utilities, clothing, IRA contributions, and other retirement savings). Either assign a percentage of your income to each category (rent: 22%) or a dollar figure (clothing: $125).

Those are your goals. Make sure they're feasible—you'll be in a lot of trouble if you spend 175% of your income each month! In fact, a major reason for budgeting is to cut expenses so that income is ahead of expenses; that way, you'll have money to save and invest. Finally, compare each month's actual spending to the goals. If you spent less, congratulations! Depending on the amount involved and your overall financial condition you could either invest the money you saved or enjoy a well-earned treat.

To budget from the bottom up, start with the actual spending figures for the previous month. Analyze each figure—was it really necessary? Will it come up again? (Odds are you won't need another new picture tube for the TV for quite a while—if ever.) Analyze continuing expenses (such as food) and see where, if anywhere, you can cut.

Here's a worksheet for doing a short-term (weekly or monthly) budget; you can customize it by substituting categories that are relevant to your own financial style. "Allowance" means the total cash that all family members get to pay for lunches, bus fares, and similar minor expenses. "P" means "projected"—the budget figure you assigned in advance; "A" means "actual"—what you really spent. "C#" means "check number"—recording this helps you keep track.

Items that don't appear every month (such as quarterly insurance premium payments) can be handled either by placing the entire item in the month it will be paid or by budgeting $\frac{1}{12}$ of the yearly amount each month.

<u>WORKSHEET</u>

Week of/Month of:_____

Income for the period: $_____ Salary(ies), $_____

Interest, $_____   Dividends, $_____

Other   (explain):_____   TOTAL: $_____

Balance on all credit cards at the beginning of the period:

$_____ At the end of the period: $_____

BUDGET ENTRIES (You can use either percentages or dollar amounts.)

	P	A	C#
Rent/Mortgage	_____	_____	_____
Fuel	_____	_____	_____
Utilities	_____	_____	_____
Groceries	_____	_____	_____
Restaurant meals	_____	_____	_____
Clothing	_____	_____	_____
Laundry/dry cleaning	_____	_____	_____
Car loan	_____	_____	_____
Gas, tolls, parking	_____	_____	_____
Auto insurance	_____	_____	_____
Commuter ticket(s)	_____	_____	_____
Allowances	_____	_____	_____
Other loan payment(s)	_____	_____	_____
Credit card payment(s)	_____	_____	_____
Tuition	_____	_____	_____
Life insurance	_____	_____	_____
Health insurance	_____	_____	_____

IRA contribution	_____	_____	_____
Alimony/Child support	_____	_____	_____
Income taxes	_____	_____	_____
Furniture, appliances	_____	_____	_____
Home repairs, maintenance	_____	_____	_____
Business expenses	_____	_____	_____
Travel	_____	_____	_____
Entertainment	_____	_____	_____
Books, records, tapes	_____	_____	_____
Charitable contributions	_____	_____	_____
Gifts	_____	_____	_____
Other (explain)	_____	_____	_____

* * *

No matter how you do your budget, you'll probably have to revise the figures downward! If you were the United States government, you could simply operate at a deficit, print some more money, or both. Private families must either balance their budgets or sink deeper and deeper into debt.

How to Stick to a Budget

Deposit each paycheck into a bank account (checking, savings, split between both, or alternate paychecks in each), keeping aside enough cash for family members' allowances. Make it clear that family members can't get more cash until the following week; save the cash machines for real emergencies. After your children have to walk to school a few times because they've spent their bus fare, they'll develop a real feeling for the need to match spending to available funds.

The discussion above assumes that you budget your expenses, and then invest what's left over. What if nothing is ever left over? Some experts suggest that you start your budgeting *after* you take out your savings and investment funds. That is, every time you get a paycheck, an interest payment, or a tax refund, take out part of the money and save it or invest it *immediately*, before you have a chance to spend it. Either set a dollar goal, such as $50 per paycheck, or a percentage (maybe 5% to 7% to start with), which you can either keep constant when you get a raise, or increase, because it takes a smaller percentage of your larger paycheck to pay the bills.

With luck, you can build this into an unbreakable habit; you won't even think of spending the money because you think of it as investment money, not spendable cash. You can further this illusion by depositing the money in a six-month CD or investing in a mutual fund that doesn't give you check-redemption privileges so that it'll take some time and trouble to get money out of the account. Another tip: Earmark your tax refund each year and use it to fund your IRA.

If, even after all that, you still find it difficult to save, "forced savings" plans could be the answer. If your employer offers a salary-reduction plan (discussed on page 29), try to have the maximum permitted amount withheld from your salary. This is especially good financial planning if your employer matches part of your contributions. Ask if there's a plan at work for buying savings bonds by payroll deduction. Even if bonds aren't the best investment available at the time you start the plan, the payroll deduction could mean the difference between a solid investment and money frittered away.

Whole-life insurance policies are another route to forced savings; you build up cash value as you pay your premiums. Investment-oriented life insurance policies such as universal-life, variable-life, and single-premium whole life combine investments with cash-value life insurance; so you can make long-term investments at the same time you protect your family.

Review Your Budget Regularly

Wouldn't it be great if you could make an annual budget and relax, knowing that you had brought your financial goals within reach? It sure would, but that's not the way things work. Budgets must be reviewed regularly to make sure they still conform to reality. If you budgeted $600 a month for rent, and your lease comes up for renewal in April, you'll probably have to reevaluate. Either your present landlord will increase your rent, or you'll have to find new living quarters (with a surprise item for moving expenses to be factored into your budget calculations).

Unexpected medical expenses, increases in food and fuel prices, and unanticipated car repairs also require the budget to be expanded upwards. But not all the news is bad. A salary increase or a bit of luck in the stock market could increase the amount of money you have to work with.

Creating a Long-Term Budget

It's tough enough to figure out what you'll need to spend next year. How can you possibly figure out what you'll spend five or ten years from now? You'll have to build a little skepticism into your estimates, but don't give up long-term planning just because your figures will need checking and correcting over time.

Long-term budgeting deals with the major improvements you hope to make in your financial situation. If you want to buy a house, set a goal (buying in two years, five years, seven years, or whatever). Then consider the price range of house you can afford (see the chart on page 171), the down payment you'll have to make, and the closing costs. More about all this in "Enjoying Your Home, Credit and Automobile," later on.

Let's say that you'll need $22,000 cash to buy the house you want, and the monthly payment will be $50 more than you now pay for rent. If you already have $10,000 of the cash and hope to buy the house three years from now, you'll need to invest at least $3,000 a year just to meet this goal. (You won't need to invest $4,000 a year, because let's hope that your investment earns some return.) Once you know this, you may decide to scale down your vacation plans or stay away from the spring white sale, and reevaluate your health club membership.

When you know whether you plan to retire early, at the normal retirement age, or to keep working past the ordinary retirement age, you can set retirement income goals. You can estimate your pension benefits by asking the employee benefits coordinator or using the pension plan materials provided by the employer. You can visit the local Social Security office and get an estimate of Social Security benefits. But take these estimates with a grain of salt. Conditions are likely to change between now and then.

It's a safe bet that you'll get pretty nervous when you imagine living on just your pension plus Social Security benefits. This might inspire you to contribute to an IRA each year, even if the contributions aren't tax-deductible. (When are contributions deductible? See page 34.)

Here are more reasons why you might need a chunk of cash, or extra monthly income, in the future.

- Buying new cars as each old one wears out
- Renovating or redecorating your home
- Starting a business
- Taking a long or luxurious vacation
- Having a baby (Not only does the mother lose income during her maternity leave, but the actual birth of a baby can cost hundreds or even thousands of dollars that are not covered by health insurance.)

Your task as a budget planner is to make sure this year's savings and investment prepare you to meet the expenses you anticipate in the future.

15. Where to Keep the Nest Egg

With your financial affairs in order, wasteful expenses cut out, and a workable budget in place, the next step is saving. Build your emergency fund of three to six months' salary; then save and accumulate funds to invest.

There's no hard and fast line between saving and investing. For purposes of this book, we'll define "saving" as putting away money for immediate needs, in bank accounts where your money can be reached in six months or less. For most people, saving is an early step in building financial security. The next step is to take saved money and find a way to invest it to earn returns that are higher than those available for savings.

"Investing" will be defined as a longer-term process: buying stocks, bonds, interests in real estate, and other media where your goal is to hold the investment for a while.

But you can keep money in a savings account for years at a time, or you can buy a stock and sell it a few days later. Furthermore, a wide variety of savings and investment media have evolved to meet a variety of needs. Money-market funds and some mutual funds give you check-writing privileges: You can sell part of your investment just by filling out an instruction slip that looks and works like a check. Let's start with savings, then move on to investments.

You do most of your saving in a bank, but what is a bank? What options do banks offer you, and how can you choose the best banks and the best accounts?

There are two main types of banks: commercial banks and thrift institutions (credit unions, savings banks, and savings and loan institutions). To be strictly accurate, there are some minor technical differences between savings banks and savings and loan institutions, in terms of the way they're set up and the amount of deposits they're allowed to lend out; but basically, the two types of institutions are very similar. Credit unions are organized by and for a group of people who have something in common (for instance, they all work for the same employer); the credit union pays interest on members' deposits and makes loans for their mortgages, car purchases, and the like.

Traditionally, there was a vast difference between the "thrifts" and commercial banks. Thrift institutions specialized in small personal bank accounts and home mortgages. Before bank deregulation, the federal government set maximum interest rates, and thrift institutions paid higher interest rates than commercial banks. Commercial banks specialized in loans to businesses, and were the only place you could get a checking account.

Today, the lines have blurred. Thrifts and commercial banks compete for consumers' bank deposits; both of them can offer mortgages and personal loans and issue credit cards. Although, technically, thrift institutions can't offer checking accounts, they *can* offer other types of accounts that work in just about the same way.

Bank Services

Banks buy and sell money. They "buy" it from depositors by offering them interest plus convenient services, and "sell" it by taking the depositors' money and lending it out. All banks provide vaults, lobbies, deposit slips, and long lines in which to stand. Most banks also provide these services.

- Savings accounts are accounts into which you deposit money and the bank promises you a certain rate of interest. Usually, the rate of interest is fixed; sometimes, it's pegged to the prime rate or other economic indicators. Usually, you have a right to withdraw money whenever the bank is open (or through an ATM service if available). However, some savings accounts require you to give the bank a certain number of days' notice before you withdraw money.
- Checking or NOW (Negotiable Order of Withdrawal) accounts are accounts into which you deposit money and can either withdraw cash from the bank itself or order the bank to pay some of your money to someone else (like the phone company). These orders are called checks, drafts, or Negotiable Orders of Withdrawal. If you have "overdraft checking," you can write checks larger than your account, and the bank will pay them, not bounce them: In effect, you borrow the extra money from the bank.

  A "money market deposit account" is a checking or NOW account that pays interest at a rate which fluctuates according to trends in interest rates.
- Certificates of Deposit (CDs) are accounts into which you deposit money and agree to leave it there for six months, a year, three years, or other length of time. If you withdraw the money beforehand, you have to pay a penalty of part of the interest earned on the CD. CDs usually require a fairly large minimum deposit (such as $1,000, or even $10,000); to compensate for this requirement, and for tying up your money, CDs pay higher rates than ordinary savings or NOW accounts.
- ATM (Automated Teller Machines) are "cash machines" connected to computers that permit you to make cash deposits, transfer funds to pay bills, and withdraw cash when all the tellers are busy, or when the bank is closed.
- Loans are the way banks earn their profits: by making mortgage loans, auto loans, personal loans, and business loans.
- Safe deposit boxes are secure, fire-proof places to keep important documents, jewelry, and other valuables.

It's pretty much up to each bank which services it will offer, what rules it will establish, and what fees it will charge. So banks are not all alike. For instance, one bank may charge $6 a month to maintain a checking account; another bank pegs its checking-account fees to the level of your balance; yet another bank won't impose charges if you maintain a minimum balance, but will impose a monthly fee and a charge for each check you write if you don't maintain that balance. To qualify for high-interest accounts (sometimes called Super NOW or Money Market Deposit Accounts) you will also have to maintain a minimum balance—$2,500 or more.

Understanding Banks

When a society's economy develops, it needs banks: If you keep your money in a mattress, it not only makes the mattress lumpy, it offers a handy target for the local burglars and brigands. When there's a sophisticated economy, people and businesses need a safe place to stash money.

Not too long into the history of banks, bankers discovered that people tend to leave their money in the bank for a while. In fact, days could go by without anyone withdrawing any money. Soon, bankers discovered that there were predictable cycles, and they could conduct normal business if they kept only a small part of the deposited money on the premises.

Sophisticated economic systems also depend largely on loans. Farmers borrow money to buy seed, hoping to repay when the crops have been sold. Business owners borrow to start or expand businesses, or to buy new inventory. Would-be homeowners get mortgages. Both sides of the banking system work together: Depositors put money in the bank, and bankers lend it to consumer and business borrowers.

Of course, if all the depositors suddenly appeared and demanded their money, and if most of the money had been loaned out, there would be a "run on the bank," a "panic," and many angry depositors. That's one reason why the banking business has traditionally been subject to a lot of legal regulation. There have been rules about who could open a bank, who had a right to look at the books, and what policies the bank could use in lending—even how much interest the bank could charge. Today, banks are going through a process of deregulation, and new forms of banking are developing—but so are new risks.

How Safe Is Your Money?

One reason why you should care about *how* your bank is chartered is the question of deposit insurance. Today, most depositors can feel confident that there will never be a run on their bank that will cause them to lose their deposits. Most banks have deposit insurance. Federally chartered commercial banks are insured by the Federal Deposit Insurance Corporation; the Federal Savings and Loan Institution Corporation insures savings and loan institutions. Some states have plans to insure state-chartered banks; some banks even have private insurance.

The purpose of these insurance plans is to bolster depositors' confidence by insuring their savings up to a certain amount (usually $100,000 per account) if and when the bank runs out of funds. The problem is that many banks (especially savings and loan institutions) have gone under or are financially troubled—and if this keeps happening, the various insurance programs won't have enough money to cover all the losses. So you're safer choosing a federally insured institution than one with state or private insurance (because the federal insurance system has more money), but be aware that you could lose part or all of your bank deposits *if* your bank goes under and *if* the insurance system doesn't have enough money to rescue all the failed banks. You can find out about a bank's insurance coverage by looking for the sticker in the window ("Insured by FDIC"), reading the bank's promotional material, or asking a bank officer.

How can a bank fail, anyway? Isn't owning a bank a guaranteed way to make money, like a gambling casino? Well, a few people have managed to "break the bank at Monte Carlo"—and banks *can* lose money. They can make bad loans—for example, to countries or oil producers who can't or won't pay them back.

Banks can also get into trouble by making perfectly *good* loans for a long term at an interest rate that proves to be far below later market conditions. Let's say a bank gives a home-buyer a thirty-year mortgage at the then-current 6% mortgage rate. When the mortgage is ten years old, the prime rate—the rate that banks charge their very best customers—is 14%. The homeowner makes payments faithfully, but the bank is losing money all the time.

In effect, the bank has to "pay" depositors a lot more than 6% to make them want to deposit money in the bank, but the bank can only collect 6% on this thirty-year mortgage and others like it. That's why so many savings and loan institutions (which specialize in home mortgages) have failed, and so many more are in trouble.

Bank failures can usually be handled quietly. The federal bank regulators find another bank, in better financial condition, that can buy out the ailing bank. Bank accounts are simply transferred to the "white knight" bank; there's no real impact on the depositors. If that can't be arranged, the federal agency (or the state agency or private insurer, if the bank is state-chartered) has to bite the bullet and pay depositors the amount in their accounts, up to the maximum amount insured.

Choosing a Bank; Choosing Accounts

Choosing a bank is a lot more complicated than it was in the days when all thrift institutions offered pretty much the same savings accounts (with the same rates) and thirty-year, fixed-rate mortgages, and all commercial banks offered the same, no-interest checking accounts. Today, there's a wider spectrum of financial services available, and banks are much more competitive than ever before. That's good because you can choose accounts tailored to your needs, and earn higher returns than in the old days; that's bad, because the menu of choices can be very confusing.

Here are some guidelines for choosing your bank—or your banks. To combine convenience and high returns, you could have a savings account and a NOW account at a bank in your home town, and use the mails to buy a six-month CD from a bank in another state—and get your credit cards from yet another bank, in yet another state.

• Convenience is tremendously important. Does the bank you're considering have branches near your home? Your office? Your spouse's office? Near shopping centers, so you can get cash for shopping? Are ATMs available at the branch? Are twenty-four-hour terminals well-lighted and on busy streets, or do you have to hike through a dark alley (where muggers may lurk) once you get your cash?

• What services, besides basic savings and checking, does the bank offer? This can be important if you need a mortgage, auto, or business loan, and the bank offers a lower interest rate to its "relationship customers" (those who have several bank accounts). Some banks also give a higher rate on CDs to customers who maintain a high minimum balance, or who have several accounts or an "all-in-one" account combining several banking functions (savings, checking, long-term deposits, etc.).

• What rates are offered on savings accounts? Does the rate depend on maintaining a minimum balance? Can you get a higher rate of interest if you agree to give the bank notice before withdrawing money from the account? What definition of "balance" is used to compute interest? Your average daily balance (computed by adding up the balance on each day and dividing by the number of days in the month)? The highest balance you have at any time during the month? The lowest balance at any time during the month?

• Is interest on savings accounts compounded daily, monthly, quarterly, or annually? The more frequently interest is compounded, the more you earn, because you earn interest on the interest already paid.

Table 3 shows what happens to a $2,500 savings account, depending on the interest rate and the compounding schedule. If you keep $2,500 in a savings account, this is what your balance will be after the specified number of years. The first column under each interest rate (M) is for monthly compounding; the second (Q) is for quarterly compounding; (A) is for annual compounding.

• If the bank offers Certificates of Deposit (CDs), does it offer only six-month CDs or a choice of six-month, one-year, three-year, or longer CDs? Is the interest rate fixed, or does it fluctuate according to market conditions? How much must you deposit to open a CD? Can you add to the CD later on—and if so, which interest rate will you get? The rate for the time you opened the account, or for the time you made the later deposit? How high is the penalty for early

TABLE 3.   INTEREST AND COMPOUNDING

Year	5.25%			5.5%			6%		
	M	Q	A	M	Q	A	M	Q	A
1	2,635	2,634	2,631	2,641	2,640	2,638	2,654	2,653	2,650
2	2,776	2,775	2,769	2,790	2,789	2,783	2,818	2,816	2,809
3	2,925	2,923	2,915	2,947	2,945	2,936	2,992	2,989	2,978
4	3,083	3,080	3,068	3,114	3,111	3,097	3,176	3,172	3,156
5	3,249	3,245	3,229	3,290	3,285	3,267	3,372	3,367	3,346
7	3,607	3,602	3,577	3,671	3,664	3,637	3,801	3,793	3,759
10	4,221	4,212	4,170	4,328	4,317	4,270	4,548	4,535	4,477
15	5,485	5,467	5,386	5,694	5,673	5,581	6,135	6,108	5,991
20	7,128	7,095	6,956	7,492	7,454	7,294	8,276	8,227	8,018

withdrawal? Will the bank let you tailor your own CD—can you deposit money for the period of time that fits your needs (such as the time between the deposit and the day you pay the caterer for your daughter's wedding)?

• Does the bank offer NOW, Super NOW, or Money Market Deposit Accounts? If so, what minimum balance do you need to open an account, and what balance must you maintain? Again, is the balance on which interest is computed your highest, lowest, or average daily balance? Can you write unlimited checks against the account, in any amount, or are you limited to a certain number of checks a month (e.g., three a month), and must each check be over a certain amount (such as $100 or $500)?

• How long does the bank take to clear checks? How long are out-of-state checks held?

• If you have a checking or NOW account, how high are the fees for "bounced" checks (checks returned because the balance in the account is insufficient to pay the check) and for stopping payment on a check?

• Does the bank charge a monthly fee and/or a fee per check written, for checking accounts? Is checking free if you maintain a minimum balance? If so, is the fee imposed if your balance dips below this amount at *any* time during the month, or only if your average daily balance is below this figure?

Writing Checks

A check is a written instruction to your bank. From the legal viewpoint, a valid check is *anything* (not just a preprinted, electronically coded check form) that contains a date, your signature, and specifies who should receive money (the "payee") and the amount to be received.

Those instructions are carried out when the payee signs the check ("endorses" it) and brings it to a bank to be cashed or deposited into an account. If a check is endorsed "For Deposit Only," it can legally be deposited into the account designated, but can't be cashed by anyone. When you go through the cancelled checks that come with your bank statement, you'll notice that many businesses stamp all the checks they receive "For Deposit Only"—that's to suppress any ambitions their employees might have to make off with the business's funds.

Checks can also be "endorsed over" from one party to another. If you get a check payable to you, and owe money to someone else, you could sign the check, add the number of your checking account, and write "Pay to the Order of . . ." to whomever you want to get the check. Then that person (or business) can cash the check, deposit it, or endorse it over to someone else.

Stop That Check!

You have a right to change your instructions to the bank—to tell the bank *not* to pay a check. This right is effective until the check has either been certified (see page 98) or paid. Once the check is paid, you have to go after the payee, not the bank, and use any legal remedies you have to get your money back. Therefore, if you're a payee and you expect a dispute to brew up, the thing to do is cash the check as soon as possible—or insist on a cashier's or certified check.

Stop-payment orders can be oral: either telephoned or told to the appropriate bank official in person. An oral stop-payment order is legally effective for fourteen days. It expires after fourteen days unless it is confirmed in writing. A written order is good for six months and can be renewed. (These are general rules; they can be changed if the bank and the checking account depositor agree to a different set.)

If you have to stop payment on a check, the best policy is to use a written order. That gives you proof of your instructions and when they were issued.

Bounced Checks

What if a bank gets back a check drawn on it, and there is no account to support the check, or there is an account but the check is bigger than the balance in the account? Unless the drawer has overdraft privileges, the bank will "dishonor" the check: It reports to the payee's bank that the account has "insufficient funds," and the check will bounce.

Not every bounced check is the result of dishonesty. You can run into trouble with your checking account if you write checks in the optimistic belief that your deposits will clear sooner than they do, or that checks will be paid in the order you wrote them, or that payees will take longer to deposit them than they really do.

If you're the victim of "wrongful dishonor"—if the bank refused to pay a valid check when funds were available—you can sue the bank and collect damages. But it's not considered dishonor and, therefore, can't be wrongful dishonor, if a bank refuses to pay a postdated check until the date written on the check, or if a bank refuses to speed up its normal crediting procedures so that you can use deposited funds faster, or if the bank refuses to pay a defective or incomplete check (such as one that is not signed or has no payee listed).

More Checks and "Sort-of" Checks

In addition to the ordinary personal checks just described, there are various kinds of checks and check-like instruments.

• Negotiable Orders of Withdrawal (NOW) work like checks, but are issued by thrift institutions. Actually, the thrift institution opens its own account with a commercial bank; the NOWs are paid from the thrift institution's account.

• Money orders are bought for cash, usually by people who don't have checking accounts. Money orders are used like checks when cash payment is undesirable, for instance, to avoid sending cash through the mail.

Money orders can be bought from the Post Office, from banks, or from private money order companies. Fees and the kind of receipt or documentation given to buyers vary.

Depending on state law and the kind of money order involved, it may either be possible to stop payment on a money order (if it's treated as equivalent to an ordinary personal check) or impossible (if it's considered the equivalent of a cashier's check). From the receiver's point of view, a money order is better than a check because it isn't necessary to trust the sender to have a checking account with adequate funds.

• Cashier's checks are issued by banks, not drawers. The drawer either pays cash or proves to the issuing bank that he or she has enough money in an account to cover the cashier's check. The issuing bank makes an unconditional promise to pay the payee the amount of the cashier's check. That means that the payee only has to trust the bank's solvency, not the purchaser's. The buyer of a cashier's check can cancel it before the payee gets it, but once the check has been delivered to the payee, there's no way to stop payment.

• A certified check is a check on the drawer's account. A bank officer certifies that the drawer really does have an account, that the account has enough funds to pay the check, and those funds will be held specifically to pay the check. There are various circumstances under which the certifying bank might be legally justified in refusing to pay a certified check, but once a check has been certified, the drawer can't stop payment on it.

If you have to get a check certified (for instance, if you're in the process of buying a house and need to disburse amazingly large amounts of money to people and institutions who don't necessarily trust your solvency), watch out for a potential problem. Your bank will, naturally, debit your account instantly for the amount of the certified check. However, your account could be debited again when the payee deposits the check, because nearly all checks are processed electronically, and the computer can't tell the difference between certified and ordinary checks.

Certified checks tend to be both large and important, so this could be a major problem! To protect yourself, you could have the electronic code on the check reprinted so that it has the bank's account ID number instead of yours, or have the certified check issued on a special blank form with the bank's ID number, or have a hole punched in the check so that the computer rejects it and the check gets hand-processed. Or you could get a cashier's check instead of a certified check.

However, don't change from certified to cashier's check without getting payee's permission. Before important transactions, find out what form of payment is required. If a contract requires you to present a certified check, offering a cashier's check (or vice versa) doesn't count as complying with the terms of the contract.

•Traveler's checks are issued by a traveler's check company; American Express is the best known. When you buy the checks, you sign one line of the check. You countersign (sign again, on another line) when you use the checks to buy something. As the name suggests, traveler's checks are especially useful when you travel to other cities or countries. They can be purchased in various currencies, so you won't have to "change" money in other countries. Most places accept traveler's checks because a restaurateur, airline, hotel, or store relies on the reputation of the traveler's check company, not the traveler's solvency.

Traveler's checks are safer for you than carrying cash because the issuer has a procedure for replacing lost or stolen checks—as long as you can prove that you bought the checks and that you didn't make yourself an easy mark for crime by countersigning the checks in advance. (Once a check is countersigned, anyone who gets possession of it can collect from the issuer.)

To use traveler's checks wisely, make a list of your check numbers; keep your purchase receipt; keep the list and the receipt in a safe place, and not with the checks; learn the procedure for getting replacement checks before you leave on your trip; and be careful when and how you countersign.

How to Avoid Check Problems

Many things can happen (whether by accident, mistake, or criminal intent) to keep the process of writing, cashing, and clearing checks from being entirely smooth. Clear legal solutions have evolved for many of the difficulties; other problems must be hashed out in court, and various states have developed different approaches.

Prevent trouble by writing the amount of each check clearly, in both words and figures—and use the entire space provided (or fill the surplus with a line or dash.) That will avoid the risk that some creative person will "raise" the check (turn a check for $80 into one for $280, for instance). The general rule is that the bank is not allowed to charge a drawer's account for the higher, raised amount—only for the amount originally intended.

But if your carelessness made it easy to raise the check, or if you took an unreasonably long time to complain about the alteration, the bank is entitled to pay the raised check and debit your account. Although it's not a strict legal requirement, it's in your best interests to protect yourself by sending the bank a written complaint, with copies of the documents. Keep the original documents and a copy of the letter. Even if you're slow about making your complaint, you may still be able to win a suit against the bank—if the bank failed to use "ordinary care" in paying an altered check or a forged check.

Outright forgery is another potential check problem: Someone signs your name to a check, without your authorization. The general rule is that the bank is out of luck if it pays a forged check; it can't debit the account of the forgery victim. But once again, if you're negligent, you can lose your remedies against the bank.

The rules are similar if a check has a forged endorsement (that is, if someone pretends to be the payee of a check in order to cash it). However, claims that a check is forged can't be made more than one year after you get your bank statement and cancelled checks; claims of forged endorsements can be made for up to three years.

The U.S. Treasury Department maintains a fund to reimburse payees whose government checks (for instance, Social Security checks) have been stolen and paid out as a result of forged endorsements. However, if you're a victim in this situation, you can't sue the bank that paid your check to the con artist.

If you're at the other end, and get a "rubber" check, you have several practical and legal alternatives. First, wait a few days and deposit the check again. Many cases of bounced checks reflect funds that were not yet available when the check was cashed or deposited—not an attempt to cheat. If that doesn't work, you will have to take steps against the drawer (you can't sue the bank on which the check was drawn unless the check is certified).

A "postdated" check is one which is written with a nominal date after the date the check was really written (that is, the check is written March 15, but dated April 10). The drawer is not promising that funds will be available until the date of the check. If a bank pays a postdated check before the date, it does so at its own risk.

Unless there's a stop order, or unless you provide specific instructions, a bank has the right to charge checks against your account in any order it finds convenient—no matter how inconvenient it is to *you*. You have no legal right to complain if the bank bounces a check or hits you with an overdraft charge. (For example, you might find that your check to the IRS bounces because the bank paid out that check before it credited the deposit that would have covered it. If the bank had paid the comparatively tiny check to your niece for her birthday first, the whole mess wouldn't have happened.)

In practice, banks usually use a "first in, first out" (FIFO) system, and subtract checks from your balance in the order they receive them (which is not necessarily the order in which you wrote them).

The only way to avoid the problem completely is to maintain a large balance in your checking account—large enough to cover all the checks you write. This can be frustrating if you have to keep money in your checking account that you'd rather be investing for a higher return; at least NOW accounts, which pay interest, lessen the pain.

A few states (California, Connecticut, Massachusetts, and New York) have laws regulating the amount of time banks are allowed to take to clear checks. For instance, Connecticut law says that an in-state check can't be held for longer than four business days; an out-of-state check can't be held for more than seven business days. But banks can hold items longer if they have reason to believe the check is going to bounce.

The limits set by these laws probably don't apply to federally chartered banks within the state. However, a bill passed by Congress in the summer of 1987 forces these banks to speed up the check-clearing process.

Banks are safe and convenient "parking places" for money; having a checking account makes it much easier to pay bills. It's hard to have a valid financial plan that doesn't include a savings account and a checking account (or an interest-paying NOW account that serves both functions), and an intelligent use of credit—a mortgage, an auto loan, a student loan, credit cards—and the credit is usually provided by a bank. When interest rates are high, CDs can be an excellent, safe investment. But most financial plans don't stop with saving; other investments fit in too.

16. Making an Investment Plan

Saving is a great way to make sure that you will be able to handle ordinary bills and cope with at least minor financial emergencies. However, the rate of interest you can earn on your savings is tied to the level of interest rates in the economy as a whole. In most cases, the interest you earn on your savings is taxable; often, the rate of return on savings lags behind inflation. So if you put all your money after expenses have been paid into savings, you may be disappointed in what remains after taxes and inflation.

That's why investing in stocks, bonds (or mutual funds that invest in them), real estate, and other investment media fits into most financial plans. If you choose well, and if the economic factors are favorable, you can get investments that are tax-exempt, or that have a high yield even after taxes are paid—and that keep you ahead of inflation. For instance, if you invest in a growth stock (one which gains favor with the stock market over several years), you might buy shares for $11 apiece and find that five years later your shares now sell for $27 each.

By the same token, you could find that you bought a stock for $14 a share and now, when you want to sell it, no one will give you more than 87¢ a share. Investing involves risk: The possibility of growth in the value of your investment carries with it the possibility of shrinkage in value.

There are no perfect investments. All investments have risks and costs (such as brokerage fees). Nor are there simple formulas for choosing investments. But there are basic rules you can use to make a personalized investment plan.

An investor, like the pilot of a plane, needs to understand the terrain and the "weather report": the kinds of investments available, the basic financial and economic climate, and how changes in climate could affect the safety and return of your investments. So this chapter starts with a consideration of basic economic factors and then discusses some of the investments that might be right for your financial plan—their pros and cons.

Basic Economic Factors

Investments don't exist in a vacuum. The stocks, bonds, mutual fund shares, or real estate investments you buy are part of the United States economy—in fact, part of the world economy. Unless you have at least some understanding of economic conditions, you won't be able to make intelligent choices.

Why Inflation Matters

Inflation is one of the most important of these economic factors. When there's more money in circulation (either because the government prints more, or because banks are allowed to "create" more money by making more loans), or when there are fewer goods and services to buy, prices go up and confidence goes down. People fear that if they want to buy something later on, they won't be able to afford it because prices will have spiraled upward.

Inflation hits hardest on those with "fixed incomes"—retirees whose pension is a set amount that does not fluctuate based on the cost of living. So, if you expect high inflation, you'll be interested in investments such as variable annuities that respond to changes in the stock market and the cost of living.

When inflation is high, workers press for higher wages. If they succeed, the workers have more money, which is good news for businesses selling consumer goods but bad news for the employers; it costs the employers more to do business, and they may become less profitable, which means they can't pay high dividends to stockholders.

However, inflation isn't all bad. Borrowers like inflation because they can pay off their debts with "cheaper" money. They don't like high interest rates, though, and these tend to go along with inflation. But if you're a lender (for instance, if you own bonds), you love high interest rates because they put more money in your pocket.

Why Interest Rates Matter

In a way, money is a kind of merchandise, like fabric or two-by-fours. To operate, businesses have to "buy" money; much of their working funds come from borrowing, not out of profits. If money is "expensive" (that is, if interest rates are high), companies can either "buy" less of it (and cut back on research and expansion), charge more for their products, or cut their profits.

If high interest rates discourage businesses from buying new equipment and creating new jobs, that has a "ripple" effect: When Company A buys less merchandise from Company B, Company B can't hire new workers, pay high dividends to its stockholders, or buy as much from Company C.

Therefore, low interest rates are good for businesses, and are usually good for the stock market. After all, stock prices in general tend to go up when the economy is booming—and an individual company's stock price tends to go up when its balance sheet is healthy.

However, on the simplest level, low interest rates are not so good for the bond market. When interest rates are low, bonds are not too attractive. Why earn 6% on your money when you could earn 10% or more by buying stock? You can probably guess what's coming—that things are more complicated than that. Bond buyers don't always buy "brand new" bonds that were just issued and, therefore, reflect current interest rates. Often, they buy older bonds, issued at a time when rates were higher (or lower).

There are two ways you can make money with an investment. First, you can get income from it (stock dividends, bond interest, rent paid by tenants for use of real estate you own). Second, you can earn a profit by selling your investment for more than you paid for it. (Of course, the risk is that you could lose money by selling it when prices have dropped.)

As current interest rates fall, the price of older bonds rises. This apparently crazy result occurs because if you can buy two otherwise identical bonds—one of them paying 10%, the other paying 7½%—it's natural to prefer (and pay more for) the one paying 10%. So, when interest rates are falling, you can probably earn a good profit selling bonds you already own, but you're likely to lose money if you sell bonds when interest rates are rising.

Interest rate trends also affect your personal financial planning. When rates are low, you can afford a larger loan and, therefore, a more luxurious home or car. When rates are high, you may not be able to buy a home or replace your car at all because you won't meet the lender's standards for qualifying for a loan. Even if you qualify, you may not be willing to shoulder heavy payments.

When interest rates are falling, it could make sense to refinance your mortgage and other loans. Lower interest rates can mean smaller monthly payments, giving you more cash to spend and invest. But this strategy doesn't always work: Sometimes the advantage of lower rates is wiped out by high fees charged to refinance the loan.

High mortgage rates are bad for both home-buyers and home-sellers. The higher the rates, the less likely it is that you can find a buyer willing to pay your price, and also able to qualify for financing. That could mean a longer wait to sell your home, or could force you to drop the price to compensate. Home-buyers benefit by these price cuts—but only if they can find affordable mortgages.

Why Taxes Matter

In the end, it's not what you get that counts—it's what you keep. Intelligent planning (whether for a business or for personal finances) balances the chance of reward against risks and transaction costs. Taxes are a major cost in many transactions.

For instance, let's say you invest $5,000 for five years, and earn an annual return of 8%. After five years, your initial $5,000 investment will have built up to $7,347. Pat yourself on the back. But you can't keep all the money unless you found a tax-exempt investment paying that much. If you're in the 15% bracket, the after-tax value of your investment will be $6,947; if you're in the 28% bracket, it'll be worth $6,616 after taxes. And if you're in the highest, 33% bracket, it'll only be worth $6,492.

The difference between tax-exempt and taxable yields is even more dramatic when the rate of earnings is higher and the term is longer. If you invest the same $5,000 for twenty years, and manage a 10% rate each year, your initial investment will climb to a heady $33,638—*before* taxes. After taxes, it's $25,560 (15% bracket) or $20,085 (28% bracket). If you're in the highest tax bracket, you get to keep only $18,292—only a little more than half the pretax amount.

WORKSHEET: TAXABLE VERSUS TAX-EXEMPT

Use the following worksheet to compare the return you can get—and keep—if you have to choose between taxable and tax-exempt investments. Tax-exempt investments (such as most municipal bonds) usually pay a lower rate of return because of the tax advantage they offer. To find out whether you'd get more spendable income from a taxable investment or from a tax-free investment with a similar degree of risk, go through the following steps.

Step 1: What is the *highest* tax bracket any of your income falls into? (Either 15%,

28%, or 33%.)   _____%

Step 2: Subtract this percentage from 100%:   _____%
Step 3: Multiply the figure from Step 2 (which will
either be 85%, 72%, or 67%) by the return on the
taxable investment: _____%

Step 4: Write the return on the tax-exempt investment: _____%
Step 5: Compare. Whichever figure is higher is the better deal for *you,* based on your tax bracket.

* * *

Before the Tax Code of 1986 became effective, you would have a major choice to make between ordinary income (such as bond interest) and capital gains (profit from selling a stock, bond, or other investment). Capital gains got favorable tax treatment. That's no longer the case (see page 139 for more on this theme).

However, you can still use investments to delay taxation. If you buy a bond that pays taxable interest, you must pay tax each year on the interest received; if you sell a stock or bond at a profit, you don't have to pay tax on the appreciation (increase in value) until you sell the investment. Of course, you can't spend the increase in value until you sell the investment, either—but it does increase your net worth, and can be used as collateral for loans.

Not only do tax rates affect your personal investment choices, they also affect business operations and the stock market. Lower taxes can mean more investment (though not always—companies can increase top executives' salaries instead of buying new machinery, and people can go to the Bahamas instead of buying stocks and bonds). See page 139 for more about the effect of taxes on investment choices.

Investments That Fit Your Needs

There's no single, perfect investment because investors vary so widely. Some enjoy taking wild risks if huge profits are a possibility; others are solidly conservative and prefer predictable, low-risk investments. Investment goals also differ. Some investors need income right now: for instance, retirees who have to supplement pensions and Social Security.

Others are interested in long-term growth. The classic case: parents of small children, who invest now for future tuition needs.

Investment Strategies

There's no *single* perfect investment: Diversification is important. There are exceptions to this rule, but you'll probably be better off with several small and diverse investments. If, for instance, you've accumulated a cushion of savings and completed your insurance portfolio, and you have $5,000 to invest, you might be better off getting a $1,000 Certificate of Deposit (CD) and investing in two or three mutual funds with different objectives (let's say, a growth and income fund and an aggressive growth fund), or buying a few shares of two or three different stocks, rather than putting the whole $5,000 into a single investment.

Assessing an Investment

• *How risky is it?* (Of course, even if there's only a one-in-a-million chance of getting hit by comet debris, you could be the unlucky one.) Risk is measured relative to the investment market as a whole.

• *What is the possibility of return?* Sometimes you know the return on an investment (for instance, the interest rate on a bond); sometimes you have to guess (how much will a stock sell for next year?). It helps to research the history of an investment (such as the ups and downs of stock and bond prices), keeping in mind that good performance in the past can't guarantee the level of future returns.

  Return is also measured relative to the whole market. There's an old Wall Street saying, "Never mistake a bull market for brains." That is, you don't have to be a genius to make money when all stock prices are rising. The converse is that you (or a mutual-fund manager) are not necessarily stupid if you lose money when the market is down. In that situation, great performance means losing less than the market as a whole.

• *Do you understand the deal?* Is it a straightforward stock purchase, or an investment in a shopping center, or a mutual fund with an investment philosophy that you can understand and agree with—or is it a complex deal involving covered calls, speculation on the Brazilian cruzeiro, and aluminum futures? Don't invest until you can understand how your money will be used, and what you can expect.

• *What's the minimum investment?* Some banks will sell $500 CDs; some mutual funds will let you open an account with $250, while others demand $1,000 or even $5,000. You can buy a hundred shares of a "penny" stock for a couple of hundred dollars plus commissions, which is what it would cost for a single share of some blue-chip stocks.

• *What are the transaction costs?* If you buy a stock or bond from a broker, there's a commission involved (the size of which depends on the firm's policy and the size of your purchase). If you buy a "no-load" mutual fund there's no sales charge, but there will be a management fee each year. If you buy a "12b-1" mutual fund, you'll be charged for the fund's marketing expenses in addition to the management fee. If you buy a "load" fund, there's a sales charge of anywhere from 1% to 8½%, plus the management fee. Furthermore, there may be a "back-end load" charged when you sell your shares, or a "switch fee" when you exchange shares in one fund for shares in another fund managed by the same "fund family."

• How quickly can you get your money out if you need it, or if you want to change investments? It could take months—say, if you want to sell a house that you bought as an investment. At the other end of the spectrum, if you invest in a money market fund or mutual fund with "check-writing" privileges, you can take out some of your money whenever you like. (The funds usually set a minimum on the "checks" you can write—$500 is typical—there may be a per-check charge; and the process of closing your account is likely to be longer and more difficult because the check-writing privilege makes it harder to determine how much is in your account.)

Investment Choices for Average People

This book deals only with investments that are suitable for an investor with limited funds, who can't plunge into wild speculations. This chapter concentrates on mutual funds, stock, bonds, and real estate. Although all of these investment media have their risks, they can be good choices for investors who start with a small amount of capital, who do not have long experience or professional education in investing, and who don't have access to private portfolio managers.

17. Mutual Funds

Mutual funds provide two major advantages: diversification and professional management. Mutual funds give you a chance to invest in many stocks for a small amount of money. Most mutual funds do require a minimum investment: $250 to $1,000 is typical, although some funds require a larger initial investment, and a few funds do not have a minimum. Many funds permit you to open an account with a lower minimum, or none at all, if your account is for an IRA.

Mutual funds are set up with a variety of objectives; the portfolio managers choose, buy, and sell investments to meet these objectives. The best-known fund types are:

• Growth funds, specializing in stocks that the portfolio managers believe are undervalued and will increase in value over time. Growth funds differ in the amount of risk they are willing to take. Some are "balanced growth" funds, with a comparatively low risk; others are "aggressive growth" funds, which are much riskier because they take bigger chances, buying very speculative stocks that could drop in value—or involved in acquisitions whose parent com-

panies could go bankrupt. An "OTC fund" invests only in, or specializes in, stocks of companies sold "over the counter" (not on a major
stock exchange). Most of these stocks are newer or smaller companies
likely to be more risky than well-established "blue chip" stocks.

• Income funds invest in stocks that pay high dividends (utility stocks
are a popular choice); some invest in both stocks and bonds. Growth
and income funds aim at selecting a portfolio that has both the potential for increase in stock prices and a steady stream of income.

• Bond funds, of course, invest in bonds. There are funds that invest
in corporate bonds ("junk bonds" are risky corporate bonds that pay
a high rate of interest—as long as they don't default), and funds that
invest in government bonds—federal, state, local, or a mixture of all
three. Some bond funds invest in tax-exempt bonds, and income
from these funds is likely to be tax-exempt. The risk level of a bond
fund depends on the rating of the bonds in which it invests—the
lower the rating, the higher the risk.

• Money market funds invest in financial instruments such as bank
CDs, short-term government obligations, and commercial paper
(short-term IOU's issued by businesses). They're low-risk because
there are hardly any defaults on instruments like these. Some money
market funds invest only in tax-exempt instruments, so they yield
income that is probably tax-free.

• Sector funds invest in only one sector of the economy: maybe mining stocks or biotechnology companies or utility companies or health
care companies. Sector funds are always risky because you're taking
on an additional layer of risk (not only that the stock market will
behave well, and that the portfolio managers will choose wisely, but
that the particular sector of the economy will do well).

• International funds invest in securities issued outside the United
States—either all over the globe or in a particular part of it (e.g.,
Japan and Korea, Australia). These are risky too because it's harder
to monitor investments in countries (language problems, differences
in accounting practices) other than the United States, and because
you're taking the risk that changes in currency values will make your
investment less valuable, or even wipe it out.

Another basic distinction you should be aware of is the difference
between "open-end" and "closed-end" funds. Most funds are open-
ended: They continue to accept new investments as long as they
think they can turn in an adequate performance. (See page 111 for
the effect of fund size on performance.) Closed-end funds are limited
to a certain amount of investment (say, half a billion dollars). Once
that amount is reached, fund shares are no longer sold to new investors. If you want to buy in, you have to buy the shares of someone
who has already invested.

There are "fund families" of mutual funds issued and sold by financial organizations such as Fidelity (the largest), Dreyfus, Scudder, and

many others. The advantage of a fund family is that you can "switch"— issue instructions to have part of your investment shifted from one fund to another. This is an easy way to adapt your investment portfolio to deal with changes in the stock market and the economy. If you think OTC stocks will boom but bonds will go bust, you can switch out of a bond fund and into an OTC fund.

Mutual Fund Returns

The subject of mutual fund returns is a very difficult one. First of all, the returns change constantly (like baseball statistics), and yesterday's champ can be today's bum. For instance, in the first quarter of 1987, some of the best mutual fund performers were precious metal funds that invested in the stocks of companies mining and refining gold and other precious metals. Some of these funds scored a return of over 60% in the first quarter. Some precious metal funds also performed well in 1986—but shares in these funds *lost* about one-quarter of their value in 1984 and 1985. (A fund's performance is usually measured by adding the value of all the securities in its portfolio, including dividends and profits earned by selling securities, dividing by the number of shares, and comparing this figure to the figure for an earlier period.)

In 1986, the best performing fund gained almost 75%—and the worst performing fund lost almost 25%. For the first quarter of 1987, the average for 648 major mutual funds was up almost 20%. That sounds terrific until you realize that that the Standard & Poor's 500 (an index of 500 major stocks) went up 21.35% during the same time period. So you would have done better just by buying shares of all the S&P 500 stocks without trying to decide which stocks would soar, which would lag. ("Index funds" do just that—they buy all the stocks in the S&P, or the Dow Jones Industrial Average, or another group of stocks used as a measuring standard.)

Another problem is that mutual funds use different assumptions in figuring out their yield. For instance, some of them quote yield on the assumption that all dividends are reinvested, but some mutual fund shareholders get their dividends paid to them in cash, instead of using them to buy more shares in the mutual fund. Funds also have different ways of handling stock splits and dividends issued to the fund by companies whose stock the fund owns in the form of stock, not cash.

Funds can also manipulate time periods—for example, by reporting their performance for a twenty-nine-month period, or other odd amount of time, chosen to make their performance look good. But all bets were off in October 1987, when the market lost over 500 points. Remember, no bull market lasts forever. If possible, find out how well the fund has done over the past ten years so that you can see how they managed when times were rough. (Of course, not every mutual fund has been in existence for ten years.)

You can get objective figures for fund yields from the financial press (try *Business Week, Fortune, Forbes,* or *Money* magazine, or stories in your favorite newspaper), or from publishers who put out annual almanacs summarizing the performance of hundreds of mutual funds in the past year.

How Much Does It Cost to Play?

Finding out how much it costs to play is another tough subject because different funds charge a confusing variety of charges for their services. All funds charge an annual management fee, which usually runs between ½ of 1% and 2% of the balance in your fund account. That's the only constant. If the mutual fund is efficient, its management fee should be somewhere around 0.6% to 0.8% of the net asset value (NAV). NAV equals the total value of all the fund's assets, divided by the number of shares in the fund.

Originally, there was a clear distinction between "no-load" funds, which were sold through the mail by the funds themselves, and "load" funds, which were sold by brokers. "Load" funds imposed a one-time charge of 8% to 8½% of the original investment to pay the broker.

Now, the lines are blurred. Mutual funds now sell "low-load" funds directly to customers, and some funds available through brokers have less than the traditional load. To make things even more confusing, some funds have added new kinds of charges.

A low-load fund imposes a one-time charge (typically 1½% to 3% of your initial investment) when you buy a fund. A "back-end load" is a one-time charge assessed when you sell shares in a mutual fund. Sometimes the back-end load diminishes or phases out if you hold your shares for more than a certain period of time (e.g., seven years); sometimes the back-end load decreases if you invest more than the "breakpoint" of $10,000, $25,000, or whatever figure the fund chooses.

A 12b-1 fund (named after SEC Rule 12b-1) charges annual "distribution fees" (typically ¼ of 1% to 2% of the balance in your account) to pay for the fund's marketing expenses.

How can you find out what a fund charges? If you're buying your fund through a broker, ask him or her to explain all the charges, and how they will affect the return on your investment. If you're buying directly from the fund, read the prospectus (the legal document that you must receive before you invest). The various types of fees will be explained there. Or, consult a reference book, a mutual fund almanac, or a magazine article that summarizes the rules for various mutual funds.

It would certainly simplify life if I could tell you to restrict your investments to no-load funds so that more of your money could be put to work for you, not the mutual fund or your broker. Very often, that's a good idea—but some of the funds with the best performance are load, low-load, or 12b-1 funds. The key is how the fund performs *after* all expenses are taken into account.

Big Fund or Small?

There are mutual funds that have a relatively small number of share-holders and a few million dollars to invest—and funds that have millions of investors and billions of dollars to invest. There's a real philosophical difference about which is a better choice.

Those who favor small funds say they're lean, mean, and ambitious, striving hard to attract investors. In this view, the larger, older funds are lazy fat cats, relying on the fact that investors tend to leave their money where it is—at least until a fund turns *really* sour. Then there's the paradox of mutual fund success. Let's say that a smart, talented mutual fund manager finds enough underappreciated stocks to make up a portfolio that scores exceptionally high returns. (Of course, there are lots of fund managers, managers of pension fund portfolios, and investment advisers who are also out beating the bushes for those un-derloved stocks, and waiting for them to soar in value.) Everybody looks at the manager's terrific returns and tries to invest in his or her mutual fund. So the manager has to find two or three times as many under-valued stocks—a task that's more than twice as difficult.

The other side of the argument is that large mutual funds can benefit by economies of scale. When they buy blocks of stock, they can negotiate for a commission rate cut to the bone. They can afford to install the most sophisticated computer systems. They can publicize a new fund by appealing to their existing customers. And, if there's a hot new stock issue, with demand exceeding supply, underwriters and brokers are much more likely to "find" a few shares for a huge fund that's done millions of dollars of business with them than for a small fund that contributed a few thousand dollars to their coffers.

A 1986 study by Lipper Analytical Services (a company that studies the performance of various kinds of investments) shows that 20 of the top 100 mutual funds for the period of July 1982 to April 1986 were small funds (those with assets under $25 million). That sounds like a clear vote of confidence for the little guys until you realize that 53% of the funds fell into the small-fund category. "Fell" is the operative word for the two-thirds of the 100 *worst* funds that were described as small.

Choosing Mutual Funds

Here are some guidelines if you want to start your investment program with mutual funds, or add some mutual fund shares to your portfolio.

- Before you invest, get all the information you can—both from the fund itself and from independent sources.
- In general, the narrower a fund, the more risky it is (but the more room for appreciation in value).
- Find out what the minimum initial investment is, and the minimum

investment you can later add to your account. The quickest way to get money into an account is to wire transfer it; that way, the fund doesn't have to wait for your check to clear.

• Find out the steps you must follow to take money *out* of your account, whether you're switching to another fund in the same family or taking out money to spend. The most convenient is telephone transfer to other funds or to banks, or "check-writing" privileges that let you transfer money to yourself or to another payee. Many disgruntled investors who do not have telephone transfer or check-writing privileges have found out that it can take a long time and lots of nagging to get mutual funds to issue checks to shareholders who sell shares in the mutual fund.

• Investing in *one* mutual fund gives you a chance to diversify because the fund invests in many different securities. You can take a further step and diversify by investing in several different types of mutual funds. For instance, if you have $5,000 to invest, and can take a little bit of risk, you can put $2,000 in a safe, high-performing growth and income fund, and $1,000 each in a bond fund, aggressive growth fund, and sector or international fund.

Monitor the performance of your funds. The fund will send you regular statements—and there's a phone number on the statements which you can call to find out the share price for the fund for the day you call. If interest rates go up, your bond fund will probably do badly (and vice versa, if interest rates go down); aggressive growth funds tend to do well if stock prices are climbing; sector funds respond to the demand for that sector's products; international funds respond to the strength of the dollar as well as the strength of the particular country's economy.

If a particular fund is performing badly, you may want to switch to another fund (or hang on because you believe that conditions will change). When you want to add to your investment later, use the results of the monitoring process to choose a fund.

Money Market Funds

Money market funds are a special kind of mutual fund. They invest only in "money market instruments"—legal mechanisms for short-term borrowing. Some money market funds invest only in federal government obligations, so they're very safe: If the U.S. government goes out of business, the status of your money market fund will be the least of your worries. Others specialize in tax-exempt instruments (such as short-term borrowing by state agencies), so the investors in these funds can escape income tax on income by the fund. (By the way, even though money market funds work a lot like bank accounts, and even though the fund's income derives from interest payments made by borrowers to lenders, the income you earn should be reported on your tax return as dividends—not as interest.)

Money market funds are always safe investments because the debt instruments they invest in are very, very unlikely to suffer default. These "money funds" are also very convenient for investors because of the check-writing privileges they offer. So why isn't this A#1 choice discussed at the beginning of the section? Because the rates that money market funds pay their investors depend completely on prevailing interest rates. When interest rates are high, money market funds are a wonderful investment. When they're low, you might as well keep your money in the bank. As Hemingway said, "Long time ago good, now no good." Alas.

18. Buying and Selling Individual Stocks

Many successful investors swear by the strategy of finding a good broker, doing solid research, then buying and selling individual stocks. You rely on your own talents, not someone else's. You won't be able to diversify as much as if you bought mutual fund shares (because you won't be able to afford as many stocks), but that could also mean there will be fewer *lousy* stocks in your portfolio.

Very few of the hundreds of thousands of American corporations sell their stock to the public. It's not so much that they don't want the money as that registration—the legal process of qualifying to sell stock publicly—is difficult, time-consuming, and very, very expensive. What should you do if you're offered the chance to buy some stock that is not registered?

This isn't the same as being offered stolen merchandise that "fell off the truck": It *is* legal to sell nonregistered stock, if a strict set of legal rules is followed. The buyer usually has to promise to hold the stock for at least two years before selling it. The theory is that the buyer is a serious investor, not a speculator seeking quick profits. If you can wait that long, this "letter stock" can be an excellent deal. Sometimes the new company does fantastically well, "goes public," and its shares explode in value. But sometimes the company just explodes, and its shares will become worthless.

But it's much more likely that you'll restrict your stock buying to publicly available shares. The advantage is that the stock of publicly traded companies can be bought or sold whenever you want: You don't have to wait a long time to find a buyer (as you might for a tangible asset such as a work of art or a house).

Publicly traded stock comes in two varieties: listed and over-the-counter. An explanation of the difference depends on a further fact: You're not allowed to buy or sell stock by yourself; you must go through a licensed broker. Even if your friend Ralph needs cash for a new garage and would be happy to sell you his Consolidated Sousaphone shares for $1,000, you still have to use a broker. But what the broker does depends on whether the stock is listed or not.

Listed stock is listed on a stock exchange. The largest exchanges are the New York Stock Exchange (the "Big Board") and the American Stock Exchange. A stock exchange is a sort of club: The exchange itself decides which stocks are important enough to be traded there; the corporation issuing the stock can either accept or reject the invitation. Sales of listed stocks are handled through the exchange, which "matches up" sellers and buyers. If you want to sell stock that no one wants to buy right at that moment, a broker called a "specialist" in that stock "makes a market" by buying the stuff from you himself, then holding onto it until an outside buyer turns up.

It's easy to find out how many shares of listed stocks were traded on a particular day, and the prices: Stock quotation pages in newspapers and financial media, such as *Barron's* and *Investor's Daily,* give price quotes for these stocks on every weekday.

However, over-the-counter stocks are bought and sold directly by brokers. Typically, these are the stocks of smaller or younger companies. Their stock is usually lower priced but riskier than the stock issued by more established companies. Furthermore, few of these stocks pay dividends, so the investor's motive is usually the hope that the stock price will go up, not the expectation of a steady stream of dividend income.

A "penny stock" is one selling for less than $5 a share. Not all OTC stocks are penny stocks, but there's a high correlation. One viewpoint is that penny stocks are great for novice investors because those investors can easily afford the shares (and can afford to suffer the loss even if the shares become absolutely worthless). The other viewpoint is that it's all too likely that the investor will have to absorb the loss, and that stock market tyros should start out with higher-quality stocks until they understand the market and its workings.

Because OTC stocks are not as heavily traded (weeks, or even months, can go by without a single share of some OTC stocks being traded), less information is available about their prices. An association of brokers, the National Association of Securities Dealers (NASD), maintains a computerized listing of the current prices of about 5,000 OTC stocks. Your broker can just tap into the NASDAQ (NASD Automated Quote) system to find out the price of any of these stocks; newspapers also print price quotes for some popular OTC stocks. Financial publishers publish "pink sheets" (daily or weekly quotes) for smaller, more obscure issues.

Types of Stock

Common Stock. The most common type of stock is common stock. Owning common stock in a corporation gives you the right to vote for the corporation's directors, and on other important issues of corporate governance. (Well, usually; but a recent development is the issuance of nonvoting common stock, which is entitled to dividends like the usual kind of common stock, but which doesn't carry a vote.)

Preferred Stock.   Preferred stock doesn't carry voting rights, but does permit its owners to be first in line when dividends are declared; the stock also sets the level of dividends to be paid and, therefore, the level of income the preferred shareholders can expect. Where do dividends come from? After a company pays all its expenses, including its taxes, it generally has money left over. The money can be plowed back into improving the business or distributed to the stockholders in the form of dividends. Companies assess their financial position, release information about their financial status to the public, and declare (or decide to skip) dividends four times a year. If a company issues preferred stock (many companies only have common stock), the common stockholders can't receive a dividend until the preferred stockholders have gotten the level of dividend promised.

Cumulative Preferred.   If things are so bad that the company can't pay dividends for one or more quarters, cumulative preferred stock promises that the preferred stockholders will get a belated payment of all the dividends that were missed before the common stockholders get any dividends. So preferred stock is the choice of investors who are more interested in current income than in long-term growth.

Convertible preferred stock, which can be exchanged for shares of the company's own common stock, offers income and a chance for appreciation. (Other possible choices: common stock in a company that has a history of paying high dividends to common shareholders and bonds.)

Stock Dividends.   A stock dividend is a dividend paid in the form of shares of stock instead of money. (It's a way to keep the stockholders happy without giving them actual cash.) A stock split occurs when the price of a company's shares goes high enough to discourage potential stockholders. If the company decides to "split" the shares, it "recalls" the shares, and gives each shareholder, let's say, three new shares for every two old ones turned in. Each of the new shares is worth less than an old share; the hope is that the price of the new, less-expensive shares will rise until the total is higher than the old total.

Short Sales.   It's not illegal to sell stock you don't own, but it *is* risky. If you believe a stock's price will go down, you can "sell the stock short." (Since the beginning of 1987, it's also possible to sell mutual fund shares short.) That is, you sell it now, and agree to produce the stock some time in the future. You "cover the short" by buying the stock when it's time to deliver. If you were right about the price trend, you can make money by buying the stock for less than what you've already sold it for. The risky part is that you could be wrong—and you have to buy the stock for *whatever* it costs, which could be much more than the selling price.

Let's say, for instance, that you pick a stock that now sells for $20 a share. You think its price will dive below $14. So you find someone naive or optimistic enough to buy the stock from you at $19. When it comes time to settle up, you discover, much to your chagrin, that it sells for $26 a share. You lost $7 per share: the $26 you must pay minus the $19 you get. But your wrong guess would have been cataclysmic if you'd had to spend $44 a share to buy the shares you sold for $19 apiece.

The traditional advice to small investors was to avoid short sales, leaving them to sophisticated investors. Today, it's more accepted as a worthwhile, if risky, strategy for the small investor. It all depends on how much faith you have in your ability to forecast the trend of stock prices—and how much trouble you'll be in if you lose money on the short sale.

Americus Trust. The Americus Trust (named after the company that originated it) is a fairly new wrinkle. The trust buys shares of stock (either from a single company or a group of stocks, such as those making up the Dow Jones Industrial Average), then issues new securities called "primes" and "scores." A "prime" gives the owner the right to receive dividends; a "score" gives the owner a profit when the stock appreciates in value. (Sometimes the prime owners get the appreciation up to a certain amount, and the score owners get the rest.) The prime holder is the one who gets to vote the shares.

The theory is that the combination of prime and score will be worth more than the underlying share of stock. It's also a way for investors to concentrate on either income or appreciation, whichever they prefer. Caution is needed: If you swap shares of stock for primes and scores offered by trusts established or registered before early 1987, there are no tax consequences to the swap. But if you buy into a "Johnny-come-lately" trust, the IRS will consider it a sale and expect you to pay tax on any profits. Check before you invest!

Choosing a Broker

If you're going to buy and sell stocks, you'll have to use a broker; and if you rely on advice from your broker, you'd better pick a good one. There can also be significant differences in fees depending on the brokerage firm you choose.

Before 1975, the last factor didn't enter into the choice of brokers. All brokers charged the same commissions, which came from a fee schedule set by organizations of securities dealers. It was considered unethical to depart from the schedule in any way—even to give customers a discount.

However, in 1975, brokers were permitted to set their own commission rates. They could adopt one of two marketing strategies: either to compete on price, becoming "discount" brokers, or compete on service, offering investment analysis, research, and advice.

However, once again, things aren't as simple as they seem. Sometimes a small trade, or a trade in inexpensive stock, may be *less* expensive when carried out by a full-service broker. Discount brokers' fee schedules are frequently geared to volume discounts, and there may be a set minimum fee that exceeds the full service broker's fee for the same transaction. To cope with this, you could open an account with one discount and one full-service brokerage house, and choose between them for each transaction to find the best deal.

Choosing a broker is also a matter of personalities. Some people want a lot of investment advice; others just want the deal pushed through as fast as possible. Some investors love to hear the broker's latest recommendations. Others suspect that the broker is pushing the stock because it's the "dog of the week," and everyone at the brokerage house is working frantically to find unfortunate investors to take it off their hands.

19. Monitoring Your Investments

Before you buy a stock, you'll want to find out about it; to decide which investments to keep and which to sell, you'll have to check dividend levels, stock prices, and the financial health of the company.

What's a Dow?

Maybe you're concerned about the fate of a particular stock you own. Has RubberGasket Bubblegum gone up or down? What are its earnings per share this quarter? What is its price/earnings (P/E) ratio? (The P/E ratio, the stock's current price divided by earnings over the past year, further divided by the number of outstanding shares, is considered highly significant in many systems of stock analysis.) How high will this quarter's dividend be?

Or, you might want to know how the stock market as a whole—and, by extension, the economy—is doing. "The Dow," or another stock index, is a useful tool. An index is made up by choosing a group of representative stocks and seeing what happens to their prices and/or dividends over time.

Although Dow Jones (a compiler and publisher of financial information) maintains several indexes, when people talk about "the Dow" they usually mean the Dow Jones Industrial Average (DJIA).

The DJIA consists of thirty industrial and related stocks. The index always has thirty stocks—but the makeup of the index has changed over the sixty years of its existence. For instance, American Express was added to the Dow in 1982. IBM joined the Dow in 1932, when it still made tabulating machines, was removed from the index in 1939, and roared back triumphantly in 1979.

The index number is calculated just by adding together the prices of all thirty stocks, then multiplying by a figure that accounts for stock splits and changes in the makeup of the index. Throughout the first quarter of 1987, the Dow stayed well over 2,000, making the average price of a Dow share about $70. This is an all-time high for the index—until inflation is considered. If prices are restated in 1966 dollars, the adjusted Dow stands at about 600—lower than the real Dow was in 1966. However, stockholders have been earning dividends all along, and when both inflation and dividends are factored in, the adjusted Dow is about 1,400. This means that the Dow beat inflation by about 3% a year. It's too soon to tell the effect of the October 1987 collapse; perhaps when the battlefield has been cleared up investors will find that their investments did not outpace inflation.

Other Indexes

The Dow tells you a lot about market trends, but not everything. It's a small sample of stocks, and not necessarily the most representative. So other indexes are used to study stock market trends. The Standard and Poor's 500 (S&P 500, or just S&P), as you'd expect, tracks the behavior of 500 stocks. Some of them are issued by companies much smaller than the thirty in the DJIA. So the S&P is more informative than the DJIA in situations where small companies and large companies are faring differently in the stock market.

How to Analyze a Stock's Performance

There are dozens of methods for analyzing a stock's performance. People use numerology, astrology, hemline lengths, Superbowl results, and the libido of male executives to figure out what the market will do next. But that's only part of the problem.

Even if, miraculously, you knew *exactly* what would happen to the Dow or the S&P 500, you still wouldn't know if the particular stocks you happen to own would behave like the market as a whole or head in the opposite direction. Either you can "buy the market," by investing in a mutual fund that tries to buy shares that come as close as possible to representing the entire stock market (or at least the S&P 500), or you can analyze the history of your stocks and what you believe will be their future behavior.

Serious analysts tend to fall into three groups: the *fundamentalists* who study economic "fundamentals" about a company (such as its earnings, the success of its product lines, the state of its physical plant) as a guide to whether to buy or sell the stock, the *technicians* or *chartists* who look at changes in a stock's price and the volume of stock sales as a predictor of its future price, and *contrarians* who are both cynical and cyclical. They go around buying up stocks no one else wants, figuring that today's unfashionable investment is bound to come back as next year's star.

Random walkers believe that no rational patterns can be found in stock prices, and that a monkey throwing darts at the stock pages would do as well as an MBA with a fifth-generation computer. This would be a big joke, except for the fact that dart board portfolios frequently do as well as carefully managed ones.

Who Can Help?

If you want advice about buying and selling specific securities, you can turn to a full-service broker (as described above). You can also get advice from a financial planner. However, the law requires that anyone who gives specific, individual advice about securities must be registered with the Securities and Exchange Commission (SEC) as an investment adviser.

If your financial planner is not registered, he or she can still give you information about integrating your investments into an overall financial plan. That is, he or she can't (legally) tell you to sell your AT&T stock and buy General Motors instead—*but* he or she can advise you about the amount of investment income you'll need to meet a financial goal such as paying off your mortgage.

The traditional sources of financial planning advice in general are brokers (who advise on specific investments), bankers (if they are personal bankers they will be familiar enough with your financial situation to offer long-range financial planning), insurance agents (who will inform you about both the protective and investment functions of insurance), accountants (who deal with taxes, financial record keeping, and valuation of assets), and lawyers (who can handle your tax and estate planning).

If you need help, then, you can turn to any of these individuals or institutions. And if you're confused about integrating all these elements, turn to a well-trained person who can give a comprehensive view of a variety of financial products and how they can be used in a long-term plan.

The new profession of financial planning aims to do this. That's the ideal; not all financial planners have the training or experience to live up to it. So, before you hire a financial planner, find out:

• What his or her training is. In most states, anyone can hang out a shingle as a financial planner. You want a person with training such as that provided by the American College (whose graduates are called chartered financial consultants) or the College for Financial Planning (where Certified Financial Planners are trained). The International Association for Financial Planning is the professional organization for financial planners.
• How the planner keeps up with new developments, once basic skills have been learned.
• How much you pay for a financial plan or for advice. Some planners work for an hourly rate, others for a flat fee, and a third group sells financial products directly and collects a commission.

There are good planners in all three groups, but each kind of compensation has its temptations. Planners paid by the hour have an incentive to drag out the process to earn more money. Flat-fee planners have the opposite temptation: to hustle you out of the office with a "canned" plan, without really exploring your personal needs and priorities. Those on commission might be tempted to recommend financial products that carry the highest commissions. Overall, you're looking to work with a long-range financial planner for years; this will help ensure that the planner will be working to keep your business, not turn a quick profit for himself or herself.

• What the planner provides in a complete plan. A really good financial plan explores what you already own (including your insurance portfolio), your income and expenses, what your long-range goals are (or helps you set goals), and makes general recommendations of investments you can make now and others for the future. (If the financial planner is licensed as a broker or registered as an investment adviser, he or she can make specific recommendations.) The plan should take taxes and transaction costs (such as brokerage commissions) into account, and should give you alternate strategies if conditions change or the planner's recommendations don't pan out.

• Whether the planner works with a team. For instance, can the planner recommend a lawyer familiar with estate planning, a good tax lawyer, if necessary, an accountant who understands pensions?

To be an informed client, you'll need to understand the financial basics and keep in touch with financial developments. And if you handle all your decision making by yourself, without professional advice, you'll certainly need sources of data.

• Then, fill out the "Big Checklist" (on page 6) before you set up an appointment

Information from the Media

There's a huge business press out there, waiting to tell you about stock market trends and to shine the spotlight on individual companies and their securities. Start with the financial coverage in your favorite newspaper and the TV news show you watch—they'll tell you what the Dow is doing; the newspaper will probably carry all the stock and bond tables you need. If that doesn't give you enough information, try investment guides and magazines for the general reader, or network or cable TV shows aimed at business people and investors.

And if you're still not satisfied, move on to the more specialized financial press (such as *Barron's*, the *Financial Times*, and the *Wall Street Journal*, which is my personal favorite and has great coverage of personal finance issues). If you need your news fast, there are monthly and bi-monthly newsletters that make investment recommendations (and newsletters that sum up the other newsletters' recommendations). There are even daily computer services, if you have to know each day's developments.

For most investors, though, the numbers are the thing. Fundamentalists revel in a company's annual report to the stockholders. If you're not a stockholder, you can request a copy anyway, or read it in a business library.

Naturally, the annual report contains words as well as numbers, such as a letter from the corporation's management to the shareholders summarizing the past year and outlining goals for the future. (It can be really instructive to compare this year's results to last year's goals.)

The "MD&A" is also worth reading. It's the "management discussion and analysis" of the success of the corporation's business activities. The corporation sums up its financial results in the income statement (also called profit and loss statement, or P&L) which contains past figures for the past three to ten years to compare money earned, costs, taxes, and finally the net income, or bottom line. Summaries of financial health also appear in the balance sheet, which itemizes the corporation's assets and liabilities as of a particular date. The footnotes to the balance sheet are especially important—they disclose everything out of the ordinary in the balance-sheet figures and the way at which they were arrived.

Many corporations—the largest ones—are SEC "registrants." They have to register with the SEC and disclose data such as yearly reports, quarterly reports, and certain important events (such as major changes in stock ownership, or a change in the accounting firm that audits the firm's books). Auditor changes can be important because the auditor may have quit or been fired because the auditor found something amiss—or just before the auditor uncovered evidence of monkey business. The SEC reports can be read at an SEC public reading room (found in the federal government building in large cities). Stockholders can order free copies of reports about corporations whose shares they own.

How to Read the Financial Pages

Newspapers publish very detailed tables of stock prices. These tables are the technician's best friend because they can be used to draw the charts that are analyzed to predict the stock's price movements. For stocks whose prices are listed in the newspaper, you can find out the highest and lowest price the stock has reached in the preceding year. Then you'll know how the stock is performing relative to its past prices.

The newspaper will also tell you the annual dividend per share, the stock's yield (the income that the dividend provides, stated as a percentage of the stock's price), and the stock's P/E ratio. The financial pages tell you the volume of trading for each stock (the number of shares sold that day) and summarize the most actively traded stocks of the day as well as the stocks with the biggest increases and declines in value. Usually, the volume figures leave out two zeros, so 450 means 45,000 shares traded—but figures that start with "z" are for low-volume stocks, and the figure on the table is the actual number of shares traded.

The last figures on the table show that day's trading: the highest and lowest prices for the day and the closing price (the stock's price when trading closed for the day). The very last figure is the change between the preceding closing price and that day's closing price. Prices are given in dollars and eighths of dollars, so 19¼, up ¼ means that the stock closed at $19.25 a share—25¢ more than the preceding day's closing price.

Stock tables for OTC stocks are less complex, giving only sales volume, the stock's bid price (what buyers offered to pay), asked price (what the sellers asked for), and the change in the bid price since the previous trading day.

When you follow the tables for stock you own, you can put the stock's price changes in context. Is the P/E ratio rising or falling? How is the stock doing compared to this time last year? Is the volume high? If so, it could either signal lots of buyers trying to take advantage of a superior stock, or lots of stockholders rushing for the exit before a total collapse. You can also compare your stock to the stock of companies founded at about the same time, in a comparable geographic area, and in more or less the same line of business.

Yes, it's a lot of work. Millions of people find trading in stocks to be a fascinating (and often profitable) combination of hobby and business. If you have too much anxiety about individual stocks, or if you're not prepared to take the time to monitor stocks and trade them actively— or if you find that the more you trade, the more commissions you have to pay without generating much profit—you don't have to give up investing.

You can pick stocks that you expect to increase in price over the long term (five to ten years), buy the stocks, and then *hold* them. You can invest in mutual funds, and leave the decisions to the fund manager. If you're more interested in earning income that can be spent right away than in seeing the value of your investment grow, you can buy bonds and hold them. Or, if you want to earn profits by anticipating interest trends, you can buy bonds, then sell them when market conditions raise their price.

Bonds

Compared to the stock market, bonds seem tremendously staid. Traditionally, bond buyers bought the bonds for a steady stream of income and held onto them until maturity. But today, with frequent changes in interest rates, you can trade actively in bonds, or even speculate, taking advantage of the price fluctuations caused by changes in interest rates. (See page 103 for an explanation of why this happens.)

How Bonds Work

A bond is an IOU. Instead of borrowing from a bank, a corporation or government agency issues bonds—a promise to pay a certain amount (the face value) on a certain date (the maturity date). There are two major ways in which bonds work. In the traditional way, the bond pays regular interest (usually every quarter); either the bond has a series of coupons, one of which must be returned to collect each interest payment, or the whole thing is handled by computer. The interest rate is set when the bond is issued.

A "zero coupon" bond doesn't pay interest. Instead, it's sold way below face value (the longer it is until maturity, the lower the price because the issuer gets to use your money for longer). At maturity, the issuer pays you the face value. Many investors like zero-coupon bonds because they're an inexpensive way to "lock in" a guaranteed return later on: when you're ready to retire or when your kids enter college, for instance.

But watch out: If you want to sell a zero-coupon bond to another investor before the bond matures, you may lose money because the market prices of zero-coupon bonds fluctuate a lot as a result of interest rate changes. Also watch out for taxes: Unless the "zero-coup" bond is a tax-free municipal bond, you must pay taxes each year on "phantom interest," which is the interest you *would* have received if the bond paid regular interest.

How to Buy Bonds

Bonds are usually purchased from a broker, who charges a commission based on the cost of the bond. You may not want to buy bonds because you have to buy (or sell) a whole bond; you can't just sell part of it if you need a little ready cash. (But see page 125 about stripped bonds.) The issuer of the bond (such as a corporation or state agency) sets the face value of the bond—usually $5,000 or $10,000, although there are some $1,000 bonds. To get over this difficulty, and to add diversity to your bond investments, you can buy shares in bond funds. Then, if you own 300 shares in a fund, you can sell 100 of them, buy 50 more, or whatever, without having to worry about the face value of the underlying bonds. Bond funds, like stock mutual funds, can either be bought from a broker or, if the fund is a "no-load" or "low load" fund, directly from the fund.

Also like stock mutual funds, bond funds differ in their fee policies. "Closed-end bond funds" (also called "unit trusts"), which buy a portfolio of bonds and just hold onto them until maturity, tend to charge lower management fees than "open-end funds," which trade actively. Fair enough: There's a lot more work and higher costs involved in active trading.

Many financial companies sell no-load or low-load open-end bond funds directly to the public; closed-end funds tend to be "load" funds, with a one-time charge of 4% to 5% of the initial investment. However, closed-end funds tend to yield about 1% more income than bond funds with a comparable risk level. So the bond fund, with its lower initial cost, tends to be more attractive to short-term investors; closed-end funds tend to be more attractive to those who are in for the long haul because the impact of the "load" can be spread out over a number of years.

Types of Bonds

T-Bonds and T-Bills.   Many bond investors are interested in current income; others are looking for very safe investments. United States government obligations fit the bill on both counts. The U.S. Treasury conducts frequent auctions (weekly for some obligations, monthly for others). Long-term securities called *T-Bonds* are sold in units of $1,000 face value (for four-year or longer terms), $5,000 for one- to four-year bonds. The shorter-term T-Bills are sold in units of $10,000 face value.

The qualification "face value" is important because the actual prices are set at these auctions by the buyers' bids. The results of the auctions are studied eagerly because they show the trends in interest rates and, therefore, have a lot of impact on the overall economy. You can go to the auctions yourself and save the broker's fee, or you can buy treasury securities from a broker.

Short-term treasury securities are called *T-Bills* and are available in three-month, six-month, and one-year terms. Longer-term treasury securities are called T-Bonds. Interest paid on T-Bonds is tricky: It's subject to federal income tax but free of state and local taxes. The way T-Bills work is even trickier. T-Bills don't pay interest in the normal sense. Instead, they're purchased for far less than their face value; when they mature, the Treasury redeems them for their full face value.

Savings Bonds.   The federal government also sells U.S. Savings Bonds. The series now available is Series EE. The bonds, which have a ten-year maturity, are sold for half their face value at banks and savings and loan institutions. You can spend anywhere from $25 to $5,000 to buy these bonds, and there's no "load" or other commission. The Treasury sets the rate of return by setting up a schedule of what you'll receive, depending on when you cash in the bond. You're encouraged to hold on for at least five years (because the rate of return is much lower if you cash in the bond in under five years), but there's no advantage in holding on to the bond for more than the ten-year face value.

Municipal Bonds.   State and city governments also issue bonds to handle everyday expenses of government operations, and also to fund projects like maintaining highways and building sports stadiums. Municipal bonds can either be backed by a government's "full faith and credit" (a commitment to apply any of its resources necessary to meet obligations) or be "revenue backed" with a specific source of funding (e.g., tax collections) earmarked to pay the bondholders. Surprisingly, revenue-backed bonds are much riskier.

Most of the time, municipal bonds are a very safe investment—although there have been some defaults (failure to pay scheduled interest and/or repay bondholders at maturity). Bonds are rated for safety and quality by S&P's and by Moody's (a similar financial information service).

Two agencies (the Municipal Bond Insurance Association and the Municipal Bond Investors Assurance Corporation) also insure municipal bonds: They say that they'll pay up if the government agency doesn't. As common sense would dictate, riskier bonds pay higher rates than safer ones, and insured bonds pay lower rates than noninsured bonds because the risk is lower.

The general rule is that interest paid on municipal bonds is free of local, state, and federal tax. (A bond fund advertised as "double" or "triple tax-free" is basically a municipal bond fund.) There are two exceptions to this rule. First, if you buy municipal bonds from states other than the state in which you're a resident, interest is still free from federal tax—but the interest can be taxed by your home state and home city if they have income taxes. Second, as a result of the Tax Code of 1986 (TC '86) the interest on "private activity" bonds (basically, bonds whose proceeds are 10% or more devoted to activities other than those of the government entity) is subject to federal tax. And don't forget that municipal bond interest is counted in determining whether a senior citizen must pay income tax on part of his or her Social Security check (see page 268).

Corporate Bonds.   Corporations also issue bonds. The interest on corporate bonds is fully taxable. Corporate bonds vary widely in risk, from AAA-rated bonds from blue-chip companies to "junk bonds" issued with little or no backing or by companies one step ahead of the bankruptcy court. Once again, the S&P or Moody's rating (which you can find at most library reference rooms) will give you a good idea about the degree of risk.

Corporate bonds are usually issued in denominations of $1,000 or more. Like municipal bonds, both closed-end and open-end bond funds are available from brokers and directly from the fund issuer.

Stripped Bonds.   As explained on page 22, most bonds have "coupons" which give the owner the right to receive regular interest payments. When a bond is "stripped," the coupons are sold separately from the bond itself. The owner of the coupons gets the interest; the owner of the bond can sell it or redeem it at maturity. There are complex tax rules about stripped bonds, so check with your tax adviser before you invest in either the coupons or the underlying bonds.

Finding Out about Bonds

Bonds are described as something like "Old Siwash 6¼'s of 2001–2009." That means that the bond is issued by Old Siwash, pays interest of 6¼% of the face value, and matures in 2009, but can be "called" (bought back) by the issuer at any time after 2001 if the issuer finds it can do better by paying off the bondholders and borrowing more money.

Bond prices are based on a "par" figure of 100. If a bond sells for exactly its face value, the bond is at par, trading at 100. But if you have to pay more because the bond's interest rate is higher than normal, it might be quoted at 103, which means you'd have to pay $1,030 for a bond with a $1,000 face value. A bond sold at a discount might be quoted at 95, 75, even 50, depending on its terms and the interest-rate environment.

Bonds in Your Investment Plan

Right now, the most popular sector of the bond market seems to be municipal bonds. These bonds are easy for middle-income people to buy and afford; and if the income from the bonds you choose is tax-exempt, this is one of the last tax shelters you can still use.

But other kinds of bonds can also be good values. Bonds can fit your investment plan if:

• You want steady, predictable income.
• You have a theory about the trend of interest rates, and you think you can make money by selling bonds as interest rates change.
• You think the stock market is too risky. In this case, buy only federal securities, insured and/or top-rated municipal bonds, and top-rated corporate bonds.
• You want high income—much higher than you can get from a bank account or CD—and don't mind accepting risk because you think the overall return will be worthwhile. In this case, try a junk-bond fund which invests in low-rated corporate bonds, which must offer high interest to get any investors to buy them.

20. Real Estate and Related Investments

If owning the home you live in is such a great investment, wouldn't it also make sense to invest in other forms of real estate—raw land that can be developed, houses you can rent out or hold for resale when the price increases, office buildings and stores? Many investors agree that real estate and related investments are an important part of a safe, well-balanced portfolio.

Just like stocks or bonds, real estate investments can produce income (for instance, the rent that tenants pay), growth (a price increase, when the house you bought for $112,000 is now worth $179,850), or both. Furthermore, although TC '86 limited or eliminated some of the tax advantages for real estate investors, real estate still offers tax benefits that other forms of investment don't.

Ways to Invest in Real Estate

The simplest way to invest in real estate—though not necessarily the best—is to go out and buy some property yourself. Depending on your budget, this could be anything from a vacant lot to a shopping mall. Some investors buy "occupied apartments"—apartments in buildings converted to co-ops or condos, whose tenants have chosen not to buy the apartment. The buyer of the apartment becomes the landlord, collects the rent, and can move into or resell the apartment when the current tenant vacates.

Your goal is to find property that either yields immediate rental income, will increase in value, or both. You'll also have to think about what it will cost to run the property (for instance, providing heat and hot water, paying real estate taxes, meeting your mortgage payments) and what tax benefits you'll qualify for (expert advice is a must here).

Many real estate investors make heavy use of "leverage"—the ability to make a small amount of money go further by borrowing. For instance, they use a small down-payment to buy property and get a mortgage for the rest. As the property becomes more valuable, and as the mortgage gets closer to being paid off, they have more and more equity in the property. Then, they can sell the property or trade it for a more valuable property, getting a mortgage for the balance—or use the property as security when they buy more and more property and mortgage it. This strategy can work spectacularly, if cash flow and tax amounts are right. It can also fail spectacularly, if interest rates rise and property values fall, and the investor can no longer afford the payments on the property already owned, much less buy more.

No question about it, operating as a real estate "lone wolf" is risky. Even investors who eat risk for breakfast may prefer to join forces with other investors. That way, they can buy more expensive, and often potentially more lucrative, properties and can hire one or more professional managers.

Limited Partnerships and REITs.   The two major ways of joining with others to invest in real estate are limited partnerships and REITs. (Of course, you can just get together with other investors and cut your own deals—but be sure you have legal and tax advice first.) Limited partnerships can invest in a wide variety of real estate—anything from buying land and developing it for residential, commercial, or mixed use to operating time-sharing vacation condos to buying buildings and turning them into condominiums.

The essence of a limited partnership is that the general partners, or sponsors, manage the project and are legally liable for all of the partnership's debts and losses. The investors—limited partners—like a corporation's stockholders, can lose all their investment but can't be forced to pay additional money if the project runs into trouble later. However, it's much easier to sell shares in a corporation than limited partnership interests. If you want to get out of a limited partnership because you decide it was a bad investment, or simply because you need cash, you can't guarantee that anyone will be willing to buy you out.

Read the prospectus carefully before investing in a limited partnership. Find out the general partners' track record. If the project isn't fully completed, try to judge if the scheduled completion dates and income projections are realistic. If it is completed, try to figure out what will happen to the project (and your return) if taxes, fuel prices, or interest rates rise, or real estate prices fall. How realistic are the general partners' projections? How much of your money goes to work at once—and how much is a fee for the general partners? What are their continuing management fees, and must you pay a fee when you sell your interest?

Most important, find out the objectives of the limited partnership. If you're in a low tax bracket and want immediate cash, you won't be happy with a limited partnership aimed at generating tax losses for high-bracket investors. (By the way, if you're offered a fabulous bargain on a limited partnership interest, it may be that the high-bracket owner is desperately trying to bail out because the new tax law makes the investment a bad choice for him or her.)

REITs, or real estate investment trusts, work a lot like mutual funds. That is, they buy and manage real estate, then divide their holdings into shares which are sold to the public. (Something called a real estate mutual fund is a conventional mutual fund investing in stock of companies that develop real estate or own a lot of real estate—or even investing in REITs.) REITs have different investment objectives. Some buy property, others lend money to real estate developers and construction companies, and some combine these strategies.

Choosing an REIT in which to invest is a lot like choosing a mutual fund. Once again, checking the prospectus is essential. What is the trust's track record? How has it fared in both up and down markets? What training and experience do its managers have? One advantage of REITs over limited partnerships: REITs are much more liquid. That is, it's a lot easier to turn your investment into cash when you want to—many REITs are traded on a stock exchange, so you can sell whenever you want (though there's no guarantee you won't lose money).

If you buy a variable annuity (see page 270) or investment-oriented life insurance policy (see page 66), you may be offered a real estate fund as an investment option. And you're probably a real estate investor without knowing it: Pension funds and insurance companies invest heavily in real estate and mortgages.

Mortgage-Related Investments. A mortgage? How can you invest in—that is, buy or sell—a mortgage, of all things? As we've seen, one of the basic economic trends is the development of increasingly abstract forms of investment in addition to plain buying and selling of merchandise.

As a simple example of mortgage investment: If you're selling your house and the buyer has trouble getting a mortgage, you might be willing to "take back" a mortgage (technically known as a purchase money mortgage). Instead of insisting on the whole purchase price in cash, you agree to lend the buyer part of the price of the house, relying on him or her to make regular payments.

But if you decide you don't quite trust the buyer, or if you need cash right away, or you're not equipped to monitor the payments, you might sell the mortgage to a bank or finance company. They give you cash, right away (less than the full amount of the mortgage, of course, to allow for their costs and profits). So a mortgage can be turned into a saleable item, and sold and resold.

Carrying it a step further, the bank may not want to hold on to the mortgage. Banks frequently "bundle" up a group of mortgages and sell them—often to government agencies. Then the agencies (or private investment companies) sell shares in the group to investors.

Ginnie Maes, Fannie Maes, and Freddie Macs.

The Government National Mortgage Association (Ginnie Mae), Federal National Mortgage Association (Fannie Mae) and Federal Home Loan Mortgage Corporation (Freddie Mac) are federal agencies whose mission is to encourage bankers to make home loans by providing guarantees. If the mortgagor (homeowner) defaults—and most people don't, no matter how grim their financial situation—the federal agency gets the bank out of the hole. The federal agency keeps itself out of the hole by selling mortgage-based securities to mutual funds and individual investors. Although the federal government backs the mortgages in the "package" and guarantees that investors will receive their principal back if they hold their interest until its due date, it does not protect investors against possible losses when they try to resell their "Ginnie Maes," "Fannie Maes," or "Freddie Macs" on the open market. That's because Ginnie Maes and the like work a lot like bond funds, and their prices have a lot to do with interest rates.

You can buy Ginnie Maes and the other mortgage-related securities directly—but you probably won't because the minimum investment is $25,000. It's more likely that you'll invest in a Ginnie Mae mutual fund, which has a lower minimum investment—usually $1,000 or $2,500, perhaps $5,000. Once you invest, you'll get a check every month, which contains some interest on your investment and some of your principal returned. That's because the "package" contains mortgages with similar, but not identical, terms, and some of the mortgages get paid off routinely every month. When the term of the package ends, so do your checks. You've already been repaid your principal, plus interest—much like a bond fund, only the principal repayment and interest payments are mingled and distributed throughout the term, not separated.

The borrowers on the underlying mortgages also have the right to prepay their mortgages, which they're likely to do as interest rates fall because the rates they're paying are higher than the prevailing market rates. When they do this, the owners of Ginnie Maes get more principal, but of course the interest stops sooner because more of the mortgages have been prepaid. The higher the "coupon rate" on a Ginnie Mae (the interest rate on the underlying mortgages), the better the chance that the mortgagors will refinance.

Private concerns (such as investment bankers) have been assembling similar pools of mortgages for many years. However, TC '86 adds tax and accounting advantages by adding provisions about Real Estate Mortgage Investment Conduits (REMICs) to the tax law. It's too early to tell how REMICs will perform; get investment advice before you actually write the check.

Real Estate Investment and Taxes

Like life insurance, real estate investment has traditionally gotten especially favorable treatment in the tax code. Also like life insurance, the treatment isn't quite as favorable now that TC '86 has been passed—but both real estate and life insurance still have tax advantages.

One of the most powerful tax benefits of real estate is that investors can claim depreciation on buildings (but not on land). That is, they get a tax deduction equal to a certain percentage of the value of the building for each of several years—even though the buildings get *more* valuable over time, not less. So a building's owners who are really making money, in terms of cash flow, may have a loss for tax purposes. The loss means that they pay less tax on their other income.

After TC '86, the game isn't quite as much fun: Depreciation deductions are smaller, and a lot of real estate activities are now called "passive" activities. (Sounds like another contradiction in terms, doesn't it?) To boil down the complex rules, it means that real estate losses might only act as tax shelters if the real estate investor also has other investments in tax shelters—"paper" losses for tax purposes may not cut the taxes the investor has to pay on his or her salary or other income. The moral: Check with your tax adviser before you make a real estate investment; find out if you'll still have a good deal once you pay your taxes.

The tax code still offers tax advantages for rehabilitating historic property—putting fine old buildings back into usable shape. Under the right circumstances, investors can get a tax credit (which reduces the amount of tax to be paid), not just a tax deduction (which reduces the amount of income on which taxes are computed).

Especially if your income is under $200,000 a year (which means you qualify for some extra tax breaks), you might consider investing in a limited partnership that rehabilitates historic properties. (The tax advantages for taxpayers with higher income are more modest.) Usually, it costs at least $10,000 to invest in one of these deals, although some allow smaller investments.

Experts say that a really good limited partnership of this type yields returns of at least 10% a year. Watch out for limited partnerships that provide too cushy a deal for the promoters who set them up; an up-front fee paid to the promoters that's much over 10% is a bad sign—so is a partnership agreement that gives more than 20% to 25% of the eventual profits to the sponsors. The more the sponsors keep for themselves, the less remains for the investors!

The Real Estate Investment Market

Real estate investments have more diversity than stock or bond investments, a wider variety of legal structures and tax consequences, and a wider spectrum of risks. So it's only possible to give a few general rules here.

• If you want to buy investment property yourself, you buy it through a real estate broker. The seller of the property pays the broker's commission directly—but naturally, the price of the property will reflect the commission. To assess risks and rewards, check public records (found in the county courthouse, city hall, or municipal building) to see how the prices, real estate taxes, and rental values of comparable properties have fared over time. (Local newspapers often print this information too.)

• Ginnie Maes, shares in REITs, REMICs, and the like are sold by securities brokers; the brokerage firm determines the level of commission the buyer must pay. If you prefer a Ginnie Mae or related mutual fund, these funds are available both through brokers and directly from the fund issuer. Like stock mutual funds, these funds vary widely in their "load" and fee policies—the prospectus will tell you what a particular fund charges.

• Depending on the legal structure of the deal, limited partnerships and interests in syndications may be sold either by securities brokers or by the sponsors of the deal; and there's a wide, confusing variety of commissions and fees involved. It's an excellent idea to check with your accountant or other tax adviser before investing in one of these deals; the tax rules are quite complex, and investors can choose deals that are theoretically okay, but wrong for their particular tax situations.

21. Other Investments

Many investors happily maintain a high-yielding, diverse portfolio made up of mutual funds, stock, bonds, and real estate. However, there are some other forms of investment that rate at least a few quick words here.

Art and Collectibles

Art and collectibles are investments you can really sink your teeth into, or at least put your finger on. You can buy paintings, photographs, prints, jewelry, antiques, fabulous fifties furniture, gold and silver bullion or coins, posters, porcelain, or anything else that gives you pleasure now and that you think will later appreciate in price.

There are three things to keep in mind here.

- To avoid getting taken, you have to become a real expert.
- These investments don't yield income until you sell them—in fact, it costs money to insure, protect, and take care of them.
- You usually buy at retail but sell at wholesale, so there must be a dramatic price appreciation for you to make money.

Commodities

Speaking of buying things, you can buy sugar, cocoa, tungsten, pork bellies, fuel oil, and many other things that are used in manufacturing or commerce. Well, if you're a commodities investor, you probably don't really want to buy them, just speculate in price changes. So, in effect, you *say* you're going to buy the coffee beans, but you find someone else who really wants them. If he or she pays more than you did (and enough more to cover brokerage commissions—you buy through a broker who is part of a commodities exchange), you win. If he or she pays less, you lose.

That's about all I'm going to say about commodities. For one thing, commodity exchanges won't let you play unless you can prove that your net worth is high enough that you can afford to lose a lot. Then again, commodity investors are divided into two groups: a very small group who have made lots and lots of money and the vast majority who have been cleaned out.

Stock Options, Rights, and Warrants

What if you're interested in the changes in the price of a stock, but don't care about earning dividends—or even owning the stock? You can speculate on price changes without ever buying a share of stock.

Stock options come in two varieties: call and put. A "call option" is the right to buy 100 shares of stock at a particular price, on or before a set date. If you buy a call, you can either use it to buy the stock yourself (if the price has gone up enough to make it worthwhile), or sell the call to someone else who thinks the stock will go up. Speaking of selling, you can sell calls to other investors. If you sell calls on stock you really own, it's a covered call; the buyer has the right to demand that you sell the stock at the set price at any time before the call expires.

If you sell calls on stock you don't own, it's a naked call, which is really a kind of short sale (see page 115). If the call buyer wants to buy the stock, you'll have to run out and buy it (at whatever the current market price is). A "put option" is similar, but this time it's the right to sell 100 shares at a particular price.

Securities brokers handle the purchase and sale of put and call options. Selling covered calls is not risky at all, and some conservative investors use it as a way to add a little extra income to their portfolio.

(The price of the call, less broker's commission, goes to the seller—the "writer"—of the call.) The only risk is that, if the call is exercised, you will have to sell your stock at a time that might be inconvenient for you; you can always buy more shares of the same stock. Selling naked calls *is* risky because if you guess wrong about the trends in the stock's price, you can lose a lot of money buying the shares of stock to deliver to the call buyer.

What about buying calls or selling put options? These can be quite risky because most options expire worthless, and the option owners lose their entire investment. That is, the right to buy shares of a particular stock at $107 a share is very valuable if the price of the stock on the open market is $122 a share—and completely valueless if anyone can buy the stock for $85 a share. But stock options are not just for high-rollers. Some small investors are willing to accept the risk because stock options are much less expensive than buying the underlying shares of stock—and a few good choices can make up for a lot of bad ones.

Warrants and rights are similar but are issued by a corporation to its own stockholders, not "written" by owners of the stock. Rights give the stockholder the right to buy a certain number of additional shares in the corporation, at a below-market price. Rights are good only for a short time (such as one month). Warrants are similar but last longer. The stockholders can either exercise the rights and warrants they receive (buy more stock at the "discount" price), or sell them to other investors through a securities broker.

Rights and warrants are cheaper than options, and much cheaper than stock. They're a way to earn a large return on a small investment—but the investment will become completely worthless if you decide not to buy the stock involved, and if you can't find someone else to buy the rights or warrants before they expire.

22. Summing Up Your Investment Choices

As you can see, there's a vast spectrum of possible investments. Table 4 gives some strategies that may appeal to you, based on your personality (whether you can cope with risk), how much you can afford to lose, your time horizon (Do you need income right now? Do you want to build up net worth without pesky, current income you don't need and will only boost your tax bill? Do you want to build an estate to leave your family comfortably endowed after your death?), and the amount of time and trouble you're willing to put into choosing investments and shifting out of nonperforming investments. The chart is followed by two case studies that show how two people used investment strategies to fit their own life-styles.

TABLE 4   INVESTMENT STRATEGIES CHART

Low Risk/Low Effort	Low Risk/High Effort
• Buy high-quality bonds and hold them until maturity. • Invest in a money market fund. • Invest in a mutual fund specializing in preservation of capital. • Buy and hold blue-chips (stocks in well-established, successful corporations), preferred stock.	• Decide the right time, then "write" covered calls on stocks you own. • Buy investment real estate that needs a lot of work and management, but that yields a rent roll high enough to cover the expenses.
Medium Risk/Low Effort	**Medium Risk/High Effort**
• Invest in a high-growth or OTC mutual fund. • Buy zero-coupon bonds—to trade, not to hold. • Invest in a Ginnie Mae mutual fund.	• Research common stocks; invest in stocks with a low P/E ratio and a history of paying dividends. • Invest in a real estate limited partnership. • Develop the expertise to invest in "collectibles."
High Risk/Low Effort	**High Risk/High Effort**
• Open a "discretionary account" giving your broker the right to make investment decisions for you. • Invest in raw land and wait for it to appreciate. • Invest in a junk bond fund.	• Write naked calls. • Invest in penny stocks and aggressive growth stocks. • Invest in rental property that needs work not covered by the rent roll. • Invest in rights, warrants.

The rest of the section deals with the issues that are important to investors who have chosen a portfolio and must manage it: monitoring investment performance, and taxation of investments.

23. REAL LIFE: MICHAEL MARK

"Hey, I'm just a kid," Michael said with an uneasy laugh. "A wild and crazy guy, you know? Always a laugh, a good time, always glad to pick up the check when we have a round of drinks."

"You're not a kid," his brother Dave said. "Except that you're kidding yourself. You make pretty good money. Even with inflation and all, you make a lot more money than Dad did when he was your age. And when he was your age, he was a married man with a family on the way. You don't have anybody to take care of but yourself. You should have money in the bank. Do you?"

"Sure. There's almost $111 in my checking account."

"And what about investments? Don't tell me your car is an investment. The minute you drove it out of the dealership—speeding, if I know you—its value went way down."

"But what a baby!" Michael exclaimed. "Great lines, acceleration, power; she's got everything!"

"I don't even want to think about a pension. Are you going to have a pension? You've been out of school for three years, you've had three jobs."

"Number one, they made a mistake. They really needed someone with more computer experience. Number two, I made a mistake. How did I know the company was going to go under? And now, I'm doing great. Joey—he's my boss—said that I am, no question, the best in the trainee program, and they'll promote me in a New York minute as soon as they're convinced that I'm steady."

Dave didn't have to say anything. The raised eyebrows on his stony face told it all.

"Anyway, why should I bother with an IRA? Isn't it no good anymore because of that new tax law?"

"Mick, you have to worry about what's going to happen to you after you retire a lot more than you have to worry about your taxes. Besides, you can have a responsible attitude about things, if you have to. I remember when you wanted that racing bike, you saved up for it for almost two years. And if you start an IRA, you won't even miss the money."

"Believe me, I'll miss it," Michael said gloomily. "My best blue suit is on its last legs—or my last legs, I guess, and it's Christina's birthday next week and I want to get her something really nice; and Ed Santana has this great video camera—you should see it—you can carry it in one hand; it's only a little bigger than the cassette. . . ."

"You sound like a kid at Christmas," Dave said wearily. "I'm tired of sounding like a Dutch uncle, but I'm even more tired of waiting for you to grow up."

The Numbers

Michael Mark earns $30,000 a year as a sales trainee for a company that videotapes in-service courses for corporations. His largest expense is for miscellaneous living costs: Food, clothing, evenings out, telephone bills, and so forth add up to $10,000 a year. His next largest expense is income tax: $8,500. He'd sure like to find a way to cut that down. Bringing up the rear, his auto loan and car insurance, weighing in at 10% of his income, or $3,000 a year.

Overall, although it usually seems that money burns a hole in his pocket on payday, Michael has a surplus of 10% of his gross income, or $3,000 a year, to save and invest.

The Answers

An IRA is a big priority here. If he invests the full $2,000 close to the beginning of the year (perhaps by using his Christmas bonus before he has a chance to fritter it away), Michael gets maximum mileage out of his investment. Because he's a young man, he can afford to take some risks in his IRA: An aggressive growth fund might be a good idea. Depending on whether or not Michael is a participant in a qualified plan, he may or may not be entitled to a deduction of part or all of his IRA investments. (See page 34 for more on IRA investing.)

The forced-saving aspect of whole-life insurance could also be valuable for Michael. However, he shouldn't go overboard on insurance—nobody's depending on his income, yet. (Depending on how things go with Christina, Michael might find himself married and a family man; then his insurance needs will increase.) Or, if he doesn't enjoy thinking (and worrying) about investments, an investment-oriented life insurance policy could take care of both insurance and investment needs by making only one decision. ("Killing two birds with one stone" doesn't sound quite right in this context.)

Like most people, Michael could use extra income; and like most people, he would like to pay lower taxes. Tax-exempt bonds (or a tax-exempt bond or money market fund) could be a good solution to both problems for Michael. As Michael sits in his darkened living room, an icebag on his head, this New Year's Day, Michael's New Year's resolutions should include a resolution to track his spending, analyze how money is used and where he could cut down without seriously hampering his life-style, and start saving (for emergencies) and investing (for a better, more secure future) right away. (See page 79 for budgeting tips and techniques.)

24. REAL LIFE: BILL HEATER

Bill couldn't get over it . . . how different the two were. When Jenny Katherine's sister Danielle was a new-born, she was always kicking, crying, screaming, always at center stage. Jenny Katherine is much quieter. She seems like a philosopher, lying in her crib with what seems to be a tiny grin, enjoying the newness of everything around her. When you picked up Danielle, she'd give you a bear hug; Jenny Katherine folds herself gently into your arms. Bill and his wife Cynthia love them both equally, and are delighted to have the whole spectrum of family life in only two kids.

The health plan at Bill's job paid most of the expenses of Jenny Katherine's birth, but the Heaters still have a bill of $1,000 to take care of. Jenny Katherine is sleeping in Danielle's crib and is wheeled around in Danielle's stroller, so the expenses of her birth were partly taken care of. Even so, Bill's raise (he's a buyer for a department store chain) came in very, very handy. Now he and Cynthia have two children to love, protect, take care of—and pay for. Their main goal is to build security for the family; their secondary goal is to accumulate some investments.

The Numbers

Bill is only 30—a young man to have so many responsibilities. He earns $35,000 a year, with the raise, and he thinks that's pretty good for a man his age. But there are a lot of demands on his income: $8,500 a year income tax, the same amount in rent. Food, clothing, and insurance add up to $11,500 a year, with $1,500 a year in miscellaneous expenses. Car payments, gas, and auto insurance take up another $2,000 a year. So they're sailing pretty close to the edge: $3,000 a year for savings, investment and, indeed, everything else.

Under the circumstances, it's impossible to start an intensive program of investments right now. It would be crazy to cut back on insurance; in fact, probably the best decision is to beef up insurance coverage, but select an investment-oriented product that permits a faster build-up of cash value. (The cash value will be available for borrowing if emergencies arise, or if the children go to camp, go to college, and the like.) Bill and Cynthia chose a variable-life policy that permits an investment choice among a balanced fund, a money market fund, a stock fund, a bond fund, and an aggressive high-growth stock fund. With the stock market booming, they've chosen to invest the entire insurance account in the stock fund.

Bill and Cynthia are painfully aware that their cash savings are slender, and could easily disappear in a few trips to the pediatrician and a modest family vacation. They've talked about treating Bill's raise as if it didn't exist—continuing to live at the same budget level, and using the raise to fund Bill's IRA or to invest in savings bonds. (They encouraged friends and family to buy savings bonds for Jenny Katherine instead of getting her some silver-plated trifle or a couple more of the terry-cloth crawlers that she outgrows even as you look at her.) But they know that it's almost impossible to scrimp and save day in and day out; sooner or later, they're going to want to break out and buy something just because it's fun, not because it fits perfectly into a niche in the budget.

25. Now That You're an Investor . . .

Welcome to the world of deals, takeovers, and Schedule D (the part of your tax return used to report investment profits). You've chosen a portfolio of investments; and if you're like most investors, you're never quite sure you made the right choices, or that you shouldn't shift your investment focus to adapt to changing conditions.

Here's a worksheet for monitoring your investments. Depending on the amount of time you want to spend, the riskiness of your investments, and whether you invested "mad money" or money you absolutely can't afford to lose, I suggest you review investments at least once a quarter; maybe every month. If you trade stocks actively, check stock prices at least once a week.

If you have a brokerage account, you'll get regular statements. Mutual funds will send you statements at least once a quarter (usually, monthly)—and the statement will include a telephone number to check the value of a share in the fund on any given day.

WORKSHEET

1. Name of investment: _____

2. Date(s) purchased: _____

3. Purchased from: _____

4. Broker's name (may be the same as Item 3): _____

5. Amount you own (number of shares, face value, etc.) _____

6. Total current value of your investment: $_____

7. Amount you paid: $_____
8. Current value of your investment per share or other relevant measure-

   ment: $_____

9. Name of most nearly comparable investment: _____
10. Current value of that investment per share or other relevant measure-

    ment: $_____
11. Rate of return on your investment in the last year, quarter, and so on, as

    reported in your statement: _____
12. Price increase/decrease for your investment since the last time you moni-

    tored the investment: $_____
13. Price increase/decrease for the Dow or other relevant index for the same

    period of time: $_____
14. How has your investment performed, in both income and price change?

    _____

15. Explain whether you think this will change, how long the change will take, and

    why: _____

    _____

16. If you are disappointed with this investment, how quickly could you dispose

    of it? _____

17. How high would the transaction costs be? _____

YOUR DECISION

☐ Keep the investment
☐ Get rid of the investment by (date): _____
☐ Buy more of the investment, if it's available at a price below $_____

* * *

26. Tax Tips for Investors

The fundamental rule about taxation of investments is that you must pay tax on dividends and interest in the year you receive them; you don't pay taxes on the increase in value of your investments until you sell the stock, bond, real estate, Oriental rug, or other form of investment. So, if you bought a stock in 1985 for $15 a share, and it's now worth $33 a share, congratulate yourself on your investment savvy—and don't pay any taxes on these "paper profits" until you turn them into actual profits (or losses) by actually selling the stock. (There's an exception to this rule—turn to page 141 for a discussion of "original issue discount.")

Before the Tax Code of 1986, the most important fact about investments was that the profit on the sale of most forms of investment was "capital gain," not "ordinary income," and was taxed at much lower rates than ordinary income (such as interest on bank accounts or salary). For instance, in 1985, the highest tax rate on ordinary income was 50%; the highest tax rate on long-term capital gains (profits from the sale of investments that had been owned for six months or more) was 20%. So people who earned large salaries definitely had an incentive to invest in ways that would yield capital gains, not ordinary income.

To oversimplify a little, the new tax code wipes out the difference between capital gains and ordinary income—both are taxed at the same rate. The rate will be either 15%, 28%, or 33%, depending on your income and your filing status as single, married, or head of household. (There's a special rule for 1987 returns—the ones you file in 1988; the maximum tax rate on capital gains is 28%, even if your income is high enough for you to pay a 38.5% tax rate on ordinary income.)

However, you still have to keep track of whether your assets are capital assets or ordinary assets because there's a limit on the amount of capital *losses* you can deduct if you have to sell an investment for less than you paid for it. You can't deduct more than $3,000 in capital losses in any year (only $1,500 if you're a married person filing a separate return). If you have the bad luck to lose more than that in a particular year, then you can "carry forward" the losses—use them to reduce your tax bills in later years.

Why would you sell investments at a loss, anyway? For several reasons.

• You might have a lot of investment gains and other income, and the losses could cut down your taxable income and, therefore, your tax bill. (This is a lot less important now than it was when tax rates were higher.)
• You might be short of money, and selling some of your investments is the best way to raise cash.

• Maybe you think that the investment was a horrible mistake, or economic conditions have changed dramatically, and you want to get *something* before the investment becomes completely worthless.

You have a taxable gain or loss whenever you sell stocks or bonds, or whenever you exchange them for other securities that are not identical. (There's no tax on a stock split—you exchange your stock certificates for equivalent certificates issued by the same company.)

Therefore, if you invest in a mutual fund family and "switch" from one fund to another, you *can* have taxable profits (or deductible losses). Let's say you bought 2,000 shares of the Fund Family's High-Income Fund for $9.95 a share. Now you think that the Fund Family's International Fund is a better bet, so you switch all 2,000 shares to the International Fund. Your High-Income Fund shares are now worth $11.12 apiece—giving you a taxable profit of $2,340 ($1.17 a share times 2,000 shares).

Figuring Profits and Losses

Your profit or loss, for tax purposes, is the difference between the basis of your investment and the price for which you sell it. (Remember, the basis of anything is its value for tax purposes.) Your basis, in turn, is what you paid for the investment—including brokers' commissions. If you got dividends in the form of extra shares of stock, or if the stock "split"— if you were asked to return your stock certificates so that you could get two, three, or more less-expensive shares for each shares surrendered— you'll have to adjust the basis of your shares to deal with these events.

What makes it really complex is the fact that investors frequently buy shares of the same stock, or similar bonds, at different times, and at different prices. Let's say you buy 100 shares of a stock in September 1986, and pay $55 a share (including brokerage commissions). You have a lot of faith in the company's management and buy 50 more shares in February 1987 (for $58 a share)—then 150 more shares at $49 a share (not everyone agrees with you about the management). In 1989, you decide to take some of your profits and sell 100 of your 300 shares, and get $6,100, less the broker's commission, for them. But what is your profit?

If you keep track of your stock and bonds (when you bought the securities, how much you paid, how many shares or bonds you bought, numbers of your share or bond certificates, stock dividends and splits), you can tell your broker *which* bonds or shares of stock to sell; the price of those securities determines your taxable profit. In the example above, if you pick shares that cost $58 a share, your profit is $300 minus commissions.

However, if you don't keep adequate records, you must apply the first in, first out (FIFO) rule. Your taxable profit or loss is computed as if you sold shares in the order that you bought them. That often means that you will have a larger taxable profit than if you had a chance to decide which securities were sold. So, like Snow White's short friends, you may whistle as you work at record keeping: "FIFO, FIFO, it's off to work we go."

Original Issue Discount

If you buy most bonds at a discount (for less than their face value) the bond has *original issue discount (OID)* for tax purposes. If you own a bond with OID, you must pay tax on part of the OID every year that you own the bond, just as you pay tax on the interest you receive. (That's why corporate zero-coupon bonds make you pay tax each year, even though you don't get any interest; what you're really paying tax on is the OID.)

However, you do not have to pay tax on OID, even if you buy bonds at a discount, if:

• The bond is tax-exempt.
• It's a U.S. savings bond (as we've seen, you buy U.S. savings bonds for far less than the face value; so without special tax treatment, you would have to pay tax on the OID).
• The bond has a fixed maturity date of one year or less.
• There is OID, but it's minimal: not more than ¼ of 1% times the number of years from the bond's issuance to its stated maturity.

The New Tax Code's Effect on Investments

On one level, it's important to understand the new tax code because you want to invest for the maximum after-tax return. On another level, you should understand business as well as personal taxes because taxes affect a company's profits (and, therefore, the size of the dividends it pays) and stock prices.

Although there are many other factors involved, one of the most important factors in a stock's price is how profitable the company is. If a company's annual report is filled with bad news, the stock price is likely to go down. If you own shares of the stock, your investment will, at least temporarily, be less valuable. Similarly, if the annual report shows ever-increasing profits, there's a good chance that the stock's price will rise.

Part of what determines profitability is the sheer number of widgets the company can sell, the price it gets per widget, and the profit margin on each. But tax and accounting rules also determine profitability. The more taxes a business has to pay, the less profit remains after taxes. The new tax law provides slightly lower tax rates for corporations—but also cuts back on, or eliminates, many deductions, and forces businesses to adopt accounting rules that can make their profits look anemic.

For instance, businesses no longer get a tax credit for investing in new machinery. This puts businesses, especially the "smokestack," heavy industries, in a bind. They can go ahead and invest, knowing that they'll have to spend a lot of money for comparatively little tax benefit—or they can by-pass the investment and try to remain efficient and competitive without the new machinery.

It's too soon to tell, but the new tax code seems likely to have these effects on the investment market.

• Some consumers will pay lower taxes, so they'll have more money to spend—making businesses, such as appliance manufacturers and department stores, more profitable.
• The smokestack industries—already troubled by high costs and foreign competition—will probably get into even deeper trouble as a result of the tax law changes. Therefore, their stock prices will probably go down. This could be a chance to invest and earn high profits—*if* you think these companies will rebound later on.
• Service industries will probably benefit because they have comparatively little investment in machinery or buildings; they won't miss the investment tax credit because they probably didn't qualify for it in the first place.
• The effect on the real estate industry will probably be mixed. It'll be harder for developers to raise money because the tax-shelter benefits for investors are less generous. But it won't be impossible: There are so few other tax shelters that investors will still climb aboard; and investors are always interested in good deals, even if they don't provide tax shelters.

Tax Aspects of Investing in Real Estate

Before the Tax Code of 1986, real estate offered a terrific tax shelter. Under current tax law, the benefits are less dramatic (deductions for depreciation must be stretched out over more years, so the deduction for each year is smaller), but most other tax shelters have been wiped out, so investing in real estate still looks good.

The new tax code also introduces brand-new rules about *passive activities* (investment that is neither portfolio income, such as stocks or interest on a bank account, nor business income from a business that you own and help run). If you lose money in a passive activity (such as investing in real estate), you can't subtract these losses from your salary income, or even from your portfolio income. All you can do is use them to reduce the tax bill for income you earn from other passive activities; or you can carry them forward if you earn money from passive activities in later tax years.

This means that real estate tax shelters—which operate by using depreciation and other tax deductions to create tax losses—are much less attractive because the tax losses are only really helpful for taxpayers who have passive income from other tax shelters.

Does this mean that real estate is no longer a good investment? No; there are still real estate deals that yield a good rate of profit on the money you invest. And if you're earning a profit, you don't care whether losses are deductible or not!

There's also a special real estate tax break that helps middle-income investors. If you earn less than $100,000 a year, are at least a 10% owner of a real estate project, and actively help manage the project, you can use up to $25,000 in losses to reduce any of your taxable income—not just passive income. The benefits of this tax break are reduced if you are a married person, but file a separate return; and to qualify, you can't be a limited partner in a real estate partnership. If you use a limited partnership to reduce the amount of risk in the deal, you also lose tax benefits.

(See page 174 for more about tax aspects of buying or selling a home; this section deals with real estate you buy for investment purposes, not as your own home.)

Part Three:
ENJOYING

For many people, the pattern is to leave the parental nest—either for a college dorm or for an apartment. For many people, owning a home (whether a co-op apartment, condo, or house) is an important financial goal. As we'll see, owning a home is often a good way to save money (it's frequently cheaper than renting an apartment), to make an investment that is likely to appreciate in value, and to save on your tax bills (the Internal Revenue Code has many provisions favorable to homeowners).

This section starts with a discussion of the practicalities and legalities of renting an apartment or house, then moves on to consider the financial aspects of buying, owning, and selling a home.

27. Tenants' Rights

Traditionally, landlord-tenant law was considered a special branch of law with a system of rules, most of which favored the landlord. The emphasis has shifted, and now most disputes between landlord and tenant are treated as matters of contract law based on the lease. That is, the landlord promises to deliver a habitable apartment (one which is safe and fit to live in); the tenant promises to pay the rent and refrain from damaging the apartment or annoying the other tenants. In general, if the tenant fails to live up to these promises, he or she can be evicted. If the landlord fails to live up to his or her side of the bargain, the tenant can withhold rent, either alone or by joining the other tenants in a "rent strike."

Rent Regulation

Some cities have a system of rent regulation for some or all apartments. In general, these systems create a method for computing the maximum rent that can be legally charged for an apartment, with adjustments for improvements in the building, taxes, fuel costs, and so on. Thus it's very worthwhile to find out if an area in which you are apartment hunting has these regulations, and which apartments are covered.

Once you have rented an apartment whose rent is regulated, it's even more worthwhile to find out the maximum rent for your particular apartment. Whether by accident or design, landlords often charge a rent higher than the legally permitted maximum. If this is true of your apartment, you may be entitled to a refund of excessive rent already paid, and a "rollback" of rent in the future.

The rent regulation system may also give you the right to renew your lease when it expires, and may protect you against eviction if the building is converted to co-op or condo form (see page 150) and/or if you're disabled or a senior citizen.

How to Read a Lease

A "handshake" deal is a very bad idea—you should insist on a written lease, even in the rare instances in which the law does not require a written lease to create the landlord-tenant relationship.

Sometimes reading the lease is made easy for you. Many areas require leases to be in plain English; even if this is not necessary, plain-English leases are easily available from legal stationers. (If you have any bargaining power at all, try buying some plain-English blank leases, bringing them with you on the apartment hunt, and offering your own form to be signed.) Sometimes, it's tough: The lease is four impenetrable pages of legal terminology. But all leases deal with the same basic problems.

- Who is the landlord?
- Who is the tenant? Not as silly a question as it seems—there could be an ever-changing cast of roommates, or spouses who divorce and both of whom want to keep the apartment.
- What is included in the lease—an apartment of course; but are heat and hot water included? Can the tenant use the laundry room, the health club, the freight elevator?
- What is the rent? When is it payable—the first of the month, at monthly intervals, on or before the 19th?
- How long is the lease term? Does the tenant have to ask for a renewal, or is it automatic unless the tenant opts out? Are there any limits on rent increases when the lease is renewed?
- Is the tenant allowed to sublet the apartment (allow someone to live in the apartment—paying rent to the tenant—during the tenant's temporary absence) and/or assign the lease (let someone take over the rest of the lease)?
- Are pets allowed? Or are small, noiseless pets allowed; big, noisy, messy ones forbidden?

Remember, before you sign the lease, you may have room for negotiation, and you may be able to have lease provisions you don't like changed to others that are more favorable. It depends on your bargaining power.

Roommates, Subleases, Assignments

There are many reasons why you, as a tenant, might want to have someone else living in the apartment with you, or instead of you. This is a changing area of landlord-tenant law, and one where local law varies a lot, but generally the best procedure is to ask the landlord's permission to have someone else live in the apartment (whether as a roommate or subtenant). From the legal standpoint, your landlord *should* grant the request unless there's a reasonable cause for turning it down.

- You could be in a fix if you ask permission, get refused, and go ahead with your plan. However, local law might come to your rescue. In New York City, for instance, tenants have a right to have members of their immediate family, plus one unrelated person, living in their apartments.
- Furthermore, a landlord who accepts rent checks from a subtenant or roommate might be held to have known that the other person was there, and to have given up any possible objections by taking his or her money.

Now, if you sublet, assign the lease, or take a roommate against the landlord's wishes, and there are no legal arguments in your favor, then you're *really* in the soup; your landlord can bring an eviction action against you, and he or she might win.

Repairs, Remedies, and Rent Strikes

Sometimes something goes wrong in your apartment, or in the building as a whole, and the landlord is slow about repairing it, or seems to be refusing outright to make the repairs. Sometimes this is because the landlord doesn't know about the problem, or because he or she is good-heartedly dithering about what to do and hasn't found a solution yet. (You'd never have caught me saying a good word about landlords before I was one.) So make sure the landlord knows what problems exist— by detailed, specific complaint letters. Make sure you keep copies, and gather any evidence you can (photographs—with dates—showing tumbled plaster, pools of water near leaky pipes, etc).

The evidence will come in handy if it turns out that your landlord is deliberately withholding repairs—either to save money or in the hope that you will move out and let the landlord use the building in some more profitable way. In either case, you have several options, both offensive and defensive.

- In many areas, you have a legal right to "repair and deduct"—that is, you can hire someone to make the necessary repairs (being sure to keep receipts and cancelled checks). Then, deduct the cost from your rent, informing your landlord by letter what you've done and why. If the landlord tries to evict you for nonpayment of rent, you can demonstrate that you applied the rent money to doing the landlord's job for him or her.
- There's probably a local agency that enforces the housing laws. Complain to them (with evidence to back you up); they'll literally get on the landlord's case. If necessary, they'll take him or her to court

to get a court order requiring the landlord to make the repairs, and perhaps fining the landlord for falling down on the job.

• As a defensive tactic, you can simply cut back or stop paying the rent—being sure to keep the withheld money in a safe place, instead of spending it! If the landlord attempts to evict you for nonpayment of rent, produce your evidence. It's very unlikely that you'll be evicted; more likely, you'll be ordered to pay the back rent—most likely of all, the landlord will be ordered to make the repairs, and you'll be ordered to pay only part of the back rent.

• When conditions are really bad, your best tactic can be to join with the other tenants. If nobody is paying rent, the landlord will have to start paying attention! If your building is without heat in the winter because the landlord economizes by not buying any fuel, you and the other tenants can join together to buy fuel yourselves and get the boiler going again.

If your rent strike ends up in housing court, the group of tenants may be able to get a court order permitting them to pay future rent (and whatever part of the back rent they're ordered to pay) directly to a special fund administered by the court. That way, the money will go toward the necessary repairs, and the landlord won't be able to earn any profit until the repairs are completed.

28. Co-op and Condo Conversions

Sometimes a real estate developer will buy land and put up a building or group of buildings on the land. Then, the developer has the choice of selling the property outright, renting the units to tenants, or operating the property in condominium form. An apartment building, whose units are rented to tenants, can be converted from rental form to co-op or condominium form. There are technical, legal, and tax differences among these forms; which one the developer chooses depends on local law, custom, and the prevailing real estate market.

The impetus for conversion from a rental building to co-op or condo form nearly always comes from the building's owner—but it's not impossible for the tenants to organize themselves and suggest to a hostile landlord, or one who claims that the building can't both be maintained decently and operated at a profit, that the tenants buy out the landlord.

In the co-op form, the building is owned by a corporation. Tenants can't buy their apartments; instead, they can buy shares of stock in the corporation entitling them to a "proprietary lease," which is somewhat similar to an ordinary tenant's apartment lease. The co-op is managed by a board of directors (elected by the tenant-shareholders) and officers (either elected directly by the tenants or appointed by the board of directors).

In practical terms, what usually happens is that the building is really managed by a professional managing agent hired by the board of directors. The managing agent does tasks like hiring elevator operators, getting broken windows replaced, and making sure the front sidewalk is shoveled after a snowstorm. Also, in practical terms, the managing agent is usually connected with the real estate company that used to own the building.

In the condominium form, the tenants do buy their own apartments; they also have the right to use "common areas" (such as the paths between townhouses, or the laundry room in an apartment building) and the obligation to pay for required repairs to the frequently used areas. Once again, a managing agent is common—and once again, no one should be surprised if the former owner of the building continues to provide management services.

Practical Differences

Most of the time, owners of co-ops and owners of condos get exactly the same advantages and face the same problems. For instance, co-op and condo owners are entitled to tax deductions for the mortgage interest and real estate taxes they pay, just like owners of conventional homes. However, there are some minor differences between the two forms of ownership.

- •A condo unit is real estate; for legal purposes, a co-op purchase is a purchase of shares of stock plus rights under a proprietary lease. The required legal formalities are different, and you can get a perfectly ordinary mortgage on a condo unit—but you must get a personal loan on a co-op because you're using the money to buy stock, not real estate. If you want to leave your co-op to someone in your will, you must refer to your proprietary lease and shares of stock in the co-op corporation; references to "real estate" do not cover co-ops.
- •Usually, proprietary leases are written so that the co-op board of directors has the right to approve (or disapprove) anyone to whom you want to sell your shares of stock. This is not a rubber stamp process—they can refuse permission, causing what you thought was a "done deal" to fall apart. However, you can sell a condo unit to anyone you like; the owners of the other units have no more right to block the sale than have the people next door to block the sale of a single-family house.
- •Under normal circumstances, a co-op corporation does not have to pay federal income taxes. But this exemption is lost if the corporation earns more than 20% of its income from sources other than maintenance and assessments paid by the stockholders, for instance, if the co-op rents out stores and professional offices. This limitation on

outside income could mean higher maintenance charges because the co-op corporation has few other options when it needs income.

•Whether you buy a co-op or a condo unit, you will have to pay a monthly maintenance fee—your share of the expenses of running the building or townhouse complex and maintaining the common elements. (This charge is over and above your mortgage, if you financed part of the cost of the unit.) You may also have to pay "assessments," which are special charges required when the roof leaks or the building's elevator operators and hall-cleaners get a raise.

The Conversion Process

Usually, the conversion to co-op or condo form begins when the owner of the building decides it would be more profitable to sell the apartments instead of keeping the building in rental form. But the conversion depends on two things: legal approval by the necessary regulatory agency (usually the one that handles stocks and other securities), and agreement by at least some of the tenants that they will buy their apartments. (To simplify, this discussion will refer to co-op buyers as buying an apartment, although technically they're really buying stock.)

From the tenants' point of view, the building's conversion to condo or co-op form is either a marvelous opportunity to buy a valuable asset at a discount ("insiders'") price; a threat of losing their home; or no danger, just a nuisance. It depends on the tenants' own financial situations and plans, and also on local law and the course the building owner has chosen to take.

Local law determines whether the owner of the building has the right to evict tenants who don't buy their apartments. Frequently, the law outlines two kinds of conversions: a "non-evict" or an "eviction" plan. If it's a non-evict plan, tenants who choose not to buy their apartments can stay on as tenants, just as if the conversion had never taken place. (The sponsor of the conversion can sell their apartments to an investor, who then becomes the landlord of whichever apartments he or she buys.)

But if an eviction plan is chosen by the sponsor and approved by the appropriate state agency, most tenants must either buy their apartments or move out. I say "most tenants" because senior citizens and disabled tenants are protected against eviction in this situation by many state laws.

From the sponsor's point of view, the main difference between the two plans is that more of the tenants must agree to buy their apartments for an eviction plan to be approved than for a noneviction plan to become effective.

What to Do

You'll probably hear a lot of rumors before your building enters the conversion process. But the first official intimation will probably be a preliminary prospectus or offering plan. These documents are sometimes called "red herrings" (although they're far from irrelevant) because they have a red legend on the front explaining that the plan has not yet been approved by the authorities.

Usually, the best strategy is for all the tenants to form a tenants' committee and raise enough money to hire a lawyer and accountant experienced in conversions. First of all, the tenants will need accurate information about their options; second, professional advice will make it possible for them to use their negotiating position to the fullest.

Hiring a lawyer and accountant is a lot like hiring a plumber: You interview a lot of them, find out if they've ever done this kind of work before (and how good the results were), and how much they charge. Sometimes a tenants' group can arrange to have part of the lawyer's fee contingent (dependent) on results achieved, such as lower insider's prices or financing offered by the sponsor. However, it's hard to put a dollar value on benefits like extra time for nonbuying tenants to relocate.

The tenants usually divide into three groups:

• Those who can't or won't buy their apartments, and hope that the conversion plan falls through
• Those who think the plan is favorable enough as it stands, and are just waiting to get out their checkbooks
• Those who might buy their apartments—but only if they're absolutely sure the deal is as good as they can make it

All three groups can benefit by working together. If the tenants aren't unified, they may find that an eviction plan has been adopted, or that they could have bought their apartments on more favorable terms if they'd bargained harder. Remember, the plan can't become effective unless it gets official approval and at least the minimum number of tenants agree to purchase. If it looks like the minimum number won't be achieved, the sponsor of the conversion has to "sweeten the pot"— perhaps by lowering the "insider's" price of the apartments, increasing the reserve fund that will remain with the building, or otherwise making the deal more attractive.

One common tactic by the sponsor is to give the tenants only a limited amount of time (usually 90 days) to buy apartments at the insider's price; after that time passes, they can still buy the apartments, but at the higher price charged to nontenants. One of the things the tenants' committee (and their lawyer) can do is to get this period extended.

The "no-buy" pledge is one of the tenants' strongest weapons. Tenants can sign an agreement, either refusing to buy their apartments at all or refusing to buy until the sponsor meets their terms. Be careful before you sign one of these agreements—some courts have held that they are legally enforceable, and you'll be stuck if you sign a no-buy pledge and then change your mind.

Should You Buy?

If you decide to house hunt, you will have to make the choice between a conventional house, co-op, or condo. If your apartment building is converted, you have to make the choice a lot faster! The test is whether you can afford to buy at the insider's price and with the best financing you can find, and how your apartment stacks up, both as an investment and as compared to the cost of other housing (minus moving costs you save by not relocating).

If you can find other housing that is better and/or financially more favorable, you can buy your apartment at the insiders' price, reap a quick profit by selling it to an outsider at a market price, and then move to cheaper or better quarters. Some offering plans (or co-op bylaws) call for a "flip tax": Insiders who sell (perhaps before a certain period of time has elapsed) have to turn over part of their profits to the co-op corporation.

Your opinion about flip taxes depends a lot on your own situation. If you want the building to retain a stable population, with no quick-buck bonanzas, you want a flip tax. If you want to sell fast and earn legitimate profits from being in the right place at the right time, you don't want one! The flip tax is controversial now; expect many court cases about it in the future.

The lawyer, and especially the accountant, for the tenant's association can give the tenants a lot of valuable information about whether the sponsor's suggested offering plan is a valid one. For instance, the sponsor may want to walk away when the building needs new elevators or other major capital improvements, with the offering plan calling for a very small capital reserve. In that case, the unlucky tenants will face big increases in their maintenance payments almost immediately.

Another point to watch: In a condo, each owner's responsibility for maintenance charges is set by the percentage of ownership he or she has in the "common elements." In a co-op, each apartment is assigned a certain number of shares. Each tenant gets one vote in co-op elections—but responsibility for maintenance increases depends on the number of shares assigned to the apartment. This leads to conflict when owners of "low-share" apartments enthusiastically vote for expensive improvements, knowing that the owners of "high-share" apartments will have to carry most of the cost.

After the Conversion

The tenants now own the stock in a co-op corporation, or the apartments or townhouses in a condo. The tenants hold a meeting to elect a board of directors; either the tenants elect the officers directly, or the board of directors appoints them. Like any other corporation, a co-op corporation has bylaws explaining its operations and stockholders' rights. The proprietary lease also outlines the apartment owner's rights and duties. Similarly, condo owners have a declaration of effectiveness of the condo conversion plan, bylaws, and house rules.

The directors and officers have an important job; they're responsible for budgeting and management of large sums of money. You will recognize the people who strive to be on the board—they're the people who always ran for student council in high school. Many people shy away from attending owners' meetings (which do, indeed, tend to be characterized by numbing forty-five-minute speeches, enlivened by occasional shouting matches or even fistfights). But remember, if you don't get involved, you will have no say if poor financial management is exercised, if repairs are delayed too long, or if necessary repairs are done extravagantly (with an impact on your maintenance charges).

29. Is It Cheaper to Buy or Rent?

Right after you leave school and get your first job, you probably won't have a choice: Either you'll have to move back in with your folks or rent an apartment or a house (perhaps with a couple of roommates to help foot the bills). But once you're better established financially, think hard about whether buying a home is a good financial move.

Here are some of the disadvantages of buying a home.

•No matter how low your monthly payments (I'll get to that in a second), it takes cash to buy a home. You'll need a down payment, closing costs (the real estate corporation Century 21 estimates closing costs for a typical $87,000 home are about $5,000), miscellaneous costs of house hunting (from the cost of a tank of gas and a sandwich and coffee during a house-hunting expedition, to an engineer's inspection and inspection for termite infestation), and the cost of moving to the new home. If you can't afford this cash commitment, you can't afford to buy a home; if you can afford it, you'll have to take the money out of savings or investments—so you'll lose investment income.

•The trend has been for the price of houses to increase faster than inflation, so most home buyers find that they've made a good investment. But some have made a disastrously poor investment—they own property in areas such as Seattle or Dallas, where the price of homes has dropped severely.

•Homeowners frequently have unexpected large (or huge) expenses: Real estate taxes can soar, and anything from dry rot to furnace death can lead to a giant repair bill.

Then there are the advantages of buying a house.

• Renters have nothing but a pile of rent receipts to show for years of faithful payment; homeowners have an asset that can be sold.
• Homes also yield tax deductions for mortgage interest and real estate taxes; certain costs of rehabbing a home may also qualify for tax advantages.
• Even if you don't want to sell your home, you can use the equity in your home to borrow money (to pay for college, your son's or daughter's wedding, a vacation, etc.).

"Let's Go to the Videotape"

According to Century 21 and the consulting firm Runzheimer International, in most cities it's actually cheaper to own a home than it is to rent one. For instance, a family that earns $42,000 can expect to spend a little more on mortgage payments than on rent (estimated at $19,028 a year for the renter, $23,843 a year for the homeowner in Los Angeles versus $12,292 and $12,770 respectively in Atlanta, $15,827 and $16,011 in Chicago, and $15,988 and $19,197 in Boston)—but the tax savings mean that the homeowner ends up with an extra $750 a year in Los Angeles, and a whopping $3,186 a year extra in Chicago.

It's estimated that a Dallas homeowner earning $37,500 a year, with a 9.75%, 30-year fixed-rate mortgage, would save $1,262 a year over a similar family spending $600 to $700 a month on rent. The monthly mortgage payment would be $779 on a typical $79,000 home purchased with a $3,950 down payment and closing costs of $5,450.

The one area where renting was found to be cheaper than buying was New York City. Rent may be a painful $1,200 to $1,300 a month, but housing prices are so astronomical that it would take an annual income of $83,500 to buy a typical $193,000 home—and mortgage payments would be $1,948 a month for a 9.75%, 30-year mortgage. Buying the house would take a down payment of almost $20,000, and closing costs would devour about $11,000 more.

The average home in the Century 21 study cost $87,290, so it would take a $33,450 income to make the monthly payments of $780 (for the 9.75%, 30-year fixed-rate mortgage)—just a few dollars more than the average $750 rent. Tax advantages (about $3,000 a year for a family in the top 38.5% bracket) make the difference. The average down payment would be about $9,000, and closing costs about $5,000.

But "home" is a sentimental concept as well as a financial one, and there's more to the rose-covered cottage than the gilt-edged securities.

30. Buying a Home—An Overview

What's it like to buy a house? Well, let me tell you about the 75¢ cashmere coat I bought at the block party. (Okay, maybe it was $1.50—something like that.) It's 100% cashmere, and it's really in pretty good shape, but the buttons were a little shabby, and the coat was sort of baggy, so I got a nice set of buttons. About three bucks.

The coat's too large, so I had the local seamstress turn it into a double-breasted coat. That took a week, cost $8, and actually she didn't do such a hot job. Now I noticed that the sleeves were droopy, and the simplest answer was to bring up the shoulders with a pair of shoulder pads: $5.35.

I still love the coat, but is it a 75¢ coat or a $15.00 coat, once you take all the "little extras" into account? By the same token, once you buy a house, you'll find that the down payment—even the full purchase price of the house—is only one element of what you'll pay.

Even the process of buying a house is expensive. There are fees involved in applying for a mortgage, closing costs, homeowner's insurance to buy. If the house isn't in perfect condition, there'll be anything from a few licks of paint to a "gut rehab" to pay for. And, of course, over the life of your mortgage, you'll pay many thousands of dollars in interest—quite possibly, more than the original selling price of the home.

The Buying Process

Buying a house is a four-step process (most of the process is exactly the same for a co-op or condo; make the necessary adjustment if that's the kind of home you're looking for).

• "Shopping" for a house—deciding your needs, contacting brokers, and looking at houses that might be suitable. Once you see a house you like, it's an excellent idea to hire an engineer to inspect it for structural defects and damage.
• Negotiating with the sellers, not just how high the price will be, but when you can move in, what items will be included in the sale (washing machine and carpeting, for instance), and whether the sellers are willing to provide some or all of the financing.
• Speaking of financing, once you've chosen a house, you'll probably need at least one mortgage—maybe two. (The exceptions are people who've just sold another house, or who have a chunk of cash from an inheritance or a lump sum from a retirement plan.) You'll have to find out which local mortgage lenders offer the best terms.
• With all that arranged, the final step is the "closing": transfer of ownership from the sellers to the buyers. Usually, the buyers put down some money ("earnest money" or "deposit") before the clos-

ing; at the closing, they pay out more of their own money (down payment) and get a mortgage or mortgages (from the sellers and/or a bank, finance company, or other financial institution). Therefore, the sellers get the full purchase price of the house at the closing.

If the seller's mortgage includes a "due-on-sale" clause, they must pay off the balance remaining on the mortgage at the closing. Otherwise, the buyers may be able to "assume" that mortgage (take it over from the sellers and continue making the payments that the sellers would have made if they'd kept the house). Assuming the seller's mortgage is a good deal if their interest rate is much lower than current interest rates, or if assumption makes it possible to avoid the hundreds of dollars it costs to apply for a mortgage.

Another important part of the closing: The sellers give the buyers the deed to the home (the legal document showing ownership). Once the deed is recorded with the appropriate authorities, the buyers are the new legal owners of the property.

31. Selling a House—An Overview

For every buyer, there must be a seller, of course. Besides, many families find themselves as *both* home sellers and home buyers at about the same time. They may decide to move out of a house that is too small, too large, or needs too much work; maybe career needs call for a transfer to another part of the country. The solution is to sell the present family home and buy another—or to sell the home and move to a rented house or apartment.

Sellers should remember that a little money and effort spent on fixing up the house (fresh paint, repairing sagging trim or cracked windowpanes) can make a big difference in the house's attractiveness—and its sale price. Besides, these expenses may help cut your tax bill: If you have to pay a tax on house profits, your taxable profits will be smaller if you have deductible "fixing-up expenses." (Ask your tax adviser, or read IRS publications to find out which expenses are deductible.)

FISBO

For the seller, one of the most important decisions is whether to use a broker or go the FISBO (For Sale by Owner) route. The advantage of using a broker is that the broker screens out people who are completely unable to afford the home; the broker also has extensive negotiation experience, and may be able to find a buyer at a higher price than the seller would have asked for on his or her own.

The disadvantage is that the broker's commission is usually 6% to 7% of the sale price (though you may be able to negotiate a lower commission rate). Either you'll have to boost the price of the house to compensate (scaring away some potential buyers), or you'll have less left over once all the expenses are paid.

If you decide to handle the sale without a broker, you must advertise the house for sale, arrange to show the house to potential buyers, and handle all the negotiations yourself. If a broker is involved, he or she handles these tasks. Of course, there's nothing to prevent you from trying to sell the house yourself, then bringing in a broker if it's too much work or you can't find a qualified buyer.

Multiple Listing?

If you do decide to use a broker, there's another choice to make: whether to give a single broker the exclusive right to show the house for a period of time (such as three months), or whether to "multiple list" the house. Under multiple listing, many brokers can send prospects to see the house. Once it's sold, the brokerage commission is divided between the broker who originally got the listing and the one who finally made the sale.

An exclusive listing may motivate the broker to work harder because he or she is not competing against a horde of other brokers for the sale. However, a multiple listing has the advantage of showing your house to more potential buyers (and the disadvantage of sending a larger army tromping through it!).

Don't be angry if the broker questions you about defects in the house. Yes, the broker works for you and is supposed to be on your side—but there's an increasing tendency for courts to permit angry home buyers to sue the broker (as well as the seller) when the purchased home turns out to be defective. The theory is that the broker, as a professional, should not only have asked the sellers about the condition of the house, but should have taken steps to find out its real condition (including problems about which the sellers were not aware).

Bridge Loans

Theoretically, all home sales work neatly. The seller sells home A, collects the funds, and then buys home B. In real life, things aren't that tidy. A seller who thought it would take six months to find a buyer gets one in three weeks—and the buyer is eager to move in at once. Or, the seller already has a new home picked out, a contract of sale signed, and a mortgage arranged—and no way to get rid of white elephant A.

In the second situation, a bridge loan can resolve an otherwise hopeless financial muddle. The bridge loan provides money for the down payment and closing costs on the new house; it's repaid in a lump sum once the old house is sold. The bridge loan usually operates as a second mortgage, so it may not be available if there's already a second mortgage in place.

Banks seldom advertise bridge loans, so you'll have to investigate—

and check with several banks because there's a wide variation in the fees charged. Some banks seem to think of bridge loans as an opportunity to make substantial profits; others think of them as a low-profit service that promotes good customer relations. Of course, you'd prefer to borrow from a bank in the second group!

Usually, the largest available bridge loan is 75% of the value of the present house, minus outstanding mortgages. However, some lenders will make bigger bridge loans because they will lend 75%, or even 80%, of the value of the new (usually more expensive) home.

Another possibility is to take out a home equity loan against the current home, and use that money as a "bridge." This strategy can also work for condos; banks, however, usually refuse to make bridge loans on co-ops because the seller just owns stock, not real estate that can be foreclosed.

32. For Buyers: What to Look For—Specifics

Real estate professionals say that the three most important things are location, location, and location. To maximize the value of your housing investment, you want "the worst house on the block": a comparatively inexpensive house whose value is boosted by the attractive homes nearby. A good location is one in a neighborhood increasing in value, or remaining stable. If you have or plan to have children, good schools are vital.

Once you've chosen a neighborhood, think about the kind of house you want—the "must have" features and the items that would make the house nicer, but can be done without if necessary. And decide both how much you'd like to pay (down payment, overall price, and monthly payment) and the amount you could afford, at a stretch.

When you see a house you like, investigate it thoroughly. Don't be put off by a dingy appearance if the house is basically sound. A coat of paint could cure the problem. On the other hand, don't be fooled by superficial "fixing up" that masks water damage, bad plumbing, and insufficient electrical wiring. Unless you plan to do extensive rehab work, or unless you can get the house at a very low price, make sure that the basic mechanical systems (heating, plumbing, electricity) are in good shape, and that the house is structurally sound—no sagging beams or tower-of-Pisa tilts. Is the basement trim with well-designed storage facilities? (Of course it isn't—it never is.) Well, okay, is it just dark and dank, or has an accidental in-ground swimming pool established itself in the house?

In the end, though, your emotions will probably prevail, and a house will tell you, "Buy me! I'm the one!"

The Legalities of Buying a Home

If you're unusually businesslike and prudent, you will hire an experienced real estate lawyer as soon as you decide to buy a house—even before you take the first tour. If you do this (and the lawyer will certainly be surprised), you can start out by learning some of the ins and outs of contract law, and the legal aspects of mortgages and deeds. Most important, your lawyer can draw up a draft contract of sale that favors *you*. When you find a house you want to buy, you can offer your own version of the contract, and explain that the seller's lawyer can contact your lawyer to iron out the details.

However, if you're like everybody else, you'll find a house, make an offer to buy it, and *then* find a lawyer. Once you express interest in buying a house, you'll probably be asked to sign a "binder"—an informal contract requiring you to make a small payment. Try not to sign a binder if you can help it. The problem is that binders—like all informal contracts—create endless legal problems because they hardly ever get the care, thought, and legal advice that should go into drafting a formal contract.

As a typical example, you could sign a binder, find out that the house is to termites what Mel's Drive-In was to the characters in *American Graffiti*, and try to walk away from the deal—then get sued by the indignant would-be seller. Or, you could craftily insist that the binder specify that it is not valid until it has been reviewed by your attorney. Then you find out that the house has been sold under your nose, to someone else who signed a contract of sale. *Your* binder, of course, never became valid because you didn't have time to have your lawyer review it.

In short, it's in everyone's best interest not to sign anything until a contract of sale has been carefully prepared and reviewed by *both* sets of lawyers. If the seller says that other eager buyers are waiting in the wings, and you'll have to sign a binder or lose the chance to buy the house, offer a nonrefundable $100 to $200 to the seller to keep the house off the market for a few days. During this time, you can get legal advice and get your version of the contract drawn up. If need be, you can walk away from the deal, losing the money, but with no other liability. Make sure you get a receipt indicating clearly that you have *not* signed a binder.

Contract of Sale

The contract of sale spells out all the terms of the sale of the house: how much the down payment will be, what kind of deed the sellers will provide (a warranty deed gives the buyers the most protection; a quit-claim deed gives them the least—the sellers just transfer whatever interest they have in the house, which may be limited or even nonexistent), and what personal property will be included with the house and land. Perhaps most important, the contract also spells out the "contingencies": If the contract is contingent, it won't be effective unless certain specified things happen.

Contingencies can protect both buyer and seller. For instance, the contract can be contingent on the buyer's getting financing in an amount at least equal to X, for a term of at least Y years, with an interest rate not higher than $Z\%$—and by a date early enough so that the closing can take place when scheduled. That way, the buyer can back out if he or she can't get affordable financing, and the seller can look for another buyer.

The contract can also be contingent upon the buyer's getting a satisfactory inspection report from an engineer and/or termite inspector. The buyer wants this part of the contract to say that the buyer can walk away if he or she is dissatisfied for *any* reason. The seller prefers a contract that limits the contingency to certain named, serious problems (such as rotting of structural members) and gives the seller the right to fix the damage, or reduce the price of the house to compensate—but still have the deal go through.

Buyers should remember that the contract is not contingent upon *anything* unless it says it is! Buyers may assume that they can forget about the purchase of a new house if they have trouble selling their present house, or if it sells at a disappointingly low price. That's not the way the law interprets the situation—unless the contract specifically states that it is contingent upon the buyer's selling his or her house at a certain price, or higher.

The period of time between the signing of the contract of sale and the closing is filled with legal and practical events. Unless it's a cash deal, the buyer has to find financing—which probably means a mortgage (or first plus second mortgage) from a bank. Other events are also going on behind the scenes.

Title Search and Insurance

In a title search, all of the public records are consulted to find out if the sellers really own the house, and if there are any claims that could be asserted against them. For instance, taxes could be owed on the house, it could have been used as security for a loan that was not paid on schedule, or unpaid workmen could assert a claim for work done on the house.

Usually, though, the title search does not reveal any problems; just in case, the buyer's lawyer orders a title insurance policy.

The *title insurance policy* compensates the insured person for damages suffered if it turns out that the seller did *not* have free and clear title to the house. The tricky part is that if there's only *one* title insurance policy in the transaction, it protects the lender who writes the mortgage on the house—not the buyer, even though the buyer pays for the policy. The buyer can (and probably should) buy a separate title insurance policy to protect his or her own interests.

What if there are problems? They could be simple matters of confusion (is the Esther Lindemon who inherited the house in 1932 the same as the Esther L. Flagg who sold it in 1947?) or mistakes that can easily be cleared up (the seller produces a cancelled check and receipt for the allegedly unpaid taxes). It's up to the lawyer to iron it all out and either resolve the problem so that the closing can take place on time, or work out another solution.

What Can Go Wrong

Sometimes the deal is off; sometimes the closing has to be delayed until the solution is worked out. For instance, the buyers might accept the house, but at a lower price; maybe the sellers will deposit money in escrow (with a neutral party, for safekeeping) until things are straightened out. The closing date may also have to be delayed if the buyers can't get a mortgage commitment before the scheduled closing date.

Sometimes buyers are frustrated because the sellers can't or won't move out of the house on time. The sellers may stay put if their new home isn't ready, or if they haven't been able to find suitable accommodations. One way to avoid the problem is to leave a little extra time in the schedule; another is to have the contract of sale specify a penalty of a certain number of dollars per day past the scheduled or actual closing date that the sellers stay in the house. Or part of the sale price can be put in escrow, to be paid to the buyers if they can't move into the house on the day of the closing.

33. Mortgage Shopping

A mortgage is something like an auto loan. In either case, you have to put down a down payment, which often comes from "trading in" an earlier car or house. You make monthly payments, as defined by a written loan agreement—and if you don't make the payments, or if you otherwise fail to live up to your agreement, the lender can "repossess" your car—or your house. Houses are "foreclosed" that is, if you default, the lender gets a court order directing that the house be sold. If the sale proceeds are less than the amount still due on the mortgage, you still owe that amount to the lender; if the proceeds are higher, you're entitled to the extra.

A "second mortgage" on a house is second in line when there's a foreclosure—so there's a real risk that there won't be any money left after the house is sold and the first lender is paid off. The lender on a second mortgage doesn't get anything until the first lender is fully paid; the lenders don't share the amount realized by selling the house. Because the risk is higher, the interest rates on second mortgages are generally higher than on first mortgages.

Mortgage Basics

Buyers today should be grateful they don't have to pay the 20% (or even higher) mortgage rates that were common in the early 1980s. In fact, a good shopper may be able to get a single-digit mortgage: one with an interest rate under 10%. To decide which mortgage to apply for, there are three real tests.

• Can you qualify for the mortgage? Lenders will check your income, your assets, and your other debts. You probably won't qualify if your mortgage payments, plus other long-term debt, will equal or exceed 36% of your gross income. Some lenders insist that long-term debt not exceed 28% of your gross income. (Later in this section, on page 171, there's a worksheet to see if you qualify for a mortgage on the house you've chosen. It comes later, instead of here, because certain financial concepts must be explained before the worksheet makes sense.)

• Can you afford the monthly payments? Paying back the lender is only part of your mortgage payment. Your real estate taxes and your homeowner's insurance premium are also paid out of your monthly mortgage payment. If real estate taxes rise, or if you need more homeowner's insurance because the value of your house has risen, you could find the increased monthly payment difficult or impossible to meet—especially if you take out a loan to repair or improve the house, or if you add a home equity loan for house-related purposes or as part of your general financial planning.

• How much does the loan cost overall? When you apply for a loan, the lender will disclose the APR (Annual Percentage Rate—the interest rate), length of the loan, monthly payments, and other terms of the loan. He or she will also tell you the uncomfortably large number that represents the total of payments to be made under the loan.

Table 5 on page 168 gives you an idea of how much your monthly payment would be, based on the size of the mortgage and the mortgage rate. The worksheet on page 171 helps you decide whether you can afford the house you like best.

Fifteen or Thirty?

You may be given a choice between a short-term mortgage (fifteen, or even five years) and a long-term mortgage (twenty or thirty years). Broadly speaking, the trade-off is that you will have higher monthly payments under a short-term mortgage, but you'll build equity in the home much faster (a real plus if you plan to use home equity loans for college tuition or medical bills)—and you'll end up paying much less interest overall.

Usually, the payments on a fifteen-year mortgage are 10% to 20% higher than the payments on a thirty-year mortgage. However, lenders usually require slightly higher rates (¼% to ½%) on thirty-year mortgages because they're tying up their money—and taking the risk that interest rates will go up—for a longer term.

However, if you've got your heart set on a house you can just barely afford, you'll be better off with a longer mortgage, and lower monthly payments. You'll also get interest deductions on your tax return for a longer period of time. The lender will allow you to qualify for the thirty-year mortgage with a lower annual income.

For instance, according to the Federal National Mortgage Agency ("Fannie Mae") it would take a family income of $34,500 to qualify for a 10%, $75,000 fifteen-year mortgage, and the monthly payment would be $806; a family with only $29,500 income would qualify for a thirty-year mortgage on the same house, and monthly payments would be only $686.

The price of lower monthly payments on the larger mortgage is that you pay far more interest overall—the house becomes far more expensive, when all the factors are taken into account. Consider a $100,000 mortgage. If the borrower takes a fifteen-year mortgage at 9.25%, he or she will pay $1,029 a month for principal and interest—and, over the fifteen years, will pay the $100,000 principal plus $85,254 in interest.

If, instead, the borrower gets a 9.5%, thirty-year mortgage in the same amount, he or she will pay back the $100,000 in 360 monthly payments of $841—but those payments will include $202,708 in interest. In short, the borrower end up paying three times the amount he or she originally borrowed.

But we've only looked at one aspect of the situation. Most homeowners can deduct mortgage interest, so the higher the homeowner's tax bracket, the more of the interest cost he or she can pass along to Uncle Sam. In our $100,000 example, a taxpayer in the lowest, 15% bracket really pays only $72,465 in interest for a fifteen-year mortgage, once tax deductions are considered. Taxpayers in the middle, 28% bracket pay $61,382 interest after taxes; those in the top, 33% bracket pay $56,267 interest after taxes.

The difference is even more dramatic for the thirty-year mortgage. Out of total interest of $202,708, a person in the 15% bracket ends up paying $172,301 after taxes; a person in the 28% bracket pays $145,949 after taxes; and a person in the highest bracket pays $133,787 after taxes.

In short, you'll pay a lot less interest with a shorter mortgage—but you'll get much bigger tax deductions with a longer one.

If you can't afford a fifteen-year mortgage, ask if your bank will set up the mortgage with a payment every two weeks, each equal to half the ordinary payment for a thirty-year mortgage. You'll make twenty-six payments a year, instead of twelve (or twenty-four half-payments)—and this small difference means that your mortgage will be paid off in only eighteen years, not thirty.

Another strategy: Find out if your mortgage allows you to prepay without a prepayment penalty. If so, get a thirty-year mortgage; when you've saved up $500 or $1,000, prepay that amount and have the bank work out a new payment schedule. Either you'll finish paying your mortgage earlier, or you'll enjoy a lower monthly payment because of the prepayment.

Fixed or Adjustable?

There's plenty to think about when you're shopping for a fixed-rate mortgage (one with a steady interest rate throughout the mortgage). To add a level of complexity, you'll also have to decide between fixed-rate and adjustable-rate mortgages.

Adjustable-rate mortgages, a fairly recent development, were created by lenders who got tired of taking a beating every time interest rates rose and they found themselves stuck with long-term, low-rate mortgages. Instead of a single rate throughout the life of the loan, adjustable-rate mortgages have an initial rate (say, 8.25%). The initial rate is good for a short time (such as one year). After that, the interest rate changes in response to changes in economic indicators. For instance, your mortgage rate might be set at 3% higher than the prime rate, with the lender permitted to change the interest rate twice a year.

If you get an adjustable-rate mortgage, you're speculating on interest rates. (Between 1983 and mid-1986, the strategy worked out well: Although 80% of borrowers chose fixed-rate mortgages, those with adjustable-rate mortgages actually paid lower interest rates.) So that this won't turn into a wild gamble, many adjustable-rate mortgages have "caps" on interest rates. One kind of cap puts a limit on the amount the interest rate can rise—let's say, 1% in any given adjustment, and not more than 6% over the term of the mortgage.

Another kind of cap limits the increase in the monthly mortgage payment. But if this kind of cap is *not* combined with a limitation on interest-rate increases, you could encounter "negative amortization." That is, instead of each mortgage payment containing part interest and part principal, each payment could be too small even to pay all the interest legally due. So you owe more money the longer you continue paying the mortgage.

Amortization

Most mortgages today are written to be "self-amortizing." That is, each monthly payment is divided between principal (repayment of your debt), interest, taxes, and insurance premiums. If it's a twenty-year mortgage, it's designed so that by the time you make the 240th payment, you've repaid the entire principal.

However, "balloon mortgages" are not self-amortizing. These mortgages are written so that at the end of the mortgage term (usually short—three to five years), you still owe a large "balloon" payment. You have two choices at the end of the mortgage term: either make the balloon payment—if you can afford it—or refinance. In effect, you're gambling that either you'll have the cash or that financing will be available on terms you can afford.

Self-amortizing mortgages are computed according to an "amortization schedule," they are *not* arranged so that each payment repays the same amount of principal. Instead, each payment has a different balance between interest and principal. Early in the mortgage, each payment is all, or almost all, interest; later on, the balance shifts and each payment repays a lot of principal.

There's a practical reason for this, and it has practical consequences. At the beginning of the loan, you haven't had a chance to repay much and, therefore, you have the use of most of the lender's money. That means that the lender is entitled to more interest. The more you repay, the less of the lender's money you're using—and the less interest the lender is entitled to.

Fixed-rate mortgages *could* be set up so that each payment represented exactly one month's share of principal, plus the interest due on the balance outstanding for that month. But it's never done that way because each payment would be different, driving both lender and borrower nuts. Anyway, this arrangement would make the loan payments much higher in the early years of the mortgage, just when young families are least able to afford it. (In fact, there's a kind of mortgage called a graduated-payment mortgage that starts out with low monthly payments; the payments increase over time, to balance the presumably increasing family income.)

Instead, amortization schedules are set up by adding up all the interest, plus the principal, and dividing by the number of payments to be made. The practical consequence for the borrowers is that the largest tax deductions come in the early years of the mortgage, when payments are almost all interest. (That's also when most people are in their lowest tax bracket—but you can't have everything.)

Another consequence is that home buyers don't build up much equity during the early years of the mortgage. Therefore, their net worth doesn't increase much during this time, and they don't have much equity to borrow against by using home equity loans. If they sell the house, much of the money they receive from the buyer goes straight to the lender.

Using the Mortgage Table

Table 5 gives the "payment factors" that show how much you'll pay each month, in principal and interest, for every $1,000 borrowed at a given interest rate. The payment factors are given in Column 1 (for fifteen-year, fixed-rate mortgages) and Column 4 (for thirty-year, fixed-rate mortgages). Columns 2 and 3 show the monthly payment for principal plus interest for two typical mortgages: $50,000 in Column 2, $75,000 in Column 3. Columns 5 and 6 do the same for thirty-year mortgages.

To use the table, find the interest rate involved (the table runs from

TABLE 5. MORTGAGE PAYMENTS*

Interest Rate (%)	Fifteen-year			Thirty-year		
	1	2	3	4	5	6
8.00	9.56	$478	$717	7.34	$367	$551
8.25	9.70	$485	$728	7.51	$376	$563
8.50	9.85	$493	$739	7.69	$385	$577
8.75	9.99	$500	$749	7.87	$394	$598
9.00	10.14	$507	$761	8.05	$403	$604
9.25	10.29	$515	$772	8.23	$412	$617
9.50	10.44	$522	$783	8.41	$421	$631
9.75	10.59	$530	$794	8.59	$430	$644
10.00	10.75	$538	$806	8.78	$439	$659
10.25	10.90	$545	$818	8.96	$448	$672
10.50	11.05	$553	$829	9.15	$458	$686
10.75	11.21	$561	$841	9.33	$467	$700
11.00	11.37	$569	$853	9.52	$476	$714
11.25	11.52	$576	$864	9.71	$486	$728
11.50	11.68	$584	$876	9.90	$495	$743
11.75	11.84	$592	$888	10.09	$505	$757
12.00	12.00	$600	$900	10.29	$515	$772
12.25	12.16	$608	$912	10.48	$524	$786
12.50	12.33	$617	$925	10.67	$534	$800
12.75	12.49	$625	$937	10.87	$544	$815
13.00	12.65	$633	$949	11.06	$553	$830

*I thank HSH Associates, Riverdale, NJ, for providing the factors in Columns 1 and 4. Dollar amounts are rounded to the next highest dollar—e.g., $829.50 is given as $830.

8% to 13% interest); multiply the factor by the amount of the mortgage. Let's say you want to know how much you'd pay for a fifteen-year, 9.25% mortgage if you make a $22,000 down payment on a $107,000 house.

The amount of the mortgage would be $85,000 (price of the house minus down payment); the factor for a fifteen-year mortgage is 10.29; the monthly payment would be $874.65. That is, it costs $10.29 per thousand dollars per month, multiplied by 85. The actual mortgage payment would be slightly higher because of real estate taxes and homeowner's insurance. The monthly payment for the same house with a 9.5%, thirty-year mortgage (remember, thirty-year mortgages usually carry a slightly higher rate) would be $714.85 (plus taxes and insurance): the factor of 8.41 times 85.

34. Applying for a Mortgage

Shopping for a mortgage can be a confusing, lengthy, and downright humbling experience (as snooty platform officers examine—and sneer at—every aspect of your financial life). It can also be a time of nerve-wracking suspense as you wonder whether you can get a loan commitment in time to keep your deal from falling through—or whether interest rates will rise in the period between your initial application and the time the bank *finally* deigns to issue a commitment. Or, you could get a commitment for a mortgage at a tolerable rate—but the commitment lasts only six weeks or two months, and expires before you can have the closing, so you have to accept higher interest rates, or even apply all over again.

Fortunately, there are steps you can take to make the whole process easier and surer (but you'll never mistake it for a ten-day Caribbean cruise).

Applying for a mortgage is also an expensive business. You'll have to pay fees for appraisal of the property, assessment of your credit record, document preparation, origination of a loan, and much more. These fees can be expressed either in dollar amounts, or as "points" (a point is 1% of the price of the house). Points are paid "up front," that is, when the house is purchased—points are not included in the mortgage or paid off over the life of the loan. (Check with your tax adviser to see if points are deductible in the year you buy the house—they usually are.)

Many of these fees are nonrefundable, even if the deal falls through, and even if the bank to which you apply refuses to give you a mortgage. Therefore, unless you're very rich or very nervous, you'll want to limit the number of applications you make.

That's why the first step is to target the best bank (or other lender—perhaps a credit union or finance company offers the best deal for you) for your first application. Read newspaper ads and telephone local lenders to find out what kinds of mortgages are available (fixed, adjustable, or both; down payment requirements; interest rates, etc.) and what fees are involved in the application. The bank may also have a set of guidelines to see if your application would be rejected out of hand.

Even if the bank doesn't have a set of guidelines ready, you can use the worksheet on page 171 to see if you're a "qualified borrower." If that's too much work, use this simple rule of thumb: If you make a 10% down payment, and interest rates are between 9.5% and 10%, you can probably afford a house that costs about twice your annual income: that is, a $25,000 annual income should qualify you for a $50,000 house if you make a $5,000 down payment.

Next, get your own house in order, financially speaking. Examine your credit report (page 195 shows you how to do this), make sure any mistakes are corrected, and do whatever you can to "polish up" your credit rating. If you've fallen into the habit of paying bills a little slowly, this is the time to catch up and get a clean bill of health.

Find your income tax returns for the past few years, to show your income and deductions. If you have a student loan, car loan, or other debt outstanding, find the loan agreements—the mortgage lenders to which you apply will want to know what your other obligations are. Last but not least, get some cash! You'll need to write stacks of checks for applications and closing costs. To say the least, it looks bad if the check bounces.

Now you're ready to apply to the bank that you think will offer the best deal. You could have smooth sailing all the way—or a host of problems. For instance, if the bank requires that the house be appraised, and the appraiser says it's worth much less than the asking price, you could be refused a mortgage as large as you need. Lenders usually refuse to lend more than a certain percentage of the appraised value of the house (typically, 80%). You'll either have to prove that the house is worth more than the appraiser says—perhaps by showing that comparable houses sold recently have fetched higher prices—find additional financing (perhaps a second mortgage, a mortgage from the seller, or a loan from a relative), or make a larger down payment.

Can You Afford That House?

Use the following worksheet to decide whether you can afford a particular house (or co-op, or condo)—or, use typical figures for the neighborhood where you're house-hunting to determine your price range.

WORKSHEET

Step 1: What is your gross income per month (for both spouses, if you're married and both are working)? $_____

Step 2: What are your monthly payments on loans and credit cards? $_____

Step 3: Subtract the figure in Step 2 from Step 1, to yield your monthly income after paying debts: $_____

Step 4: Calculate ¼ of the amount in Step 3. This is a monthly payment you can easily afford: $_____

Step 5: Calculate ⅓ of the amount in Step 3. This is the largest monthly payment that you could make, and still qualify under normal banking rules: $_____

Step 6: What is the price of the house? $_____

Step 7: How large a down payment can you make (bearing in mind that you'll have to pay closing costs)? $_____

Step 8: Subtract the down payment from the price; this is the amount of the mortgage required: $_____

Step 9: What is the mortgage rate you think you can get on a fifteen-year, fixed-rate mortgage? $_____

Step 10: For a thirty-year fixed-rate mortgage? $_____

Step 11: Turn to the mortgage table on page 168 and find the "factor" in Column 1 for the interest rate in Step 9. This is the monthly payment per $1,000 borrowed for fifteen years: $_____

Step 12: Multiply this by the amount in Step 8. This is the amount you'd pay for principal and interest on a fifteen-year, fixed-rate mortgage of this size: $_____

Step 13: Repeat the calculation with the factor in Column 4 of the mortgage table. This is the amount you'd pay for principal and interest on a thirty-year, fixed-rate mortgage of this size: $_____

Step 14: Find out the real estate taxes on the house, and divide by 12 to get a monthly figure: $_____

Step 15: Find out the annual homeowner's insurance premium on the house (or on a comparable house); divide by 12 to get a monthly figure: $_____

Step 16: Add the amounts in Steps 14 and 15 to the amount in Step 12. This is approximately what you'd pay each month for a fifteen-year, fixed-rate mortgage on the house: $_____

Step 17: Add the amounts in Steps 14 and 15 to the amount in Step 13. This is approximately what you'd pay each month for a thirty-year, fixed-rate mortgage on the house: $_____

Step 18: Compare the amounts in Steps 16 and 17 to the amounts in Steps 4 and 5. If the monthly payment is more than ⅓ of your income after paying other debts, you can't afford the house; if it's less than ¼ of your after-debt income, you can probably afford the payments and are in a good position to apply for a mortgage.

* * *

The Down Payment

The size of the down payment won't impress the seller, who gets the whole purchase price at the closing anyway, but it means a lot to the lender. One school of thought calls for the largest down payment you can possibly afford; that way, you borrow less, have more equity, have lower monthly payments, and pay a lot less interest over the length of the mortgage.

But if you have to wait until you have a spare $25,000 or even $75,000 before you buy a house, you'll *never* be able to buy if housing prices go up faster than your income. And you'll have to leave some cash for closing costs, moving expenses, and home renovation, not to mention paying your other bills and maintaining a savings cushion.

If you qualify for a Federal Housing Administration (FHA) or Veteran's Administration (VA) mortgage, you can buy a house with a small down payment—perhaps even without a down payment. And if you are a good financial risk but can't afford a large down payment, ask about private mortgage insurance (sometimes called "MAGIC loans" because the Mortgage Guarantee Insurance Corporation or other private insurer provides an insurance policy). The policy guarantees that the insurer will pay the loan if you default; mortgage insurance adds about ¼% to the interest rate on a mortgage.

You should consider your down payment as an investment, and analyze it like any other investment. Let's say you see a $115,000 house and find a bank that will lend you 90% of the purchase price on terms that are not intolerably painful. Let's also say that you have $11,500 in cash—and that you won't be down to your last nickel if you use it as a down payment. In fact, let's say you have $20,000 you can spare. Should you use it all as a down payment, put down the $11,500 the bank requires, or try to reduce the down payment even further by getting other financing or finding a bank that will make a larger mortgage loan? Well, it all depends.

The larger the down payment, the smaller your monthly mortgage payment—so a large down payment could be a good strategy if you're a free-lancer or entrepreneur with unpredictable peaks and valleys of income, or if you expect large expenses down the road. If, for instance, your kids will be in college pretty soon, you might welcome a small mortgage payment then (and a large amount of equity in your house so that you can use a home equity loan to pay tuition).

How do mortgage rates compare to the returns on reasonably safe investments? If mortgage rates are low, you could do better by making the smallest down payment you can get away with, and investing all your cash. That way, the earnings on your investments can be used to make mortgage payments—or anything else you like! (Now if you make the wrong investment choices, you'll wish you'd sunk your money safely into home equity.)

The federal government has a number of programs that make it possible for homebuyers to make small down payments, or even to buy homes with no down payment at all. The FHA provides "mortgage insurance" to lenders, not to borrowers. The FHA promises to repay the lender if the home buyer defaults, so lenders are taking much less risk. An FHA loan can be as high as 97% of the home's appraised value (which is often lower than its market price). Qualified veterans can get either a loan guarantee or a small direct loan from the Veterans Administration and buy homes with no down payment at all.

There are trade-offs on both these programs, for the lender and the borrower. Lenders like government-insured loans, of course, because their risk is reduced—but they don't like them because extra paperwork is required and because the government limits the amount of origination and other fees the lender can charge the borrower. (A common response is for the lender to require the *seller* to pay "points"— one or more percent of the sale price of the house, payable in a lump sum at the time of the sale. But the sellers can figure this out—*their* response is to increase the price of the house to compensate for the points they must pay.) Buyers who get an FHA-insured loan must also pay an extra half-percent in interest as an insurance premium.

The federal Department of Housing and Urban Development has, at least theoretically, a number of programs that provide loans to buy and fix up homes. I say "at least theoretically" because, although these programs are on the books, they aren't always given funds by Congress. And even if a program has money to lend or give out, there are apt to be many, many people and government agencies in line ahead of you. But it's worth asking your banker, your lawyer, your accountant, and community groups in your new neighborhood to see if funds *are* available, and how you can apply for them.

Also find out if your home state has a program, similar to New York's Sonny Mae (State of New York Mortgage Agency) or New Jersey's Housing and Finance Mortgage Agency. These state agencies (which typically sell bonds to finance their activities) provide mortgages— usually fixed-rate mortgages. These agencies may impose income limits (so that low- and moderate-income, but not high-income, home buyers can qualify) or set a maximum amount that can be financed (such as Connecticut's limit of a $38,000 income for a three-person family, and $110,000 maximum home price—$130,000 in Fairfield County).

Disclosure

Federal law gives you the right to get a tremendous amount of information about credit before you get a mortgage—maybe too much information to absorb easily. However, don't follow your original impulse and ignore the documents! If you can't understand them by reading through the attached instructions a few times, and if this account doesn't help, pester your lawyer until you understand.

Within three days of the time you apply for a loan (and apply means agree to pay the many, many fees involved in an application, and submit to an investigation of your credit rating), the lender must give you all the information required by the Truth-in-Lending laws. To sum up (the full version is on page 191), the lender must tell you the APR (the interest rate); the finance charge (the amount of interest and other charges); the amount you'll be borrowing; the total of payments; and, for an adjustable-rate loan, the conditions under which the rate can be adjusted.

This is all important information, but it won't necessarily tell you how high your closing costs will be. Many closing costs are not included in the APR or finance charge. Fortunately, a federal law called the Real Estate Settlement Procedures Act (RESPA) requires the lender to give you a detailed statement of closing costs. The lender, however, isn't required to do this until the day before the closing, which doesn't give you much time to raise extra cash! Therefore, you'll have to keep in touch with your lawyer about estimated closing costs, how the estimates change over time, and how the sums must be paid. (A personal check will be fine for some costs—others require certified or cashier's checks.)

35. Tax Aspects of Home Buying and Selling

If you sell stock at a profit, you'll probably have to pay taxes on the profit; if you sell your house at a profit, the profit may escape taxation under special rules. But the profit for tax purposes is not necessarily the figure you think of as your profit.

Tax calculations start with the "basis" of an asset—its value for tax purposes. The basis of a house starts out as its purchase price, but can change over time. Improvements to the house can increase its basis. If you deduct depreciation on the house when you compute your taxes (say, if you have a home office), you may have to lower the basis when the house is sold, to compensate for the tax advantages you got thanks to the depreciation rules.

The basis of the house you buy or sell is very important because the basis determines if you'll have to pay taxes on the transaction, and the size of the tax bill. It's important to maintain *all* records on a house for as long as you own it so that you can compute the basis accurately.

If this is your first house, the purchase will not be a taxable event. Just make sure you have the records to set your basis for the eventual sale. If you sell a house, however, you face a major job of tax computation, and maybe a hefty tax liability. Theoretically, your entire profit on the house is taxable gain, and, as a result of the Tax Code of 1986, you *don't* get special, low rates for capital gains, and you *don't* get to use income averaging to "smooth out" the differences in income from one year to the next. You'd have an awfully large tax liability—except . . .

Except for special provisions of the tax code that survive the 1986 tax reform bill. First of all, if you sell a house and buy a more expensive house during a period stretching from two years before the home sale to two years after it, you can "roll over" any profits on the home sale. They may lower your basis for the new house (and thus create more potentially taxable profits)—but you won't have to pay taxes on the profit at the time of the sale. There are special rules for figuring your profits. The basic question is whether the price you get for your house exceeds its basis, but you can use some of the costs of the sale and certain "fixing up expenses" (money spent to make the house more attractive to buyers: a new paint job, for instance) to reduce the "profits" as defined for tax purposes.

Now, if you sell a house and move into an apartment, or into a relative's or new spouse's house, or rent a house instead of buying one, then you will probably have to pay income tax on the profit, except . . .

Except for a tax-relief provision for senior citizens, and citizens not all that senior at that. Homeowners over the age of 55 get a special, one-time tax break, and are permitted to escape taxation on up to $125,000 of home-sale profits even if they don't buy a new home with the proceeds of the sale. You can use the rollover provision as often as you want, but you can use the "over-55" provision only once.

Many families use the strategy of buying a relatively inexpensive "starter" house, fixing it up, selling it at a profit, and buying a better house to shelter profits from tax as well as sheltering the family more opulently. They keep this up until they're ready for the "senior citizen" exclusion. This could be a very workable wealth-building technique for you too. But remember to think seriously about Medicaid eligibility (see page 285) before you sell your house and move to an apartment or retirement community. Home ownership could be your best chance to protect family assets against the very high costs of chronic illness.

Don't forget, if you have to move for reasons related to your job (whether you buy or sell a house, or move from one apartment to another), you may qualify for a tax deduction for moving expenses, house-hunting expenses, and temporary lodging en route to your new home. Be sure to keep records of these expenses, and show them to your lawyer or tax preparer for advice about whether you're entitled to a deduction; if so, how large that deduction is.

36. Tips for Newly Built Houses

So far, this discussion has assumed that the house you're buying already exists. But this isn't always the case. You could buy land and have a house built on it; you could buy a house or condo in a new development that's still under construction.

The advantage of a brand-new house is that nothing has had time to go wrong yet! However, it's important to make sure that the house is being well constructed; modern techniques sometimes go beyond efficient labor-saving to the outright sloppy. Another advantage is that you can have much more control over the house, and can have things done to suit your taste. (Remember, though, that you will almost certainly have to pay extra for any deviation from the developer's plans.)

Investigate before you sign; find out the practical and legal steps you can take if your home isn't ready on time. Find out if the architect and contractors, or developer, have a good track record. Have they worked on similar projects in the past? If so, did they finish (pretty close to) on time, (pretty close to) on budget, and without serious disputes with workers and suppliers of materials? Leave enough room in the schedule so that a few days of rain or a late delivery of materials won't leave you up in the air—with no place to live until your new home is completed.

Builders frequently ask for very large deposits (10% to 15% of the cost of the home); then the builder holds the money for months. The buyer doesn't get interest on the money for this time—and if the builder goes out of business, the buyer can lose the deposit.

The best protection for the home buyer is to have this money held in escrow (a special account)—but the builder probably won't agree, saying that the money is required to buy supplies and pay workers. In that case, press for a "bond" (special insurance that will refund the deposit if the builder goes under or fails to finish the house) or a "letter of credit" (part of the builder's construction loan is made available to refund deposits, if necessary).

A danger that sometimes besets purchasers of units in not-yet-completed condominium complexes is that the developer sometimes runs out of money before the promised "amenities" are completed. What will you do if the parking lot, laundry room, health club, and so forth, aren't completed?

If you buy a house or condo unit from a developer, all you need is a conventional mortgage (or first plus second mortgage). But if you're building a house or having it built for you, in effect, you're your own developer, and you need two kinds of financing. Your mortgage(s)—the "permanent" financing—take effect once the house is built. Then there's something to mortgage. In the interim, you need "temporary" financing—a construction loan.

37. Renovation

In spring, a homeowner's fancy turns to thoughts of renovation. Fixing up clanky furnaces or leaky roofs, adding extra bedrooms, adding whirlpool baths—they don't just make the house more pleasant to live in, they can add substantially to the resale value. In fact, keep an eye on resale value when you put substantial money and effort into home renovation. Buyers like comfortable bathrooms and kitchens, but they won't increase the price of the house enough to pay back the cost of extremely elaborate cabinets or bathroom fixtures. Also watch out for very unusual or eccentric home improvements that could turn off potential home buyers.

Renovation is also important for home buyers who get a "fixer-upper" house that needs extensive work. If you fall into this category, make two lists of work to be done. One list details the items that are necessary for the house to be worth living in. The second list—the priority list—includes the work that either must be done before the house is in minimal move-in condition, or that you will regret heartily not having done *before* you move in. I was too chintzy to have my floors refinished before I moved in. Now, I dread the thought of moving all the (expletive deleted) furniture.

For major renovation, you'll need professional help. So the question is, who should be involved in the renovation? In addition to the electricians, Sheetrock installers, tile layers, and other craftspeople who'll do the day-to-day work, the cast of characters could include any combination of these:

• The architect, who draws up the plans and supervises both the artistic and practical dimensions of the job. Certainly, an architect is required if major structural work will be done: changing the number and placement of the rooms, adding bay windows, and so on. You may be able to do without an architect if you keep the shell of the house intact and merely repair or replace existing fixtures.
• The interior designer, who is concerned with things like wall finishes and floor treatments. The boundaries between architecture and interior design are blurry; probably, only a very large (read, "expensive") renovation project would employ both.
• The general contractor, who sets up a schedule and is responsible for making sure the plumber arrives to install the new bathtub *after* the carpenter has strengthened the floor joists to hold it up—and that the bathtub itself has arrived, with separately ordered faucets that fit the bathtub and the water supply.

Many homeowners save money (it can be up to one-third the cost of the renovation) by acting as their own general contractors. But you should be warned that this is a very difficult, nerve-wracking, and time-consuming job. Furthermore, a good general contractor (and let me know if you know one in the Jersey City area) can save time and money by assembling a crew of skilled, hard-working subcontractors and by finding economical sources for quality materials. A bad general contractor, through inefficiency or dishonesty, will get you embroiled in a maze of materials that arrive late (or never) or that don't live up to specifications, bumbling workers who think a job is good enough if the walls only lean a little, and financial disputes with unpaid workers and suppliers.

In a renovation project, vagueness is fatal. You must have a detailed contract with the general contractor (or with the subcontractors, if you act as your own general contractor). Specify not only how much you'll pay, but also the procedure for making changes (what to do if a subfloor is rotten, and the new parquet flooring can't be installed as planned, for instance), when your approval is needed (the tile that arrives is #419, Glowing Puce, not the #914, Desert Sand, that you ordered—should the #419 be installed, or should something be done to get the correct tile?).

Make sure that the general contractor carries adequate workers' compensation and liability insurance; you don't want it to be your problem if a worker is injured while under contract for your renovation project. It's embarrassing to ask, but it's good strategy to make sure the general contractor is bonded. If he or she is, at least you can collect from the surety company if the general contractor skips town with your money in his or her pocket and much of the work undone. (This has been known to happen.)

Perhaps the most important part of the contract is the schedule of payments. The more money that remains to be paid to the general contractor, the more power you have over the progress of the job. Once all the money has been paid, it's tough to get sloppy work done over or leisurely work speeded up so that you can stop huddling in sleeping bags in the attic and start living in relatively civilized fashion. So negotiate hard on this point.

How do you choose a general contractor (or subcontractors, if you're the general contractor)? Get recommendations from people in the neighborhood. Ask the contractors you interview for pictures of work they've done (and done recently—there's a tendency for an up-and-coming young contractor to do a few splendid jobs at ridiculously low prices, then to let quality slide as prices go up). Try to talk to past customers. Was the work done on time? Were there financial disputes? Check with the local Better Business Bureau, but be aware that disgruntled clients may be too tired and cynical to contact the BBB.

A rule of thumb in the construction industry is to get a number of bids, and immediately discard both the highest and lowest as unrealistic; work with the others. The contractor who bids the lowest is not necessarily a good choice. He or she could be deliberately *lowballing* (making an impossibly low bid to get the job, then finding "changes" to up the price). On the other hand, the low estimate could be perfectly honest—and highly revealing about the general contractor's naïveté about what's really involved in rehabbing a house.

Once you hire a contractor, keep in close touch. Is the schedule being followed? If not, why is it behind, and how long are the delays expected to last? Make sure the contractor is paying all the bills and getting receipts to indicate that payment has been made.

Rehab Money

An early step in the rehab process is to make a detailed budget. Little things surely add up: say, thirty-five cabinet handles at $1.25 each, twelve $22 brass doorknobs, and so on. The next step is to be prepared to tear up the budget. Even if everyone involved in the job is highly skilled and positively saintly, surprises are inevitable. For example, if your house was built in the nineteenth century, before modern construction techniques were standardized, you may find that gas pipes are in peculiar places, floors are insufficiently supported, or heavy plaster ceilings are hanging by a thread.

So be prepared for cost overruns that would make the Pentagon proud. Once you know how much money is likely to be involved, where do you get the money? With luck, you have it all saved up, or you can sell a little stock or collect the profits from a canny real estate deal. Otherwise, you'll need to borrow.

If you're in the process of buying a house that you know needs a lot of rehab work, you may be able to borrow *more* than the price of the house less your down payment. The extra money will be available for renovations. Or, you could apply for a second mortgage while you're applying for the first, and use the second mortgage money to fix up the house.

Homeowners who've been in the house for a while before the work starts have several more options. If they have substantial equity, they can use a home equity loan or credit line to finance the work. Funds (loans, or even grants) may be available through federal or state programs to assist the low- and middle-income homeowner and renovate older housing stock. Again, local bankers and community groups (or your representative in local government) should have this information.

Experienced homeowners can get a second mortgage (or a first mortgage, if the original mortgage has been paid off); or, they can refinance and get a single, larger mortgage that covers the existing mortgage with funds left over for renovation work. (More about refinancing on page 180.) Or, they can get a short-term rehab loan that is basically a personal loan. Because it is unsecured, the interest rates will probably be higher than those on a mortgage (even a second mortgage); however, the loan will be paid off relatively quickly, so the overall interest burden will be lower.

Watch out for scams: Some dishonest contractors not only overcharge, but have homeowners sign fine-print-choked documents that subject the home to an unwanted second mortgage. Then the contractor sells the second mortgage to a bank, which begins to collect from the unwary homeowner.

38. Should You Refinance?

People who want to buy homes always face a dilemma: buy now, perhaps when mortgage rates are stratospheric, or buy later, when attractive properties may be unavailable or priced way out of reach? If you choose to buy at a time when mortgage rates are high, don't despair; you may be able to save a lot of money by refinancing your mortgage later on, when interest rates decline.

However, refinancing is not always the best choice. You may not qualify for the new mortgage. Maybe you applied for the mortgage when there were two incomes in the family, and now you have one income and additional mouths to feed. You could be going through a temporary spell of unemployment, or paying medical or tuition bills, or accepting a salary cut to go back to school while working part-time or at a less demanding job.

Even if you qualify, the process of refinancing is very similar to that of getting an original mortgage. Much of the process of investigating your credit (which you pay for, of course) will be repeated—even if you refinance through the lender that issued the original loan. You'll face many of the same appraisal, origination, and other fees: typically, 2% to 6% of the new mortgage. Therefore, you'll need several hundred to several thousand dollars in cash just to refinance.

As a rule of thumb, it probably doesn't pay to refinance unless the new mortgage's interest rate is 2% or more lower than the old mortgage, or unless the other terms of the mortgage improve significantly (a more protective cap on interest rate variations, for instance). It also matters how soon you plan to sell the house and move on. You can put up with a year or two of high mortgage payments, but if you'll be living there for twenty more years, a more favorable mortgage makes a big difference.

Another possibility before you refinance is to approach the original lender and ask if the mortgage can be renegotiated without a new application or origination fees, at a lower rate more responsive to market conditions. The lender may be willing to do this if the mortgage rate is so high above current rates that you're likely to refinance elsewhere. The lender may be willing to drop the rate a little to keep you from going to another lender.

39. Homeowner's Insurance

Owning a house makes you realize the extraordinary number and variety of things that could go wrong—and how one thing going wrong can set off a chain reaction. So it's almost certain that you'll want homeowner's insurance to protect the family finances against at least some of the disasters the homeowner's fertile imagination can encompass.

And even if you couldn't care less, if you have a mortgage, the bank will require you to maintain insurance—if not complete coverage, then at least fire insurance, and at least equal in value to 80% of the home's current value. If you don't do this (and if you don't make sure your coverage expands as the home's value increases), you're in default on your mortgage, and there's a small, but very real, chance that the bank will take legal action against you.

Homeowner's insurance policies tend to be very similar because there are eleven basic "perils" (things that could go wrong) that all policies cover, and seven additional perils that can be covered by broader policies. Most insurers stick closely to the standard language developed by the Insurance Services Organization (the ISO is a group maintained by insurance companies to set standards within the industry). So when you're shopping, concentrate on the price of the policy and on the company's promptness and courtesy in settling claims; you won't find a policy with startlingly new provisions.

Types of Policies

Homeowner's policies (something of a misnomer—there's a policy for people who rent apartments, and one for condo owners) are usually identified by the letters HO and a number: HO-1 through HO-8, except that there's no such thing as an HO-7 policy.

The "basic" policy, HO-1, is sort of the plain-vanilla version. It covers eleven perils.

- Fire or lightning
- Loss of property caused when you remove it from the house if there is a fire or other dangerous condition
- Windstorm or hail
- Explosion
- Riot or civil commotion
- Damage caused by aircraft
- Damage caused by vehicles
- Smoke damage
- Vandalism and malicious mischief
- Theft
- Breakage of glass that is part of the building—for example, windows, sliding doors.

Note that some new policies—whether HO-1 or other versions—don't cover loss of property removed from the house.

The HO-2, "broad" form policy adds seven more perils against which you are insured.

- Damage caused by falling objects
- The effects of the weight of ice, snow, and sleet (e.g., roof collapses)
- Collapse of any part of the building, or the whole building
- "Sudden and accidental" blow-up of a steam or hot-water furnace, or of a water heater (however, if the problem is caused by gradual deterioration, this provision doesn't cover it)
- Accidental discharge, overflow, or leakage of water or steam from appliances, plumbing, or the heating and cooling system of the house
- Freezing of pipes, appliances, or heating or cooling systems
- "Sudden and accidental injury" from current to electrical appliances or wiring (TV and radio tubes are not included)

The HO-3 policy, the "special" form, covers the house itself for *anything* that can happen (except flood, earthquake, war, and nuclear accident, and except anything specifically ruled out in the policy itself)—but only covers the contents of the house against the eighteen perils named in the HO-2 policy.

The HO-5 "comprehensive" policy covers both house and contents for all imaginable disasters, except for flood, earthquake, war, meltdown, and specifically excluded perils. However, if you have an HO-5 policy and make a claim, you can collect *unless* the insurance company can show that the damage was caused by something excluded from the policy. But if you claim under an HO-3 policy, it's your job to prove that the damage was caused by something specifically covered by the policy. Naturally, it's easier to collect under an HO-5 policy, so some companies have stopped selling them, offering instead HO-3s with extra coverage for the contents of the house.

HO-4s (apartment renter's policies) and HO-6s (for condo unit owners) cover *only* the contents of the apartment, for all eighteen perils named in the HO-3 policy. (The condominium corporation carries insurance on the actual building apart from the individual condo units.)

That leaves only the HO-8, a policy for the older home. It has the same coverage as the basic HO-1 policy; the only difference is in the way the maximum amount of coverage is figured. Most homeowner's policies provide "replacement cost" coverage (see below for reference), but the replacement cost of an older home is usually above its market value, so the HO-8 policy provides coverage up to the actual cash value of the house.

Cash Value Versus Replacement Cost

The first thing you should know is that homeowner's policies usually have half as much coverage for the contents of the house as for the structure itself, so a $100,000 policy may provide a maximum of $50,000 coverage for your property within the house. (Many policies also provide more coverage if the damage is caused by fire as opposed to other perils—the "endorsement page," or summary page at the front of the policy, will tell you if your policy falls into this category.)

Then there's your *deductible* (the amount of risk that you must assume yourself each time you make a claim). A standard deductible is $100, so if you make a claim based on $600 worth of damage covered by the property, and you have a $100 deductible, you can recover a maximum of $500. The lower your deductible, the higher your premium because it's more likely that the insurer will have to pay off.

Experts suggest that the best planning move is to cut your premiums by accepting a higher deductible. After all, you'll have to pay the insurance premiums every year, but most years will pass by without a claim. And anyway, the insurance should protect you against major calamities, not the inconvenience of repairing minor damage.

It's normal for homeowner's policies to contain a coinsurance clause, which is a sort of super-deductible. Unless you maintain adequate coverage—at least 80% of the contemporary value of the house—the insurer will only be obligated to pay a percentage of your loss based on the ratio between your actual coverage and 80% of the value.

The final limitation on claims is the way your coverage is written. The usual policy replaces cash value, that is, the value that the damaged property (which had already been subject to a number of years' wear and tear) would fetch on the open market. If your eight-year-old couch is totally destroyed, and you have cash-value coverage, you'd collect the value of an eight-year-old couch, less the deductible. Replacement value coverage, which naturally is more expensive, pays what it would cost to buy a comparable new couch (less your deductible).

In order to be prepared to make a claim, you must be able to prove that you owned the allegedly damaged property in the first place, what it was worth, and the extent of the damage (frauds in all three areas are not unknown). This task can be handled in more or less elaborate ways. For instance, you can stuff receipts and instruction booklets for major purchases into a file folder for each year. You can keep a logbook (you can find blank books at most stationery stores) listing the prices of major purchases. Or, you can buy a similar book to inventory all your property, perhaps illustrating it with photographs of the more valuable items, or even use your video camera (or hire a photographer) to travel through your house, filming your possessions in their natural settings. The more valuable your possessions, the more documentation you should have.

Floaters

Most homeowner's insurance policies put limitations on certain categories of personal property: for instance, jewelry and furs, securities, silverware, and firearms. If your policy places a $1,000 limit on the jewelry/furs/gems category, and your grandfather's gold pocketwatch melts in the same fire where your mink coat was destroyed by water from the fire hoses, all you can collect is $1,000, no matter how total the loss or the value of coat and watch.

The solution is not grinding your teeth, but buying the necessary Personal Articles Floaters (PAFs), which are minipolicies that supplement your coverage for especially valuable articles. You can buy "floaters" at the same time you get your regular coverage. It pays to be prepared: Before you order the coverage, have an idea (backed up by professional appraisals, for especially valuable or controversial items) of how much you need.

Supplements to Private Coverage

Speaking of floating, few conventional homeowner's policies cover flood damage. If you live in one of the 213 communities in 31 states that are eligible for federally subsidized flood insurance, you can get the necessary coverage at low rates. And if you don't bother to get a policy, you may be denied federal disaster assistance (or recover only a reduced amount).

Some communities have such high crime and arson rates that private insurers shy away from writing policies there. If you live in such a community, and also in one of the twenty-six states that has a FAIR (Fair Access to Insurance Requirements) plan, you can get fire insurance at affordable rates (but not other forms of homeowner's insurance). In the states with FAIR plans, the federal government "assigns risks" to insurance companies, much the way drivers with bad records are "assigned risks" for auto insurers. In order to do business in states with FAIR plans, the insurers must accept the risks and issue fire insurance policies. In these high-crime urban areas, ask your real estate broker about federal crime insurance, which issues low-cost policies insuring against burglary and related crimes. They're also available for business owners.

40. Home Sweet Money-Maker

Buying a home gives you someplace to live, of course; and a home is an asset, which will probably appreciate in value each year until you're ready to sell it. Home ownership also gives you some tax advantages: You can deduct your real estate taxes and mortgage interest (provided you follow the rules added by the Tax Code of 1986).

In the right circumstances, buying a home provides income each month. For instance (as long as you don't violate the zoning laws), you might be able to work out of your home. Not only are you earning money, but you also get additional tax advantages if you conform to the Internal Revenue Code's definition of a "home office." If you do, you can "depreciate" part of the home's cost each year and take a tax deduction. (Depreciation is a tax concept that assumes that business assets deteriorate over time, and that business people must save to replace the assets. If you follow the rules, you can depreciate your home office—even if the home actually gets more valuable each year.)

Another popular strategy—and one which may be the *only* way low-income families can afford to buy a house—is to buy a multifamily house, live in one unit, and rent out the rest. First of all, banks look more favorably on mortgage applications if they know that rental payments, and not just your salary, are available as a source of mortgage repayment. Second, the tenants supply you with cash flow every month by paying their rent (well, most of them pay—some late, some never). Third, an apartment that is rented to others is a business asset, not just a personal one. Therefore, you are entitled to tax deductions for sums you spend to maintain the apartment, and you can claim depreciation deductions for the apartment itself and for certain improvements you make to the apartment.

These tax deductions can be so large that you may have a loss, for tax purposes, when you're actually making money on the apartment (or apartments). As long as your own family income is less than $100,000 a year and as long as you actively manage the apartment, the Tax Code of 1986 lets you use up to $25,000 a year in these tax losses to offset other income, including your salary. This is quite an advantage—most other kinds of tax shelters have lost their usefulness under tax reform.

Most first-time landlords choose small properties: a two, three, or four family house. That way, the property isn't impossibly expensive, and it probably won't be necessary to hire a "super" to take care of the property. The FHA mortgage program is set up so that borrowers can buy homes for up to four families.

Being a landlord is not without its disadvantages. If the tenants have a loud all-night party, you'll know it. If the apartment needs repairs, you'll find that out too—and you can't just call the super or the management company. You have to find a plumber (perhaps at two in the morning) and pay for the repair. But the combination of getting most or all of your mortgage payment from the rent each month, plus tax advantages, can be an irresistible one.

See page 187 for the Home Strategies Chart which quickly sums up the advantages and disadvantages of renting and investing in real estate.

41. R EAL LIFE: MARGARET AND TOM FITZGERALD

We'll just bleep out what Tom Fitzgerald said when he discovered, after burrowing through six boxes labelled "kitchen" and three labelled "living room," that he could find the coffee and two mugs (one with a cracked handle), and that

Margaret had remembered to buy half-and-half at the corner grocery—but that he couldn't find the coffee pot.

It was his first day as a homeowner. The furniture was in place (the wrong place, in some cases). Some of the boxes were unpacked; some had been opened, glanced at, and deferred for later consideration (like the Christmas tree ornaments—it was April); some hadn't even been opened. Tom sort of wondered where his gray suit was. Had anybody remembered to pick it up from the cleaner's, clear across town near their old apartment?

His signature, and Margaret's, appeared on a stack of papers—more auto-graphs than a best-selling author, it seemed. They had signed a deed, and a mortgage, and agreed to buy homeowner's insurance and mortgage insurance, and maintain fire insurance in an amount equal to at least 80% of the value of the house; they had agreed not to do anything illegal, and to maintain the premises in decent condition, pay their real estate taxes, and otherwise act like fine, upstanding homeowners.

Well, now they had a house and, therefore, had one major investment. Their down payment gave them thousands of dollars of equity in the house; their equity would grow over time, as they repaid mortgage principal and as inflation and changes in real-estate values made the house more valuable. The problem was to pay for it—and to make it part of a well-planned program of investments.

The Numbers

Actually, the Fitzgeralds saved money by buying the house. Instead of paying $1,200 a month for a two-bedroom apartment, they paid $14,000 a year for mortgage payments, property tax, and homeowner's insurance. Not much of a saving, you might think, but the mortgage interest (the major part of each pay-ment) and real estate taxes are deductible, yielding tax savings.

Tax savings were important because the Fitzgeralds paid a hefty $8,200 a year in income taxes (federal, state, FICA) on a combined income of $42,000 a year in salary (Tom, as an accountant, Margaret as a seventh-grade teacher), plus a $2,000 bonus for Tom. Other living costs totalled about $1,450 a month ($17,400 a year). Altogether, the Fitzgeralds had $44,000 income, and spent $39,600 of it—yielding a nice amount to invest.

The Answers

Even for childless couples like the Fitzgeralds, owning a house instills feelings of solidity, financial maturity—and long-term obligations. So they arranged with their insurance agent for regular appointments to review their homeowner's coverage—not just to meet their obligations under the "coinsurance" clause of the mortgage (see page 183), but to make sure they would be protected if anything happened to the house.

What if anything happened to one of them? Both had excellent health and disability coverage provided by their employers: Tom had a small group-term life insurance policy. Their financial representative did a capital needs analysis and decided they needed life insurance on each of their lives amounting to three years of the surviving spouse's salary. (How else would one of them cover the mortgage payments?)

Both were qualified-plan participants (see page 34), so IRA deductions were limited. However, both decided to open IRAs and contribute $1,200 a year each, figuring they'd never miss $25 a week, and because the increase in value of their IRA accounts would not be taxed until retirement. Margaret went with an aggressive-growth mutual fund because she believed that the stock market's long-term prospects were excellent; the more conservative Tom invested in bank CDs because he felt that retirement security was too important to take risks.

In addition to IRA investing, the Fitzgeralds consulted with a financial adviser and decided to set up a regular investment program. They took an investment seminar, subscribed to *Money* and *Fortune* magazines (although they noticed, guiltily, that the magazines tended to pile up unread), bought some high-income utility stocks, and then decided that investing in individual stocks took too much time and effort. So they set an investment goal of $2,000 a year, $500 quarterly. After extensive discussion, they decided that a good growth-and-income fund would satisfy both Margaret's desire for long-term financial growth, and Tom's instincts for caution. They read prospectuses, compared returns, and chose a fund that had compiled a good track record in both bull market years and years when the stock market was sagging.

HOME STRATEGIES

Low Risk/Low Effort	*Low Risk/High Effort*
• Rent an apartment in a building owned by a conscientious, solvent management. • Use home sale funds and savings to buy a new home, co-op apartment, or condo unit for cash or with a small mortgage.	• Buy a two- or three-family house in livable condition, but needing a lot of work—and make sure the rent payments in the other unit(s) cover the mortgage and real estate taxes for the whole house.
Medium Risk/Low Effort	*Medium Risk/High Effort*
• Invest in an REIT or real estate limited partnership with a good track record.	• Buy a one-family house in a neighborhood where gentrification is already under way, or where house prices are heading upward.
High Risk/Low Effort	*High Risk/High Effort*
• Buy occupied apartments in buildings that have been converted to co-ops or condos. • Invest in real estate in depressed areas that are very overbuilt, and prices are down—wait for the rebound.	• Buy a very run-down house in a neighborhood that *might* become gentrified; borrow as much as you can against your equity in this house, and buy more real estate. Repeat the process. • Get the largest home equity loan you can; invest the proceeds for aggressive growth.

42. Enjoying Credit

It used to be scandalous to "be in debt": to borrow money or use credit. Today, even the best of families know that responsible use of credit is one of the keys to successful financial planning. Intelligent use of credit allows a family to shop for home mortgages; to get loans for home improvements, college costs, cars or boats, or family vacations; to take advantage of sales, and buy things at the lowest available price; "spread out" the cost of major purchases such as appliances over the year; and decrease the risk of becoming a crime victim by using credit instead of carrying excessive amounts of cash.

"Responsible" use is vital because it's easy to get in over your head—borrowing more than you can afford to repay, buying things you don't really need or want because they seem "free" when you can use a credit card or a line of credit instead of cash. When you understand how much you can afford, you can budget; and when you use the very substantial protection that federal law gives you, you can "comparison shop" among the many forms of credit that are available.

Forms of Credit

Depending on your situation and what you want the credit for, you may be able to use any of the following kinds of credit, or a combination of various forms. The form you choose will depend on which forms are available, how convenient each one is to get and to use, whether there are fees for applications, and how high the interest rate and monthly payment will be.

Loans

Loans are made by banks and finance companies. The lender advances you a certain amount of money, or sets up a line of credit that you can draw on when you want, up to the credit limit. To qualify for a loan, you must make a formal application and show the lender that your income and assets are high enough to make it likely that you'll repay— and that your past history demonstrates that you're responsible about paying back the money you owe.

Why would you pick a bank rather than a finance company, or vice versa? Generally, finance companies make loans to people who have lower credit ratings and, therefore, they charge higher interest rates; so it makes sense to apply to a bank first, and then turn to a finance company if you can't borrow the money you need from a bank. (If you own a life insurance policy that has accumulated cash value, you can borrow against this cash value. Consult your insurance policy or insurance agent.)

Loans take many forms: mortgages, auto loans, student loans, and personal loans, for instance. The disadvantage of loans is that the borrowing process can be inconvenient; you have to fill out a detailed application and wait for approval from the lender. Even applying for a loan can be expensive; the lender often charges a number of fees for processing the application, checking your credit, and the like. (See page 191 for more about credit costs.)

Loans can be divided into two categories: secured and unsecured. Secured loans are "secured" by collateral—a possession of the borrower's that can be repossessed and sold if the borrower defaults (fails to meet obligations under the loan). Unsecured, or personal, loans do not have collateral. Again, this means higher interest rates because the lender takes a bigger risk.

Home Equity Loans

Home equity loans allow you to benefit from the increase in value of your home—without selling your home. That is, the lender lets you borrow an amount equal to a certain percentage of the "equity" in your house (the house's current market value, minus any mortgage balance you still owe). Most banks won't lend you more than 75% to 80% of your equity under a home equity loan.

These loans became popular in the 1980s because the rapid increase in home prices gave many homeowners a surprisingly large amount of equity. Their popularity increased after the Tax Code of 1986 (TC '86) because the tax deduction for interest to buy consumer goods is being phased out. But interest on mortgages (including home equity loans) is still deductible, within limits—even if you spend the money for reasons that are not related to your home, such as for your children's college tuition or a vacation. Therefore, you may prefer a home equity loan to another source of credit if you can deduct the interest you pay on the home equity loan on your tax return.

Home equity loans can be set up as conventional second mortgages (you get the amount you want to borrow immediately and start making regular monthly payments of interest and principal right away) or as "lines of credit." If you have a line of credit, you make an agreement with the lender about the amount you can borrow (say, any amount up to $50,000), interest rates, and other terms.

A line of credit gives you the right to borrow if and when you need it. For instance, if you have a $50,000 line of credit, you could borrow $3,000 for a new furnace in one year, make regular payments starting right after you get the $3,000, and borrow $5,000 five years later when your second child enters college. The advantage of a home equity line of credit over an ordinary bank loan is that once you qualify for the line of credit, you can get money quickly, with no further applications or need for approval. (Not all lines of credit come from home equity loans; many credit card issuers allow you to set up a line of credit and borrow if and when you need cash.)

Policy Loans

If you have a cash-value life insurance policy (see page 66), you can borrow the cash value that has accumulated in the policy at a low interest rate. In fact, sometimes you don't have to pay interest at all because the cash value grows so fast that the increase in value is greater than the interest rate you must pay.

Dealer Financing

If you buy a car, major appliance, or other large purchase, dealer financing may be available. That is, the dealer who sells you the item also lends the money to pay for it; you make a down payment and regular (usually monthly) payments. The advantage of this form of financing is that it's convenient; the disadvantage is that interest rates are usually very high. (One exception: You may be able to get financing at very low rates if you want to buy a car model that is part of an incentive program—see page 203.)

Revolving Charge Accounts

Many stores offer "revolving charge accounts." You agree to pay a certain rate of interest and to make at least a minimum payment every month you owe any money to the store. You can then decide how much to charge in any month; as long as you make the minimum payment, you can also decide how long you'll take to pay off your balance. Here again, the advantage is convenience; the disadvantage is high interest rates.

Credit Cards

Bank credit cards, such as VISA and MasterCard, work like store charge accounts, but permit you to buy goods and services from many more sources. Many different banks issue these cards, and sometimes they compete based on annual fees and interest rates, so shopping for a card can save you a considerable amount of money. Depending on the card issuer and your credit rating, you may also be able to get "cash advances" using a credit card; in effect, you have a preapproved line of credit. The credit issuer may also accept your directions to transfer money to third parties, that is, to pay other bills using the card.

A "prestige," "gold," or "platinum" card has a higher credit limit and may have other advantages (such as access to airplane reservation service) in return for a higher annual fee.

"Travel and entertainment" cards (e.g., American Express, Diner's Club) require the cardholder to pay the full balance each month in most circumstances; the agreement between the issuer and the cardholder may allow large purchases, such as plane tickets, to be paid off in installments.

43. Comparing Forms of Credit

The average family has access to most or all of the forms of credit just described. When it's time to buy something, the choice is between spending savings (and losing the interest that the money is earning) and using some form of credit (which usually involves interest and may involve other fees). I say "usually" because if you charge something on a credit card and pay your entire balance by the date given on your bill, no interest will be charged. This is a major financial planning tool. Let's say that the "billing cycle" for your card ends on the fifteenth of the month. If you buy anything on the sixteenth, or later, it won't appear on the bill for more than a month. Then, you have a grace period (a period of time to pay the bill before interest is imposed). So you can get up to two months' free credit by timing purchases wisely.

But watch out: Some card issuers cut back on the grace period, and there will probably be no grace period on cash advances; interest will be charged from the date you get the cash advance.

These are the criteria to use when you choose between using savings and the many forms of credit.

- If you pay cash, sell stock, or otherwise use your savings and investments, how much interest or appreciation will you lose?
- Will you have to pay taxes on your profits?
- Will you have to pay brokerage commissions or other fees?
- If you do pay cash, will you deplete your cash cushion so that nothing is left in case of emergencies?

Once you understand that, you can balance it against the cost of credit.

- What is the interest rate? (See page 192 for a discussion of the federal laws that govern credit.)
- How many monthly payments must you make (if the contract calls for a certain number of payments), or how long do you think it would take to pay off your credit-card balance?
- Must you make a down payment? If so, how large?
- When you add the principal to the interest, how much must you pay in total?
- Does the lender charge fees when you apply for credit? Are there additional fees once you get the credit, or every time you get a cash advance or make a transfer?
- If you're comparing various credit cards, how high is the annual fee for each?

TABLE 6. CREDIT

	8¾%	10%	15%	18%	21%
$500	$ 15.85	$ 16.14	$ 17.34	$ 18.08	$ 18.84
$1,000	$ 31.69	$ 32.27	$ 34.67	$ 36.16	$ 37.68
$1,500	$ 47.54	$ 48.40	$ 52.04	$ 54.24	$ 56.52
$2,000	$ 63.37	$ 64.54	$ 69.34	$ 72.31	$ 75.36
$2,500	$ 79.21	$ 80.68	$ 86.68	$ 90.39	$ 94.20
$3,000	$ 95.06	$ 96.81	$104.00	$108.46	$113.03
$4,000	$126.74	$129.07	$138.67	$144.61	$150.71

Table 6 shows the monthly payment you'd have to make to pay off your balance within three years. The column on the left shows the amount of credit; the table compares monthly payments at interest rates of 8¾% (a rate you might pay if you get a home equity loan or line of credit when interest rates are low—or the amount of income you would lose if you sold an investment earning 8¾% and used the cash instead of borrowing), 10% (a rate you might pay on a personal loan when interest rates are low—or that you might pay on a home equity loan when interest rates are moderate), 15% (the rate you might pay on a personal loan when rates are high—or when you pay with a credit card that charges a low rate of interest), 18% (a moderate rate for credit cards), and 21% (a high rate for credit cards).

Looking at the question from the other side, if you owe $2,000, it will take five and a half years to repay the debt if the interest rate is 21% and you pay $50 a month; it would only take about four and a half years at an interest rate of 15%. The higher your monthly payment, the less impact the interest rate has. For instance, to pay off the same $2,000 debt with a $400 monthly payment takes about five to six months, no matter what the interest rate; if you can pay only $200 a month, it'll take ten to twelve months at 15%, eleven to twelve months at 21%.

44. Truth in Lending

The federal government doesn't control the interest rates that can be charged to consumers, but it *does* control "disclosure": the amount of information consumers must get, and the form in which the information must be presented. (Most states do have "usury" laws setting interest rates—but permitted interest rates are usually high enough to cause discomfort to the consumers that have to pay them! There are states that permit especially high interest rates, or that have no usury laws, which explains why many credit card issuers center their operations in places like Fargo, North Dakota—otherwise outside the financial mainstream.)

The federal Truth-in-Lending laws require creditors (whether lenders, like banks, or sellers, like furniture stores) to give consumers a tremendous amount of information—perhaps so much that consumers find it difficult to absorb it all. You can keep your head by remembering a few basic concepts.

- *All* creditors must use the same method for computing and quoting an interest rate. They must quote interest rates only as "APR" (Annual Percentage Rate). The formulas for computing the APR aren't really relevant here; the important thing is that a uniform system is used. A 10¼% APR is always lower than a 12% APR, and you can make the comparisons accordingly.
- Creditors must also disclose interest plus fees and other costs in the form of a "finance charge." Once again, complex calculations are required, but *you* don't have to make them; they're the responsibility of the creditor. Federal law determines which fees are included in the finance charge and which have to be disclosed separately. Be sure you find out exactly how much each of those charges will be.
- The "amount financed," plus the "finance charge," will always equal the amount you must repay.
- Credit transactions involve a number of legal documents; the required disclosures are contained in the credit documents.

Credit Cards

When you open a credit card or charge account, you'll sign a detailed agreement explaining the APR (both monthly and annual), your credit limit, minimum monthly payments, fees for late payments, and your rights if there is a dispute about goods and services purchased with the card.

Each monthly bill will also include disclosures: your previous balance (amount outstanding at the beginning of the cycle), new balance (amounts added during the cycle), APR, minimum payment, interest charged on your previous balance, and any late fees charged if you fall behind on payments.

When you buy merchandise on credit or get a loan from a bank, there will be other documents to sign: a "loan note," which creates a legal obligation to repay and states the terms of the agreement. Once again, you're entitled to know the APR, the amount financed, the finance charge, and the total of payments. If the loan is secured (if you provide collateral), there will also be a "security agreement" to sign. It explains the circumstances under which the creditor will be allowed to take possession of the collateral. Usually, the collateral is the item that you're buying (car, refrigerator, or whatever), but sometimes buyers or borrowers grant a security interest in their other property.

It's important to review the security agreement carefully. Sometimes it's drafted so that the borrower is in "default" (has failed to meet obligations) for reasons other than failure to make payments on time. For instance, you might be considered in default if you lose your job or declare bankruptcy—or even if a person who guarantees the loan declares bankruptcy or dies.

Other Federal Laws

Several other federal laws give rights to consumers who apply for or use credit.

•The Equal Credit Opportunity Act (ECOA) makes it illegal to discriminate in granting credit based on a person's race, color, sex, marital status, age (over 62), or his or her receipt of public assistance. Creditors can still turn down people who are not credit-worthy (those who don't have the assets or the payment history to qualify), but the denial must be based on objective factors, not prejudices. However, the ECOA applies only to personal credit, not business credit.

•The Fair Credit Billing Act (FCBA) gives consumers a right to challenge credit card bills that they believe are incorrect (for instance, you're charged for something you never ordered) or that are in dispute (you order the 122-piece Slice 'em Up knife set from a mail order house, and receive nary a knife or you buy a defective product). Your right to withhold payment applies as long as the amount in dispute is over $50 and the credit transaction took place in your home state or within 100 miles of your home; the FCBA can be used to correct clerical mistakes in your bill, no matter where the credit card was used or how much is involved.

To exercise FCBA rights, write to the card issuer as soon as you get the first bill containing the item you think is wrong, or that is the subject of a dispute with the seller. You can telephone, if you want the immediate satisfaction of yelling at someone, but only a letter will preserve your legal rights. Explain the source of the problem; include copies (but never the originals) of any supporting documents (such as a sales slip giving the true total of $19.26 when your credit card bill says $79.26).

The credit card issuer has a legal duty to investigate; during the investigation, it is not permitted to charge a finance charge or late charge for the disputed part of the bill, to close your account because of nonpayment of the disputed bill, or to report the disputed amount as unpaid to a credit reporting agency. (See next page for more about your rights under the Fair Credit Reporting Act.)

•The Fair Debt Collection Practices Act (FDCPA) protects consumers in two ways. Collection agencies (and anyone else in the business of collecting debts) are not allowed to deceive consumers, for instance, by sending letters that look like official court summonses (or, for that matter, official court summonses that look like mere, easy-to-ignore letters). Nor can they threaten debtors, hassle them by repeated phone calls or phone calls at unreasonable times, or attempt to embarrass them by contacting other people (i.e., asking the boss or family members how they feel about knowing a "deadbeat").

•Nineteen eighty-four has come and gone, but there are still plenty of files maintained on average citizens. The Fair Credit Reporting Act (FCRA) puts limits on the way these files can be used. The FCRA is really broader than its name; it covers inquiries made by prospective employers as well as prospective grantors of credit. One thing the act does is to require information in the files to be fresh; most items of information over seven years old must not be reported. Even bankruptcy usually can't be reported after ten years. And adverse (negative) information can't be reported to an employer or credit grantor unless it was either received or verified within three months of the report. (Matters of public record can be reported indefinitely.)

If you're turned down for credit or employment because of something negative in a credit report, whoever turns you down has a legal obligation to tell you the name of the credit reporting agency that provided the information. You can contact the agency, which must provide you with a copy of your file at no charge if you ask within thirty days of the turndown.

You're entitled to know who has requested a report for credit purposes within the past six months, or for employment purposes within the past two years. Then you can review the file to see if there are any inaccuracies—stale information, incomplete or inaccurate information (such as a report of a conviction for felonious assault when you've never even been arrested for anything).

The agency has a legal duty to investigate your claims within a reasonable time. If it agrees with you, it must remove inaccurate—or even unverifiable—information from your dossier. Even if the agency disagrees, you can put a short statement (under 100 words) in your credit file. Any report given out in the future must refer to the dispute and include or summarize your statement.

It's also possible to review your credit file routinely, just to find out what the file says and to correct any mistakes that could harm you later. (The credit bureau is allowed to charge a reasonable fee for these routine inquiries.) Checking your credit file is a good first step if you plan to apply for credit soon.

45. Who Qualifies for Credit?

Creditors have a legitimate interest in getting paid, so they have to find out which applicants have income and resources large enough to qualify them for the credit they want, and which applicants have a history of paying bills, and which have a tendency to be slow or skip out altogether.

Many creditors use a "point" or "scoring" system, which assigns points for six to fifteen factors such as income, length of time at the same job, and freedom from other debts. Applicants with more than a certain number of points qualify for credit; others get turned down.

It's wise to do your shopping before you apply for credit. Find out how the creditor's terms (such as interest rates, required payments, remedies if you fall behind) compare to the terms offered by other creditors. There may be application fees; in any case, why fill out a long, confusing set of papers only to discover you'd rather apply somewhere else?

If you plan a major purchase (such as a car or home) in the next few years, it helps to "groom" your personal balance sheet by paying off overdue balances, and reducing your credit card balance. Get your financial affairs in order; if you apply for a loan, the lender is likely to ask to see tax forms (or, at least, W-2 forms proving you have the income you claim). If you already have a mortgage or other loans, dig out the loan notes and security agreements. The new potential creditor will probably want to see what the old creditor's rights are.

Credit Insurance

No, credit insurance doesn't insure that you'll get credit, but it could make an uncertain creditor decide that you qualify. For instance, your income and resources could be just on the borderline between the creditor's standards for granting credit and for turning down the applicant. Credit insurance makes it more likely that the creditor will be repaid and, therefore, makes the loan or sale less risky, thereby making you a better prospect.

Credit insurance is life or disability insurance that the borrower takes out, naming the creditor as the beneficiary. If it's credit life insurance, the creditor gets paid the balance of the debt if the debtor dies before the entire debt is paid. Credit life insurance is really a kind of decreasing term insurance (see page 64 for more about term insurance). Credit disability insurance does the same thing, if the debtor becomes disabled while a balance remains outstanding.

Credit insurance is not always a good deal for the borrower. It depends on how much it costs, both in the abstract and as compared to other insurance that the borrower could get. For instance, if you're an older consumer, or have serious health problems, you may find it hard to get insurance at all, and the credit insurance premium could be lower than the premium of other available term insurance.

The next point for discussion is how credit insurance fits into your financial plan. If you leave many assets, your survivors may have no difficulty in keeping up payments to your creditors. Or, if you have plenty of insurance, payable to your family or estate rather than to your creditors, your survivors can decide whether or not to pay off your debts after you die. Credit insurance, however, locks them into a single alternative: immediate repayment.

Credit insurance is usually a good deal for the creditor because it reduces the risk that the debt will not be repaid. It's an especially good deal if the creditor itself sells the credit insurance (or owns the company that does)—that way, it collects all the premiums, *and* any payoffs when a debtor dies or becomes disabled. If you think credit insurance is a good idea, you have a legal right to get it from any insurance company you like—you don't have to take the creditor's "sweetheart deal."

46. How to Avoid Credit Problems

You're in real credit trouble if you can't make payments, and things you've bought are repossessed, and/or the creditor sues you. (The creditor can sue you even after something is repossessed, if the sale of the merchandise doesn't yield enough to satisfy the amount you still owe.)

You're flirting with trouble if you somehow manage to make minimum payments on credit cards, but never get close to paying off the balance; if you make the required payments on your mortgage, auto loan, student loan, and other loans, but never have anything left over for saving or investing. In this situation, you won't be dragged into court; in fact as long as you stay within your credit limits, you won't even have your accounts cancelled. But you *will* pay heavy interest on their credit purchases. In fact, when you add it all up, you may find that you pay several times the original cost of the items. For instance, Table 6 on page 192 shows that if you buy $4,000 worth of furniture on credit (or get a $4,000 loan for the same purpose), take three years to repay, and the interest rate is 10%, you'll pay a total of $4,646.52 for the furniture (thirty-six payments of $129.07 each). At an interest rate of 21%, the same furniture would cost a total of $5,425.56.

Sometimes you can solve your credit problems by stricter budgeting: cut back on entertainment and vacations, use the extra money to reduce your debts or credit card balance, and/or restrict the amount you borrow or charge in the future. If that doesn't do it, more drastic measures may be required. Sometimes the only thing to do is slice up the credit cards (or lock them up until your debts are under control).

Maybe you can consolidate several debts, if a less expensive form of credit can be found. For instance, home equity lines of credit usually carry an interest rate lower than credit cards; you might be able to save money by getting a home equity loan, then paying off your credit card balances with the loan proceeds. However, this form of borrowing is not without costs (like a first mortgage you get when you buy a house, there may be hundreds or thousands of dollars in application fees involved), and not without risks. You could lose your house if home equity loan payments aren't made on time.

If you're threatened with lawsuits or with the loss of your possessions, maybe the best step is to agree to a "voluntary income execution": You agree to have part of your salary withheld and paid to your creditors. If you're overwhelmed with credit problems, you can get help from not-for-profit agencies that counsel about credit alternatives. But watch out for commercial "debt consolidators" who can charge high fees for providing information readily available without charge, or who can ensnare debtors in "consolidation loans" that carry excessively high interest rates and unfair terms.

Sometimes the best solution is personal bankruptcy. Although it's not a step to be taken lightly, bankruptcy gives you a chance to clear the slate and start again. There's a special set of rules for "wage-earner" plans: People who are steadily employed can make a plan for paying their debts out of their future salary. It may be possible to arrange to pay only a part of some debts, and not to pay any of certain debts. It takes advice from a skilled bankruptcy lawyer to find out if bankruptcy is the best solution to your financial problems.

Credit Card Security

Another potential credit problem is the risk that you will become a victim of credit-related crime. Dishonest people can make a "big score" when they get hold of a credit card—or even a credit card number. So protect yourself.

- Keep your credit cards safe—preferably separate from your wallet. That way, a determined mugger may get them, but a pickpocket probably won't. Keep a list of credit card numbers and telephone numbers to call in case of loss or theft—and keep the list itself secure.
- Be very careful about releasing your credit card number. Don't give it over the phone to a "surveyor" who "needs to check it to send you your valuable prize."
- Keep your receipts for each transaction (they'll come in handy at tax time, if you charged any deductible amounts; and they're invaluable in preparing a family budget). Tear up or destroy all the carbons of the receipt; otherwise, thieves can garner card numbers and use them to buy merchandise by phone.
- It's also a good idea to keep a list of all credit card purchases, especially if several family members use the same card. The general rule is that a credit cardholder is legally responsible for all charges made to his or her account by an authorized user (someone whom the cardholder permitted to use the card). This is true even if the user was told to buy a new winter coat, and then went ahead and bought the coat, a pair of jogging shoes, a tennis racquet, a hairdryer, and much, much more.
- A tip for readers in the process of divorce: An estranged spouse who has access to credit cards has at least apparent authority to use

them—so merchants who have not been notified of the lack of authority can collect from either spouse (on a joint account) or from the spouse whose name is on the card. One possibility is to get hold of the cards (though a very hostile spouse could still charge up a storm over the phone), or cancel all the accounts on which you are the sole person responsible and open new accounts which do not permit the estranged spouse to use the card.

And don't use credit cards as a form of revenge; irresponsible financial behavior will be taken into account in dividing the couple's property, and may even constitute economic misconduct that will limit equitable distribution and maintenance, or even make maintenance unavailable to the irresponsible spouse.

• When a credit card is used by an *unauthorized* person (such as a thief or someone who finds a lost credit card and decides to take advantage of the windfall), the cardholder's maximum liability is $50 worth of use before the card issuer is notified. (After notice is given, it's the card issuer's problem; it's supposed to maintain procedures to prevent use of lost or stolen cards.) The issuer must provide cardholders with a simple method of giving notice, such as providing an address to write to or a number to call.

47. Summing Up: Credit in the Financial Plan

The negative side of credit is the nightmare swamp of unpaid and unpayable bills—or bills that come in every month for things long since used and used up, even forgotten—and get paid, but by dint of grim scraping and saving.

That's not the whole picture. The positive side of credit: a young family buying a first home with a small down payment, a student attending the college of his or her choice thanks to student loans (without credit, he or she might not be able to attend *any* college). With credit, many people enjoy better furniture, a more stylish wardrobe, more enjoyable vacations, and other good things of life that would be unavailable if they insisted on paying cash for everything (and if sellers demanded cash). The difference between the two scenarios is that credit is a positive force when credit users understand how much credit will cost them (fees, the APR, the finance charge for as long as a balance is outstanding).

It makes good sense to match the length of credit to the useful life of the thing financed (for instance, you wouldn't want to make car payments for ten years if the car lasts only four), to restrict home equity loans (which could result in the foreclosure of your mortgage and the loss of your home) to important purchases, and to choose short loan terms and pay off high-interest credit card balances as soon as you can without completely choking your cash flow.

For instance, if you borrow $10,000 (or have total credit outstanding, including all loans and credit balances, equal to $10,000) and get the debt squared away in two years, your monthly payment will be $470.73, if your interest rate is 12%. If you take three years to pay at an 11% interest rate, you can cut the monthly payment to $327.39—but you'll pay more interest overall. If you can only afford $150.00 a month, it'll take ten years to pay off a $10,000 debt with a 12% interest charge.

Credit isn't frightening, but it is powerful. Decide how much you can really handle; review your insurance coverage in light of your new financial obligations; be ready to refinance when interest rates drop (as long as you don't have to pay fees high enough to wipe out the advantage). Make credit work for you, not against you.

48. Enjoying Your Automobile

Most singles and families need a car—perhaps more than one car, to get family members to work, school, the mall, hockey games, or ballet class. But the days of paying a few dollars and trading in the family chariot every year for a brand-new car are over, probably forever. An automobile (even a used car) is a major financial investment.

This section covers some basic financial aspects of automobile ownership: choosing a car, making the best deal you can, getting financing once the price has been set, warranties and lemon laws, automobile insurance and no-fault laws.

Choosing a Car

Just as everyone has a personal investment profile, everyone has a different list of priorities in choosing a car: the number of passengers normally carried, two or four doors, air-conditioning, front-wheel drive, six or eight cylinders, a large trunk or hatchback, a roomy car versus an easy-to-park subcompact.

The first step is to research available car models, choosing the ones in your price range that are best for your needs. Car magazines (such as *Road and Track* and *Car and Driver*) specialize in detailed reviews of the performance, styling, and engineering of various models. Consumer publications like *Consumer Reports* discuss safety, value, and fuel economy.

Use the following worksheet to "profile" your dream car. For each factor, use a red pen or marker to circle the number that shows the

importance you give to it. ("5" is "crucial," "1" is "big fat hairy deal.")
Then, for the car model you're thinking about, use a blue pen to circle
the number that best represents the model's performance. (For instance, a car with limited trunk space rates only a "1" for this factor.)
Add up the point value for your dream car and the real car under
consideration, and see how closely the pros and cons of the real car
match your vision of the perfect car by comparing the items circled for
each.

WORKSHEET

1. Price under $_____	1	2	3	4	5
2. Advanced styling	1	2	3	4	5
3. Seating space for_____	1	2	3	4	5
4. Exceptionally good safety record	1	2	3	4	5
5. Trunk/hatchback capacity	1	2	3	4	5
6. High trade-in value	1	2	3	4	5
7. Exceptionally good repair record	1	2	3	4	5
8. Good dealer service	1	2	3	4	5
9. Exceptionally long warranty	1	2	3	4	5
10. Fast delivery	1	2	3	4	5
11. Availability of rebate	1	2	3	4	5
12. Low-rate financing from dealer	1	2	3	4	5

Score for dream car:_____

Score for this model:_____

* * *

Find out whether the manufacturer sells what is essentially the same car (same chassis, engine, detailing) under several different names, and at several different price ranges. And talk to an insurance agent before you buy—some models carry extra-high automobile insurance rates because they tend to be owned by incautious drivers, or because the car's own safety record is poor.

Another important factor is the availability of parts and service. Luxury cars often must be serviced by true artists (who charge accordingly). Unusual models—especially imports—may have to spend days or weeks in the shop until parts can be shipped from the factory. And if you run into car trouble far from home, the local mechanics may not be familiar with your car.

How to Buy a New Car

Once you've settled on a few models that interest you, find out the wholesale price. You can get the information from consumer publications, from specialty publishers who publish annual guides to car prices, or from computer services that furnish up-to-the-minute price quotes (for a fee).

This figure is essential for informed negotiating. Your goal should be to make a deal that's fair to the dealer—perhaps providing a $250 to $500 profit above his or her cost—and also fits your budget. Don't let the dealer reap excess profits by selling you options that you don't really want or need, or that you could get at a lower price outside the dealership.

The "sticker price" is only the starting point in negotiations. It's the manufacturer's suggested retail price for the basic car. The dealer can either discount this price (your objective, of course) or increase it by selling whatever options he or she can convince you to buy. So keep your eye on the wholesale price, not the sticker price.

However, it may be worth paying a little extra to buy from a dealership offering prompt, courteous, skilled service. Saving money on the initial purchase of the car is great, but not if it involves you in extra costs and annoyances after the car is on the road.

The law of supply and demand is in full swing when you're buying a car. If you want a popular model, expect to wait for delivery—and expect to be given a choice between a "fully loaded" model with many expensive options, and no car at all.

However, if you want an unpopular model, expect to be lured with cut-rate financing from the manufacturer, cash rebates, your own choice of options, and the chance to drive away in your chosen car as soon as the papers are signed. Just remember that the dealer's eagerness to sell a particular car is likely to be based either on its unusual profitability, or the fact that no one else wants the thing.

Here's a garland of negotiating tips, garnered from various sources. Don't be afraid to press for the best deal; you don't have to make the car salesman like you.

•The best time to make a good deal is the time when car sales are lowest: right after Christmas through late April. The combination of wintry weather, Christmas bills, and income tax is tough on car dealers. The worst times to shop: glorious summer days and right after the new models come out. However, the dealer may get a rebate from the manufacturer on unsold cars of the previous model year when the new models come out. You may be able to buy one of the "leftovers"—and share the rebate.

•Try to treat buying a car, financing, and trade-in as three separate transactions. Don't get involved in a confusing situation where the options, trade-in price, and purchase price keep changing. An unscrupulous salesperson could tempt you with a trade-in price so great that you're prepared to overlook an overcharge on the price of the car. And then—what a surprise!—the sales manager refuses to allow such a high trade-in price. By then, you've fallen in love with the car (or you're sick and tired of negotiating), so you accept the deal even though it's far less favorable than you thought it would be. Instead, keep repeating, "What is the best deal I can get on that today?" Then, figure out what the final cost will be based on the best deal you can get.

How to Buy a Used Car

You can buy a used car either from a used-car dealer or a private seller. The trade-off here is quite simple. Private sellers frequently offer a lower price, in return for buying the car as is. Private sellers are usually amateurs—people who want to get more money for their cars than they'd get by trading them in at the dealership. They don't provide warranties, parts, service, or financing, and there's no selection of cars from which to choose.

Used-car dealers, on the other hand, are professionals. Depending on the dealer, they may have anything from a casual relationship with a mechanic who looks over the cars to a fully equipped service department. Sometimes, private individuals who sell a used car can grossly underprice it because they don't understand its true value (or they're in a hurry to get some cash). You can bet that won't happen at a used car lot!

A dealer can offer you a choice between many cars—often a full range of automotive vintages, makes, models, and conditions, at a wide range of prices. Furthermore, the dealer can provide financing (and probably wants to because this can be a major profit source). But it costs the dealer money to maintain an inventory of cars, and to provide services; the price of the cars will reflect these costs.

Buying a used car involves risks: The car will have defects that the seller doesn't tell you about—or defects that even the seller doesn't know about. If you're buying from a used-car dealer, you risk being subjected to high-pressure salesmanship; by the time your head clears, you find you've bought a car.

If you're buying from a private seller, the first thing to be sure of is that he or she really owns the car! It's easy for car thieves to "earn" a few quick dollars by placing a newspaper ad and selling their ill-gotten gains. Make sure that the seller has a legitimate registration form (usually called a "pink slip") for the car. Ask to see his or her auto insurance policy, and make sure the identification of the car corresponds to the car you're thinking of buying.

Even if the sale is legitimate, the car could be in rotten condition. Negotiate to have the deal depend on the seller's fixing whatever you know is wrong after you inspect the car yourself or (even better) have a skilled mechanic look at it.

Several publishers issue "bluebooks": books that give values for various years, makes, and models of cars, depending on their condition. Check the bluebooks first (your library should have them, if you don't want to buy them), and use these figures as a benchmark for negotiations. If the price of the car is higher than the bluebook price, find out why.

What to Do with Your Current Car

Find out the bluebook value for the car you now own and want to replace. You'll need it as a negotiating tool whether you trade in your current car (which limits your options: you'll have to buy your next car from a dealer, not a private seller), or sell it privately and apply the sales proceeds to buying your next car.

In either case, invest elbow-grease and perhaps a little money in fixing up the old banger. Get minor mechanical problems corrected, and make sure the car is clean and shining enough to entice potential buyers or enhance the trade-in value.

If you're selling your car privately, you may be able to arrange a deal with a friend, or make a few inquiries to see if anyone you know is interested in buying a car or has a friend or relative who's shopping for a car. However, probably what you'll do is place a newspaper ad.

Protect yourself—you're giving out your telephone number to the general public (which has some very disreputable members). When would-be buyers call, take their phone number and call back. Don't let someone just drive away in your car. At the least, examine and copy down the driver's license number before you allow a self-styled potential buyer to take a test drive. If you can, hold on to the license and a credit card until the test drive is complete. (On the other hand, it's not always a good idea to go along on the test drive: your "buyer" could be a robber, or could be part of a gang of burglars who'll "drop in" at your home as soon as you leave.)

Before you sell, check your state's law about transferring title to a car. (If you don't have the information, call the Department of Motor Vehicles.) Be ready to carry out the transfer as soon as the sale is made. Give the buyer a receipt, but don't turn over title until the check has cleared; or, insist on a cashier's or certified check so that you won't take the risk that your buyer's check—like a brand-new spare tire—is all-natural, springy rubber.

49. Financing an Automobile Purchase

The two major sources for financing an automobile purchase are automobile dealers and banks.

Dealer Financing

The first thing you probably think about in connection with dealer financing are the very low rates (2.9%, 3.9% APR) advertised for dealer financing. The major car manufacturers have "financing" subsidiaries that lend money to car buyers, with the dealer as an intermediary; the manufacturer may offer extra-low interest rates to motivate sales, but only for models whose sales are slow. The super-low rates won't necessarily be available for the model you want.

Even if the car you want doesn't qualify for the special low rates, the dealer may be able to arrange a loan from the manufacturer at rates comparable to ordinary market rates; a prosperous dealer may even have its own credit operation, as an additional way to earn money. When you're negotiating the price of the car, the dealer may offer a lower price on the car if you get dealer financing than if you pay cash—that way, the dealer can also earn money on the loan.

Bank Financing

The interest rates that local banks charge for car loans can vary. Some banks are actively seeking new customers and more loans; others treat car loans as just an accommodation to their customers. Check the ads and make a few phone calls before applying. (In fact, check before the serious search for a car begins. That way, you can make realistic comparisons between bank financing and dealer financing, once you find the car you want.)

Sometimes "relationship banking" helps: Banks may give better rates to those who maintain one or more accounts with the bank, or who have already borrowed from the bank. (For one thing, if you fall behind on your payments, they may be able to subtract the overdue amount from your account; this is easier than repossessing your car.)

If your union or employer offers a credit union, think seriously about joining the credit union well before you look for a new car. Credit unions frequently offer car loans at a much lower interest rate than do banks—but only to credit union members; there may be a requirement that you be a member for a certain length of time before getting an auto loan.

The standard term for a car loan used to be two or three years; four years is now standard, five is not uncommon. Try not to have a loan that lasts longer than the car!

What Will a Loan Cost?

The following are factors to consider in comparing sources of financing.

- How large a down payment or trade-in can you afford to make? What is the minimum down payment or trade-in that will be accepted for the car you want? (Usually, you must put down 10% to 25% to participate in a low-rate incentive program.)
- How many payments must you make on the loan?
- How large will each payment be?
- What is the APR (see page 193 for a definition)?
- If you make all payments on time (so you won't have to pay any late charges), what is the total of all the payments you must make?
- Which is more important to you: cutting the overall amount due or cutting the monthly payment?

Table 7 shows how much it will cost to borrow, and compares a 4% loan (which might be available as part of an incentive program) to 9%, 10%, and 11% loans (which are more typical of nonincentive dealer financing and bank loans; the rate you can get depends on interest rate conditions and on how actively the lender is looking for new loans).

The table shows the monthly payment (MP), total payments (TP), and total interest (TI) for three-, four-, and five-year loans: a $5,000 loan is compared to a $7,000 and $9,000 loan. (The size of the loan is the

TABLE 7. AUTO LOAN

	4%			9%		
$5,000 loan	3	4	5	3	4	5
MP	$ 147.62	113.41	92.08	159.00	124.43	103.80
TP	$ 5,314	5,444	5,525	5,724	5,968	6,228
TI	$ 314	444	525	724	968	1,228
$7,000 loan						
MP	$ 206.67	158.84	129.62	222.60	174.20	145.31
TP	$ 7,440	7,624	7,777	8,014	8,362	8,719
TI	$ 440	624	777	1,014	1,362	1,719
$9,000 loan						
MP	$ 265.72	204.22	165.75	286.20	223.97	186.83
TP	$ 9,566	9,803	9,945	10,303	10,751	11,210
TI	$ 566	803	945	1,303	1,751	1,210

	10%			11%		
$5,000 loan	3	4	5	3	4	5
MP	$ 161.34	126.82	106.24	163.70	129.23	108.72
TP	$ 5,808	6,087	6,374	5,893	6,203	6,523
TI	$ 808	1,087	1,374	893	1,203	1,523
$7,000 loan						
MP	$ 225.88	177.54	148.73	229.18	180.92	152.20
TP	$ 8,132	8,522	8,923	8,250	8,684	9,132
TI	$ 1,132	1,522	1,923	1,250	1,684	2,132
$9,000 loan						
MP	$ 290.41	228.27	191.23	294.65	232.61	195.69
TP	$ 10,455	10,957	11,474	10,607	11,165	11,741
TI	$ 1,455	1,957	2,474	1,607	2,165	2,741

price of the car, including fees and taxes, minus your trade-in and/or down payment.)

Sobering, isn't it? Your monthly car payment will probably be between $100 (if you qualify for low-rate financing on a modest car, and stretch out payments for five years) and $300 (a three-year, 11% loan of more than $9,000); the total amount of interest may range from about $300 over the life of the loan to close to $3,000.

50. Lemon Laws

Alas, not every car works the way it's supposed to. Car problems usually show up shortly after purchase (so extended warranties aren't a big risk for auto makers). If you're the unlucky owner of a problem car, the first line of defense is to have it repaired by the dealer who sold it. If the dealer balks, protest to the manufacturer.

The next step is arbitration. The federal law regulating warranties (the Magnuson-Moss Act) requires consumers to use the manufacturer's own arbitration process before suing a dealer or manufacturer. Ford and Chrysler have their own arbitration systems; most other manufacturers use the Better Business Bureau's arbitration system.

Still dissatisfied? Most of the states have "lemon laws" dealing with cars that are born losers, that were just built badly, and can't be fixed. A "lemon" is often defined as a car that had four repair attempts for the same reason, or spent thirty days in the shop in its first year or 12,000 miles.

These laws usually give the lemon buyer a choice between a full refund and a new car (although he or she may not trust the manufacturer much after this experience). The catch is that the lemon law may require the car owner to go through arbitration process before the car can be written off as hopeless; the arbitrators' standards for "lemons" may be stricter than car owners would like.

If you're still dissatisfied after the whole process, you have a right to sue the dealer and/or manufacturer, but suits involve trouble and expense, with no guarantee of winning.

51. Automobile Insurance

Once you've chosen a car, made a deal, and paid for it, you'll probably have to carry some insurance in order to drive it legally. Nearly all of the states require drivers to carry liability insurance, which compensates the victims of accidents caused by negligent driving. (Some states have "financial responsibility laws," which require drivers to carry liability insurance—but only *after* they've been involved in an accident.) Liability insurance, like other kinds of auto insurance, is sold by insurance agents who specialize in property and casualty insurance rather than life and health insurance.

States set their own requirements for liability insurance. Usually, the requirement is quite modest (such as $25,000). That requirement is "modest" because if you are at fault in an automobile accident, you could have to pay hundreds of thousands of dollars in damages to the people you harm.

But even if you can scrape by and register your car without having liability insurance, don't do it! The risk of being at fault in an accident is high; if you are negligent, the sums you could be ordered to pay are astronomical. So check with your insurance agent about insurance costs and the amount of liability insurance you should carry.

Fortunately for insurance buyers, the cost per thousand dollars of liability coverage decreases dramatically as you add coverage. A $500,000 liability policy typically costs only about 50% more than a $25,000 policy.

And after you have the required amount of liability insurance, plus the additional liability insurance you need to avoid financial ruin after an automobile accident, you may want to protect yourself by maintaining coverage that pays medical bills if you (or your passengers) are hurt, and coverage that pays benefits if your car is damaged or stolen.

Although they're not legally required, these forms of insurance (see page 211 for details) can play an important part in your financial plan. The theory behind insurance is "management of risk": You pay a comparatively small amount that you know and can budget for so that you won't have to cope with a huge loss that might happen at any time.

Fault and No-Fault: Who Pays?

If there were no such thing as auto insurance, you'd have a real problem if your car was stolen or damaged in an accident. You certainly couldn't collect from the insurance company. Depending on the facts, you might be able to sue the person who caused the problem (if it had been your own fault, you'd be up the creek). And if you won the case, you could try to collect the amount that the defendant was ordered to pay. But if auto insurance didn't exist, there'd be a good chance that he or she would not have the resources to pay the kind of sizable judgment that would be involved if you (or one of your passengers) were badly hurt.

Of course, auto insurance *does* exist, and copes with many of these problems. If you have medical benefits coverage, collision, or comprehensive coverage, you can collect from the company that sold you your auto insurance, if you suffer the kind of damage covered by the policy. That is, when some so-and-so dents your fender or crumples the rear end of your car, you may be able to collect part or all of the cost of repairs (or an amount that corresponds to the decrease in the value of your car) from your own insurance company. (I say "may be able" because the terms of policies vary, and because of the effect of "deductibles," which are discussed on page 211.)

What if it's a terrible accident, and you're severely injured? You'll have medical and hospital bills to pay, and you'll lose time from work in addition to the damage to your car. If the other driver's negligence caused the accident, you'll probably sue, asking the other driver to compensate you for your pain and suffering as well as your medical expenses and damage to your car.

If the other driver has liability insurance, his or her insurance company will provide him or her with a defense attorney; and if he or she loses the case, the insurance company will pay the judgment—up to the amount of liability coverage carried.

What if the driver who caused the accident can't be found, or he or she lacks adequate assets or adequate insurance to pay for the damage? Some states require automobile insurance policies to have an "uninsured motorist endorsement" (a special addition to the policy), so injured drivers can collect from their own insurance companies when the culprit can't be pinned. Other states collect money from motorists and/or insurance companies, and set up an "unsatisfied judgment" fund that pays off when a defendant loses in court and can't pay up.

Well, of course, it could happen that, on the contrary, you cause the accident (or at least, the other driver thinks you did)—and you get sued. If you have liability insurance, your insurance company will defend the case; if you lose, your insurer will pay the judgment, up to *the limit of your liability coverage.*

The court system and automobile insurance work together to compensate people who suffer physical injury or property damage. But there are problems with relying on litigation to deal with automobile accidents. Unless the plaintiff and defendant can settle the case, a long and expensive trial will be required to decide whose fault the accident was. The plaintiff won't get any money for years, and much of the recovery will go to the plaintiff's lawyer.

Therefore, at the end of 1986, about half the states (Arkansas, Colorado, Connecticut, Delaware, Florida, Georgia, Hawaii, Kansas, Kentucky, Maryland, Massachusetts, Michigan, Minnesota, Nevada, New Jersey, New York, North Dakota, Oregon, Pennsylvania, South Carolina, South Dakota, Texas, Utah, and Virginia) and the District of Columbia had some form of "no-fault" system. "Some form" is an important qualification. Not all state's no-fault laws are alike. In some states, lawsuits arising out of automobile accidents are barred entirely; the no-fault system is the *only* way for an injured person to recover costs that his or her own insurance policy doesn't cover. In other no-fault states, small claims are handled by no-fault, but larger claims can still be taken to court. A third group of states allows a lawsuit if an accident has caused a death, but not if only injuries were caused.

However, critics say that the no-fault system is inadequate because the no-fault laws often limit the damages that can be recovered to economic losses (such as medical bills, lost days at work, damage to the car). In such cases, damages for pain and suffering are not granted to the injured person. But if the injured person had been hurt in a state that did not have a no-fault law, he or she might have gotten thousands, or even hundreds of thousands of dollars' damages for pain and suffering.

Do you still need liability insurance, if you live in a state with a no-fault law? Probably, yes. In "no-fault" states, the basic insurance policy is the "no-fault" policy, with rates set to deal with the fact that you would file a claim with your own insurance company if you were in an accident caused by someone else's negligence—instead of suing the other driver, and indirectly looking to his or her insurance company to compensate you. However, you may have to supplement this policy with conventional liability insurance in case your state does allow suits in serious cases, or in case you're involved in an accident while driving in another state.

Types of Auto Insurance Coverage

As already explained, most states require all drivers to have at least a specified minimum of liability insurance in order to register their cars. You'll probably want much more insurance to protect yourself and your family.

•*Liability insurance.* When you discuss liability insurance with your insurance agent, figures like "50/100/25" will be flying around. What that means is that the first number is the amount of coverage for injuries to any one person, the second number is the total coverage for injuries to everyone hurt in an accident, and the last number is the limit the insurance company will pay for damage to other people's property if you cause an accident. (All figures refer to thousands of dollars. In the case of 50/100/25, your policy will reimburse you for up to $50,000 that you are required to pay a person who is hurt because of your negligence, up to $100,000 for *all* injuries to *anyone* hurt in that accident, and up to $25,000 worth of property damage.)

In addition to liability insurance, several other kinds of auto insurance are available. There is no legal requirement that you buy them; the choice of coverage is a purely practical one. It depends on how much auto insurance you can afford—and on the condition of your car. (As will be explained, collision insurance is not always a good financial choice if your car is old and battered.)

•*Collision coverage* pays, of course, for damage caused by a collision. You don't have to sue anyone; you can collect even if the damage was nobody's fault—even if it was your fault. However, there are powerful reasons to deter you from filing a parade of trivial claims, one each time your car gets a microscopic dent. First, there's the fact that your premium will rise based on the number and size of the claims you collect under your policy.

Then, there's the deductible. Most collision coverage is issued subject to a deductible. If you have, say, a $100 deductible, you must absorb the first $100 of cost whenever your car is damaged by collision; you file an insurance claim for the rest. (However, the insurance company won't pay more than the actual cash value of your car, even if it costs more than that to fix it, so a low cash value means that you can't ever collect a large insurance claim.) A higher deductible means a lower premium because you take on more risk; the insurer takes on less.

Another option is "convertible collision" coverage. If you choose this coverage, you start out by paying only half the premium for full collision coverage. If your car is involved in a collision for which a claim could be made, you have to come up with the other half of the premium—but you can collect as if you had carried the full collision coverage all along.

• *Comprehensive coverage* pays for damage that is not caused by a collision—damage such as theft, vandalism, or the effects of a tree branch blown through your windshield by high winds. This, too, usually has a deductible.

As a matter of insurance company policy, you usually get a choice between getting collision and comprehensive, or just comprehensive coverage—usually, collision insurance won't be sold on its own.

Again, it doesn't matter whose fault (if anyone's) the damage was.

If your state has a no-fault law, you probably should carry more collision and/or comprehensive coverage than you would if you lived in a "fault" state because it'll be harder (or impossible) to sue someone else for damaging your car; you'll need a healthy dose of coverage from your own insurer.

• *Medical coverage* pays medical bills for people who are hurt while riding in your car. This coverage may not be needed if you have plenty of medical insurance, and no one but your family ever rides in your car. Otherwise, think seriously about carrying this coverage.

Depending on state law, the people injured while they are in your car may be able to sue you (some states have no-fault; others restrict suits by family members against other family members, or by guests in cars against the hosts who were driving them.) If you live in one of these states, you may need extra liability insurance as well as medical coverage to cope with this situation.

• *DOC (Drive Other Cars)* coverage gives you liability insurance if you are involved in an accident while driving a borrowed, rented, or company car.

How to Save Money on Auto Insurance

It's a false economy to skimp on the coverage you need—especially liability insurance coverage. In fact, it can be an economy move to increase your liability coverage, either directly or by buying an inexpensive "umbrella" policy that supplements both homeowner's insurance and automobile insurance liability coverage. A million dollars' worth of "umbrella" coverage can cost as little as $100 a year.

So how do you save insurance dollars sensibly? One way is to accept a higher deductible (some experts suggest that one week's salary is an appropriate deductible—it would be painful, but not tragic, to suffer a loss of that size). Another way is to shop for special rates. It's up to each insurance company to set rates and decide on the factors involved in setting the rates. To summarize this complex subject, insurers often give lower rates to:

- People over 65 (although they may suffer vision and hearing problems, they're unlikely to be "hot-rodders")
- Nonsmokers
- People who have successfuly completed "defensive driving" courses
- Owners of several cars covered under the same policy—if several cars share the driving load, the odds are lower that each one will get into an accident
- Owners of cars that have good safety and repair records

Parents of teenage drivers know enough to expect bad news when the auto insurance bill arrives—but some relief may be at hand: Some companies offer lower rates to the families of teenage drivers with B averages or higher, or who pass driver-training courses.

Auto insurance rates tend to be lowest for automobiles used exclusively for farm work (What are you going to do—collide with a cow? And if you do, the cow won't sue), higher for automobiles for personal and family use (which tend to be parked during the working day, and out of trouble), and highest for cars used in business (which tend to get intensive use, including rush hours—when the roads are crowded with potential participants in an accident).

Insurers pay a lot of attention to your driving record; if you're convicted of a traffic offense, were involved in an accident with major damage recently, or were involved in several minor accidents recently, you will probably have to pay much higher auto insurance rates than someone with a better record.

Finally, you can be a superb driver and a person who embodies every one of the virtues and none of the vices—but you may have to pay high auto insurance rates because you live in a place where there are a lot of terrible drivers, or where many of your fellow citizens amuse themselves by stealing your car or your car radio.

Use the following worksheet to analyze your insurance needs and get quotes from various insurance companies for the coverage you do need.

WORKSHEET

1. List the year, make, model, and current "bluebook" value of the car(s) to be

   covered:_____

2. For each car, give the number of miles driven in an average year:_____and

   the percentage of time for which it is used for business:_____% and personal

   or family use: _____ %

3. Give the name, age, and sex of all authorized driver(s) of the car(s):

   _____

4. List every driver who is a nonsmoker:_____
5. List every driver who has passed a driver-training or defensive-driving

   course:_____
6. Explain other factors that qualify the driver(s) for rate reductions—or rate

   increases:_____
7. If the car has been involved in an accident in the past three years, explain the

   circumstances:_____
8. If any driver(s) has/have "points" on his/her/their driver's license, explain the

   circumstances:_____

9. Do you want collision insurance? ☐ Yes ☐ No

10. Size of deductible(s) you want: $_____ collision $_____ comprehensive.

11. Amount of liability coverage you want:_____/_____/_____.

                                   *   *   *

Get quotes based on these facts—and also find out how the rates
would change if you took a larger or smaller deductible, and added or
subtracted liability coverage.

After an Accident

Insurance is an interesting product: You buy basketball tickets because
you want to go to a basketball game, but you buy accident insurance
even though you don't want an accident. So, if and when the moment
you dreaded has finally occurred, here's how to deal with your legal
obligations, and here's how to preserve your rights under your policy.

   The natural—but ruinous—impulse is to high-tail out of the way
after an accident. What you must do is stay put, exchange information

with the other driver(s) (names, addresses, insurers, etc.), and cooperate with any police investigation of the accident.

Once the investigation is over and you've driven home, you must protect your car against further damage (for instance, repairing an accident-cracked window that could make it easier for thieves or vandals to attack the car). Phone your insurance agent immediately, then follow up with a letter as soon as possible, giving details of the accident and information such as the names and addresses of witnesses and injured persons.

Claims Procedure

If your state is a "fault" state, you have three choices when your car is damaged in an accident. You can sue the other driver, hoping to win the case, or settle with the other driver's insurance company. Or, you can make a claim under your own collision coverage (for the amount of the damage, less the deductible). Auto insurance policies can be written so that if your insurance company wins a suit against the other driver's insurance company, your insurer will use part of what it collects from the other insurer to refund any deductible you paid.

What if you're the one to get sued by the driver of the other car or by its passengers? Contact your insurer as soon as you are served with a summons. The insurance company will provide you with a lawyer. If you lose the case, the insurer will pay the amount of the court's judgment against you—up to your policy limits, of course.

A claim against your own insurance company is made by filing a sworn "proof of loss" with your insurance company, which can examine the damaged car and/or ask you to give sworn testimony about the accident and the damage to your car.

If you make a claim under your medical coverage, you must file a written "proof of claim" with your insurance company. (You may have to do this under oath.) You must also sign an authorization allowing the insurance company to see your medical records; if the insurance company asks, you must let its doctor examine you.

If you live in a no-fault state, check with your insurance agent or get legal advice about any special claims procedures you must follow after an accident.

Claims Adjustment

Insurance companies use "adjusters" to decide if the insurance company has a legal responsibility to pay the claim, and if so, how much it must pay. Adjusters can either be insurance company employees, freelancers, or workers for special claims adjustment bureaus.

The insurance company uses the adjuster's report to set a maximum amount it is willing to pay; the adjuster then negotiates with the insured person. If you're in this situation, and you and the adjuster can't agree how much the claim is worth, a panel of three arbitrators makes the decision.

An "adjustment" is an agreement between the insured person and the insurer, negotiated by the adjuster. If you sign an "adjustment," you get a check, and release the insurer from any further claims. You must also agree that, if you later win a lawsuit based on the damage already adjusted, the insurer will be entitled to any amount you collect. The basic legal rule is that people are entitled to be compensated *once* for certain injuries—not to make a profit by collecting several times for the same damage.

Important: If you accept money from the other driver, or from his or her insurance company without getting your insurance company's permission first, you could hurt your legal position in any future suit—*and* you could be giving your own insurance company the legal right to turn down your claims.

52. Automobile Leasing

If you want to get a car, buying it isn't always the best way to go. No, I'm not advocating grand theft auto—just pointing out that leasing a car may be a better strategy than buying a car, just as some people find that renting an apartment is a better strategy than buying a house. Whether buying a house or a car, the buyer has to tie up money in a down payment, and has the headaches of taking care of the asset—but also has the advantages of ownership.

Automobile leases usually last four years. There are two kinds of lease that are commonly available: closed-end and open-end. A closed-end lease is sometimes called a walk-away lease because the person leasing the car makes monthly payments over the lease term, then hands over the car at the end of the term.

The contract for an open-end lease includes an estimate of what the car will be worth at the end of the lease term. The lessee (person leasing the car) makes regular monthly payments for the lease term; when it ends, the lessee returns the car and the lessor either sells the car right away or gets an appraisal of its value. If the paid or appraised value equals the estimate given in the lease, the lessee's connection with the car is over. But if the value is less than the estimate, the lessee must make an "end of lease payment" to make up for the loss of value. (You won't be entitled to a refund if the car is more valuable than the estimate, unless the lease contract includes this provision—so make sure it's written in, if you enter into an open-end lease.) You may want to buy the car yourself, at the end of the term—if so, make sure the contract gives you the option to do this at a reasonable price.

Federal law requires leasing companies to make extensive disclosures about the costs and terms of the lease. Make sure you understand this material before you sign anything.

Leasing can be a good choice if you want a car more luxurious than one for which you can make a cash down payment, if you don't want to be responsible for car maintenance, or if you think that the heavy depreciation that cars undergo right after purchase makes them a bad investment.

For instance, *The New York Times* advertised leases costing $160 per month for a car that would cost $11,500 to buy. If you made a $2,500 down payment (or your trade-in was worth $2,500), and borrowed the remaining $9,000 at 10% for four years, you'd have to pay $228.27 a month. The lease payment for a car that cost almost $17,000 was $260 a month—about what you'd pay on a three-year, $9,000, 4% loan. So leasing would save you cash—but buying a car gives you an asset that boosts your net worth and can be resold or traded in.

The Tax Code of 1986 has made leasing more attractive to some people: State sales taxes (such as the large tax charged on cars) are no longer deductible, and the deduction for consumer interest is being phased out. So you won't lose tax deductions by leasing instead of buying. Leasing can also be a useful tax strategy for businesses, or for people who use their cars for work. Check with your accountant.

Part Four:
PROBLEM SOLVING

53. College Costs

Financing college education is one of the greatest financial challenges most families will ever face. The key is that the *family* must face it. In today's financial environment, students must make a major contribution to their own education, whether by working part-time and summers, deferring college for a few years to take a full-time job and save money, choosing a less expensive college, or taking on the maximum student loans available.

The earlier parents start saving and investing for college, and the better they do at selecting long-term, low-risk investments, the easier their part of the task will be. As children get closer to college age, parents must estimate the "gap" between family resources already available (savings, current income, scholarships, loans to the student) and the costs of college (not just tuition and room and board, but clothes, books, perhaps a computer, phone calls home, and trips between school and the old homestead).

There are plenty of ways to fill the gap: PLUS loans (federally guaranteed loans to parents), personal loans from banks, policy loans taken against the cash value of life insurance, and home-equity loans. The challenge is tough, but not impossible.

Table 8 shows you the amount you must save or invest each month to accumulate $60,000 for college expenses—depending on when you start (with four to eighteen years' head start) and whether you earn 5.5%, 8%, or 10% on your investment.

54. Investing for Future College Costs

Your job is much tougher if the student is already in high school. Even if the student works part time, even if loans are used to the fullest, even if scholarship possibilities are canvassed to the ultimate, it can seem impossible to find $5,000, $10,000, even $15,000 all at once.

However, if the future B.A. is now on the honor roll at nursery school—or hasn't even been born yet—the job is much more manageable. It's true that parents fear that tuition, room, and board at a top-flight private college will eventually cost more than $20,000 a year. And

TABLE 8.   COLLEGE FUND

Number	Monthly Investment		
of Years	5.5%	8%	10%
4	$1,126.08	$1,064.76	$1,021.74
5	876.66	816.60	774.84
6	710.76	652.02	611.58
7	592.62	535.20	496.08
8	504.24	448.20	410.46
9	435.78	381.12	344.70
10	381.24	327.96	292.92
11	336.84	284.94	251.22
12	300.00	249.48	217.02
13	268.98	219.84	188.70
14	242.58	194.82	164.94
15	219.84	173.40	144.78
16	200.04	154.98	127.56
17	182.76	138.96	112.74
18	167.46	124.98	99.90

their fears are not irrational. But even this terrifying sum can be accumulated by nonmillionaires—if they have plenty of time to work on it.

College costs are related to inflation and the cost of living, though they've soared higher and faster than inflation in general. So, if college costs are exploding, interest rates are zooming up too. That fact, which sounds depressing, is really your ace in the hole. Why? If you're an investor in income-related instruments (such as bonds and certificates of deposit), high interest rates mean a high return on your investment.

Basic Strategies

Only general tips can be given here because it's tough to predict what the stock market, bond market, and economy will be doing tomorrow, much less what'll happen in ten to fifteen years.

• Depending on your own needs and spending patterns, investing for college can either be part of your general investment system or entirely separate. If your self-discipline is low, you're better off keeping the college funds entirely separate. Since the separation will be purely psychological, "college" funds will still be available if there's a genuine emergency.
• Remember, the longer you have, the less you need to invest each week or each month to guarantee that tuition funds will be available.
• Don't worry—you don't have to have every nickel saved up before your child enrolls as a freshman. It helps a lot to have $40,000, $20,000, even $10,000 saved up.
• Another comforting fact: Even after freshman-year tuition is paid, the rest of Junior's college fund continues to earn interest for three more years. After sophomore year, the balance earns interest for two, and so on. If anything is left over, it can be used for the younger

children's tuition, for general family needs, to launch the graduate on his or her career—or just for a spree of gratitude.

What should your investment choices be? Well, investing for college costs, like investing for retirement, is an investment in security. So you probably won't want to take big risks. Conservative investments like government securities funds can look very soothing.

But income investments aren't the only choices. You don't need (or even want) current income from the invested money when your child is growing up. What you really need is solid appreciation in value.

• Growth stocks (stocks whose shares can be purchased inexpensively, then gain in value over time) might interest you. Of course, growth stocks are risky. Very few stocks can achieve and sustain major gains in value. So, you might prefer to invest in mutual funds that have a good track record in picking growth companies. But remember, last year's star mutual fund could be in this year's doghouse.

• Zero-coupon bonds offer another answer to the problem of accumulating a fund of a desired size to be ready at a definite time in the future. These U.S. government, municipal, or corporate bonds are sold at a deep, deep discount. They can be redeemed at face value on their due date. You pick bonds that mature when your son or daughter enters college (or pick a bond bouquet, with maturities each year for four years). The longer you can wait, the less you have to pay for bonds that will meet your investment goal.

Why doesn't everybody invest in "zeros"? Because they're far from perfect. First, unless you get tax-free municipal bond zeros, you must pay taxes on the "phantom interest" that *would* have been paid if the zero-coupon bonds had paid interest like ordinary bonds. You have to pay taxes, even though you haven't gotten any income with which to pay the taxes.

For another thing, zero-coupon bond prices fluctuate even more wildly than the prices of other bonds. If you have to sell some zeros before they mature, you could find yourself losing quite a bit of money.

Speaking of investments and taxes, the Tax Code of 1986 (TC '86) creates serious problems for a lot of middle- and upper-middle-class parents. They used to meet family tax planning objectives by "income shifting": giving away assets to the children so that income from the assets would be taxed at the children's lower rates.

TC '86 spikes those guns. For one thing, when children under 14 have investment income, the tax code usually makes them pay taxes at their parents' highest tax rate. (This is a complex subject—check with your tax adviser to see if you can fit into one of the exceptions.)

The tax reform bill also eliminates the tax advantages of the "Clifford trust"—which *used* to be a terrific way to transfer assets to a trust for a comparatively short time (at least ten years), have their income taxed at low rates for the length of the trust, and then get the assets back when the trust term ended. But it's worth mentioning here because I suspect that influential parents will lobby to get the advantages of Clifford trusts added back into the tax code.

TC '86 does allow children *over* 14, who have investment income, to pay taxes at rates based on their own income, not their parents' income. So it can still be worthwhile to transfer assets to high-school-aged children; let them pay the tax (at rates lower than if you did), and let them use the assets to pay their own tuition. Get professional advice as to whether this will work for your family.

Families usually don't need life insurance on their children because children are not responsible for the family's economic support. However, buying and maintaining a whole-life policy for a child gives the parent(s) access to low-cost policy loans on the cash value. And guarantees your child's insurability in the future.

Grants and Scholarships

Unless you think way in advance, have plenty of money to save and invest, and have good investment judgment, there will probably be a gap between your assets and what's needed to pay college bills. It makes sense to start filling the gap with funds that don't have to be repaid. So, you should become familiar with grant and scholarship programs, their requirements, and how your child can qualify.

(A warning: This discussion was written in early 1987, when the Reagan administration proposed cuts in federal scholarship and student loan funds as a step toward cutting the deficit. The rules may have changed—probably in a direction you won't much like—by the time you read this.)

Federal Grant Programs

Federal grant funds are becoming scarcer and harder to catch. In 1975, for instance, 80% of federal higher education funds went toward grants; in 1987, the proportion was down to 48%.

The two major programs, both based on financial need, are the Pell Grant and SEOG (Supplemental Educational Opportunity Grant) programs. The maximum grant under each is about $2,000; both programs are run by colleges, who get funding from the Department of Education.

To apply for either, parents must fill out forms disclosing their income and assets. Then, the college compiles a Student Aid Report based on these disclosures, and assigns the student a Student Aid Index Number. The number is used to determine eligibility for both government and private funding. To get a Pell Grant, for instance, a student's index number must be 1,900 or lower.

The forms that parents fill out are also used to calculate the "expected family contribution" that must be made before grants will be available. There's an elaborate system of calculations, based on the family's income and assets, the student's own income, the size of the family, and the number of children in school at the same time. The additional expenses of single parents, and of two-parent, two-career families, can also be taken into account.

The federal government also gives the states money to award State Student Incentive Grants to students with very high financial needs.

Colleges themselves provide financial aid; the process of deciding whether a student qualifies also involves a consideration of the student's and family's income and assets—including the family home, small business owned by family members, and retirement benefits.

The college has a formula for deciding how much "discretionary income" a family has (income after necessary expenses have been met), and assigns a percentage of discretionary income that it feels the parents should contribute (such as 33% of discretionary income). The college may provide financial aid if, after all other sources have been tapped, the tuition and room and board still exceed the parental contribution that the college expects. However, colleges have their financial problems too; many colleges can't afford to give financial aid to every needy—and academically qualified—applicant.

Scholarships

Grants are based on financial need; scholarships are usually based on the student's achievements, or on contributions he or she can make to the school (for instance, athletic scholarships).

- National Merit Scholarships are based on high school grades and performance on standardized tests.
- Some states (New York is one) have scholarship programs for high achievers who attend college within the state—which can make the state university, or a private college within the state, especially attractive.
- Students willing to make a commitment to serve in the military can get ROTC scholarships.
- Those interested in health care, and willing to work for a while in areas short of health care personnel, can get scholarships under the Public Health Service Act, or loans under the Health Professions Student Loans and Health Education Assistance Loan programs. (All of these are sponsored by the federal government.)

  Under the right circumstances, these can turn into a kind of scholarship—if the student becomes a doctor, dentist, pharmacist, or other health professional and practices for two or more years in an area short of health manpower. Nursing students can get their loans forgiven completely if they work for two or more years in a health personnel shortage area.
- Colleges have their own scholarship programs, perhaps derived from the college's endowment, or funded by grateful alumni or cor-

porations. Once your children are in high school, guidance counselors or college advisers should be able to tell them about scholarship availability.

More bad news from the Tax Code of 1986: If a student does manage to get a scholarship, part of it (the part that represents aid for room and board instead of tuition, books, or supplies) will be taxable income. So, the value of the scholarship is reduced by the taxes the recipient will have to pay on the scholarship money.

Student Loans

The term "student loan" really covers two related concepts: loans made to students and loans made to their parents. Most students are poor loan prospects, so they have to do their borrowing from special government programs, from the school itself, or from banks reassured by government guarantees that the government will take over payments if the student defaults. Depending on their income and resources, parents may qualify for bank loans; they may also be able to borrow from government programs.

NDSL. A limited amount of loan money is available from the National Direct Student Loan (NDSL; "Perkins loan") program—"direct" means direct from the federal government. Availability depends on the "expected contribution" the government feels the student's family can make and on the cost of attending the school that the student selects.

There's also a maximum cumulative total of National Direct Student Loans that students are allowed to run up: $3,000 for freshmen and sophomores, $6,000 for juniors and seniors, $12,000 for graduate and professional school students.

Repayment is supposed to start six months after the student leaves school (as a graduate or otherwise) and normally stretches out for ten years. However, the loans can be cancelled if the student spends some time teaching underprivileged or handicapped children. (Like the health programs already described, this is a way to motivate young people to spend at least part of their career in highly necessary but understaffed occupations.)

GSL. Guaranteed Student Loans (GSL) are made by banks to students at below-market interest rates. Currently, the maximum interest rate the banks can charge is 8% (for the first four years of repayment and 10% afterwards), but under some circumstances part of the interest can be added to the principal that must be repaid.

There's a ceiling on the maximum amount that students can borrow under the GSL program: $2,500 a year for college education, with an overall limit of $7,500 for undergraduate education; $5,000 a year for graduate education; $15,000 for undergraduate plus graduate schooling.

Students must also pay a 5% "origination fee," which is subtracted from the amount students receive (they must repay the whole amount, including the origination fee). The fee goes to the federal government, not to the lender, and it's used to cope with the perpetual problem of people who default on their student loans.

Theoretically, students begin to repay their GSLs within nine months after they graduate or otherwise leave school. The student is supposed to contact the lender to set up a five to ten year repayment schedule. Repayments can be deferred while the student is in graduate school, serving in the military or the Peace Corps, or completing a medical internship. Deferments are also available if the borrower or his or her spouse becomes disabled—or if the borrower, despite honest efforts to get a job, suffers long-term unemployment.

Some students never get around to either the notification or the repayments. Others pass up jobs they really want in favor of other, more lucrative professions; struggle to make ends meet; or otherwise find some way to meet their average debt of $6,685 (for students who attend publicly supported institutions such as state universities) or $8,950 (for graduates of private colleges).

Life just got tougher for student loan deadbeats. Starting in 1986, the IRS is cooperating with the GSL program, and income tax refunds that are owed to GSL defaulters will be seized and forwarded to the government toward the repayment. In 1986 and part of 1987, more than 200,000 tax refunds were withheld, and 30,000 borrowers dug into their pockets and produced $16,500,000 in repayments to avoid the seizure.

PLUS Loans. PLUS loans are loans at normal or higher-than-normal rates (the lender can charge an extra 1% as an insurance premium) made either to parents or to students who are financially independent of parents (such as those who start college or grad school late in life). You can get a PLUS loan even if you're not financially needy— but there are limits on the maximum PLUS loan available.

The PLUS maximum is $2,500 per year, $15,000 per child when a parent borrows for a child's undergraduate education. But if the student has a GSL, the total of PLUS and GSL is not allowed to exceed the GSL maximum. The parent-borrower has sixty days from the time of the loan (*not* from the time the student leaves school) to start making repayments.

A student who has a PLUS loan must begin paying interest within sixty days of getting the loan, unless the lender allows him or her to defer payments. The principal doesn't have to be repaid until the student leaves school. Deferments are also available during graduate school, internship, military or Peace Corps service, long-term unemployment, or disability.

The rules are different for graduate students: $3,000 a year, up to a total of $15,000, can be borrowed over and above amounts borrowed under GSL.

Some states offer loan programs. Usually, they're restricted to students who attend college or grad school within the state; but some, such as Minnesota, even lend money to students who attend out-of-state schools.

Don't neglect the college itself as a source of loan funds. Some colleges make long-term, low-rate or variable-rate loans to parents, students, or both. But make this a last, not a first, resort. Colleges themselves are facing some tough times, given increases in salaries and costs, decreased federal funding—and decreased contributions from alumni.

Borrowing from Banks

Banks were making personal loans and writing second mortgages many years before federal loan programs existed. Bank borrowing is still an option for affluent parents. So are policy loans for parents who have insurance policies with cash value. (Just remember that unpaid policy loans reduce the amount of insurance proceeds available to survivors—so make sure your coverage is adequate over and above the amount borrowed, or be sure that there are plenty of other assets to meet family needs.)

Maybe Congress is embarrassed by how tough TC '86 has been on parents saving for college. (If they're not, they should be.) The deduction for consumer interest is being phased out over the five-year period from 1986 to 1991. Therefore, GSL and PLUS borrowers will not get a tax deduction for all the interest they pay; part will be nondeductible.

However, the tax code adds a category called "qualified residence interest." Interest on home equity loans (whether conventional mortgages or lines of credit secured by the house, but used for purposes that are not related to the house) *is* tax-deductible.

There's a limit, though. The largest loan on which tax-deductible qualified residence interest will be allowed equals:

- The taxpayer's basis (tax value) in the house, plus
- The cost of improvements the taxpayer made to the house (even if the improvements were not financed by this, or any, loan), plus
- Medical and educational expenses financed by the loan

This is obviously a gesture aimed at letting parents use home equity loans to finance their children's education, while locking in a tax deduction for the interest. It eases the pain of high college costs a *little,* but it's no more a long-term cure than an aspirin is for a broken leg. Anyway, the new tax law also lowers tax brackets, so tax deductions are less valuable than they used to be. If you're in the 70% bracket, an extra dollar of deductions saves you 70 cents; but if you're in the 28% bracket, that deductible dollar saves a mere 28 cents.

Innovations

Conventional scholarships and loans aren't always enough to cope with
the problem, and some intriguing new mechanisms have evolved.
They're not for everyone, so consider them carefully.

"Tuition futures" let parents pay a comparatively small lump sum
when the future student is a baby, to "reserve" four years' tuition when
the child is ready for college. This idea was pioneered by Duquesne
University; some colleges have followed, and others sell "gift certificates" providing nonrefundable payments to be used toward future
semesters' tuition.

In 1986, for instance, Canisius College (in upstate New York) would
guarantee four years' tuition if parents of an infant paid a lump sum of
$7,000; it would take $17,500 to do the same for a fifteen-year-old. The
college invests the money, hoping to earn more than the tuition. The
parents benefit by knowing that once the payment is made, the matter
is taken care of.

But there are a few risks. The college itself could be out of business
by the time the children are ready to attend. If the child's transcript
isn't as good as the parents' check, the college could reject the child's
application. Schools that offer "tuition futures" say that they'll monitor
the students' precollege academic performance, and allow some of the
"tuition" money to be used for remedial work if necessary. (Cynics say
that it's tough to turn down an applicant who's already paid for the full
course.)

Maybe some of the "futures" funds will be transferrable if the student transfers to another school after a year or two. But if the child
doesn't want to go to college at all, or picks another school as a first
choice, the "futures" program will probably refund only the actual
amount the parent contributed, with the "rejected" college hanging on
to the investment income to soothe its wounded feelings.

The idea of tuition futures is spreading into the public sector too.
The state of Michigan is considering a plan that would cover all the units
of the state university system, and would allow a student's parents to
transfer the appreciated value of the futures money to any private
college inside the state.

Combining College and Work

The most obvious way to combine college and work is the College
Work-Study Program, which is a federal program that provides part-
time jobs on or off campus for needy college students. The jobs can't be
mere make-work; they must be real jobs the employer would normally
pay for. Some work-study jobs even provide college credit, helping the
student in two ways.

The federal government also sponsors a cooperative education program, funding "projects in which students engage in alternating or
parallel periods of study and employment." That is, students can either

work one semester, study one semester, or combine study and paid work.

However, these work-study programs may lose their federal funding to the shears of budget cutters, so check with guidance counselors or financial aid personnel at the college to see if they are still available when you need them.

Most students, with or without help from Washington, should be able to earn at least part of their college costs. However, few students can "work their way through college" these days—it's just too expensive.

Precollege students should consider developing temporary job skills that are easily transferrable. That way, they can work part-time during the school year and get summer jobs. A kid who types well can always earn money typing other students' term papers. A kid who understands computers can work as a word processing operator for a temporary agency. The same thing goes for students who can drive cabs, wait on tables (the tips at La Maison Très Chère are better than those at Eddie's Diner), work in department stores or boutiques. Entrepreneurially minded students can set up low-capital college businesses (pizza delivery, laundry service, résumé counseling).

Summing Up

Is college a good investment? Well, only about one-fifth of all American families are headed by college graduates, but these families earn one-third of all the income and *half* of the disposable income (income minus basic expenses). This is true because the more a family earns, the smaller the percentage of its income goes to the necessities of life—the rest can be used for investment or for luxuries. In 1985, heads of households who had college degrees earned an average of 54% more than high school graduates heading households.

So college could be a good career move for your children; most high-paying jobs require a college degree, and many require postcollege education. If you can't afford to send your children to college right after they graduate from high school, don't despair. Maybe they can attend a two-year college while working part-time, earning enough to transfer to a four-year college. Maybe they can work full-time for a year or so and study a course or two per semester at night. Perhaps they can work for a firm that offers tuition assistance. By mobilizing family assets—including creativity—the family can work together and make sure that the costs of higher education are paid.

55. REAL LIFE: LINDA FULLER

Linda thinks she always took things slow and easy—and today, kids are always in a hurry. She and Blake didn't get married until Linda was 31; they didn't have Tamsin until Linda was 35. And now, the marriage is over; Tamsin's two—and the day-care center decked her out in a little cap and gown for a "graduation" ceremony now that Tamsin's there every day, three hours a day.

That made Linda think about college. It's tough enough to support a child on an assistant librarian's salary ($20,000). The child-support payments, $500 a month, help a lot, but Linda has heard enough stories in the laundromat and around the coffee machine at work to know that not every ex-husband makes child-support payments on time. So the two things preying on Linda's mind are how she can possibly provide a *real* cap and gown, and how Linda herself can protect herself from a lonely and poverty-stricken old age. Well, the lonely part doesn't worry her so much—she's always been outgoing and fairly optimistic. It's the poverty-stricken part that bothers her. Linda is far from extravagant, and she always has a cushion of savings in the bank. But she knows that raising a child is expensive—the expenses go up as the child grows. And she knows that her salary is just about the only resource to take care of herself and of Tamsin.

The Numbers

Linda's financial life is pretty straightforward. As mentioned, Linda earns $20,000 as assistant librarian of a branch library, and gets $6,000 a year in child-support payments. Her biggest expenses each year are income tax: $4,000, and $6,000 for food and clothing. Rent on the apartment is $383 a month, and Linda pays $150 a year for insurance on the contents of the apartment.

This isn't just sentimental, or paranoid: One of her biggest assets, her collection of photographs (worth about $4,000), is kept in the apartment. The furnishings are worth about $6,000—the divorce settlement awarded most of the furniture and other household goods to Linda. The savings account fluctuates; right now, it stands at $4,150.

It also costs Linda $2,000 a year to pay for Tamsin's day care. Insuring Linda's Subaru, and paying off the loan, costs $1,700 a year. Finally, no matter how she scrimps and saves, Linda finds that she must budget $3,000 a year for miscellany: newspaper subscriptions, an occasional movie, maybe a dutch-treat date with a fellow-librarian or someone she met at her church's singles coffee hour. Not to mention laundry and dry-cleaning, toys for Tamsin, birthday presents for her large and affectionate family . . .

The Answers

Insurance is crucial for a single parent like Linda, who's operating on the slimmest of margins and skating on ice that's none too thick. So she is careful to maintain a disability income policy because the financial situation would be just as grim if she were disabled as if she were to die.

But life insurance is also a necessity. Linda prefers a conventional whole-life because security and guarantees are most important to her.

Linda is not interested in active investing. She knows that she has to save money, and she also knows that savings accounts don't exactly pay the highest rate of return in town. But she feels that she can't afford to take any risk at all. She is a very conservative, very income-oriented investor. Growth stocks don't appeal to her. She wants more cash now, not the promise of pie in the sky. Therefore, once she has met her savings goal, she plans to invest in a closed-end bond fund. That way, she can make a single decision and stick to it. She'll also be able to get regular income from her investment.

56. Dealing with the Financial Aspects of Divorce

A divorce is not only the legal termination of a marriage relationship, with significant emotional consequences for the married couple and their children; it's also a major financial event, as the couple's property has to be identified and divided between the two new households that are created.

Even after the marriage relationship ends, the financial relationship frequently continues: It may take time to distribute the property; one spouse may be ordered to make continuing payments to support the other spouse, the family's children, or both. And if the payments aren't made on time, it may be necessary to use legal remedies to collect them.

How Divorce Law Evolved

One reason why the number of divorces keeps increasing is that laws have changed, making it dramatically easier to get a divorce. If divorce is close to impossible, then even the most miserable of couples will stick it out; if divorce is easy, couples who might have only minor disagreements may split up.

Until recently, American divorce law treated marriage as a deal in which the husband promised to support his wife and children, and the wife promised to give her domestic services in the husband's home. This deal could be cancelled if one of the parties was guilty of some kind of serious marital fault such as adultery or cruelty.

If the husband was the guilty one, he would have to pay alimony as a continuation of his obligation to support his wife. If she was the guilty party, she would lose her right to support. In this analysis, wives didn't have to support their husbands unless there was a risk that the husbands would become a public charge.

To get a "fault" divorce, the "innocent" party would have to prove that the "guilty" one had committed one of the grounds for divorce named in the state's law—furthermore, no divorce would be granted if the "innocent" party was also guilty of fault, or if he or she knew about the fault and failed to take prompt action to get a divorce. So an unhappily married person could lose badly by trying to be forgiving and patch up the marriage; and a couple who were both guilty of outrageous misconduct could find that although their marriage was impossible from the practical point of view, divorce was impossible from the legal.

As for the couple's property, unless they lived in one of the community property states (where the community property was treated as if it belonged equally to both spouses), the property would be divided up based on "title" (which spouse's name was on the deed). The practical consequence was that the husband was usually treated as the sole owner of the property.

Since World War II, the trend has been to move from fault divorce to a system in which divorce is available both on a fault and a no-fault basis, or strictly on a no-fault basis.

No-Fault Divorce

To get a no-fault divorce, a couple need only state that their marriage has deteriorated irreparably. For a "conversion" divorce, they only have to say that they've been separated for a certain amount of time, and that they've been following the provisions of a separation agreement that they negotiated.

In short, divorce has shifted from a court-based system with one party accusing the other (and having to prove the accusation) to a contractual basis, where the parties negotiate a contract (the separation agreement) and the court approves this contract (or adjusts it, if it's unfair or fails to meet the requirements of state law). Now, there are three financial aspects to divorce: a one-time division of property around the time of the divorce, continuing support payments from one spouse to the other, and continuing payments from the noncustodial parent to the custodial parent to support the children.

Before the Divorce

First, find out if your state permits "summary" divorces: a divorce without court proceedings for couples who both want a divorce and who agree on all important matters relative to the divorce (property division, support, custody). A summary divorce takes less time and is cheaper (because there's no need to pay for extensive court proceedings)—so more of the couple's resources can be used for family needs.

If your state doesn't allow summary divorces, or if you don't meet the requirements (summary divorce may not be available for couples with children), the next step is to preserve the financial status quo and arrange the postdivorce financial situation.

If you need support money for the time between the filing of the case and its final resolution, you can apply for alimony *pendente lite* (pending the suit) and/or temporary child support. You apply to the court that has jurisdiction of the divorce case; the court can make an order that runs until the time of the divorce proceedings.

You can also apply for an injunction to prevent your spouse from selling family assets, or doing anything else to dispose of them (except for carrying on ordinary business or meeting family needs). This is very important to prevent one spouse from emptying the bank account, selling stock, or otherwise keeping assets out of the hands of the other spouse.

In a state that uses the principle of equitable distribution, the process can only work if both spouses (and the court) know the real state of family finances. So each spouse must fill out sworn disclosure forms about separate and family assets. However, many people lie about this—so you may want to hire a private investigator, accountant, or appraiser to trace income and assets.

Many times, a spouse who is planning a divorce may "forget" to mention a raise or a bonus, and put the money in a hidden account. Careful examination of the couple's tax return can show a lot. For instance, if you discover that the amount of interest or dividends on the return is larger than could be accounted for by the accounts or stock you know about, it could mean that your spouse has secret accounts— secret from you, but not hidden from the IRS, which has ways of finding out about them.

If your spouse owns a business, or practices a profession, it's also important to examine the business records. Don't be surprised if the business-owning spouse pleads poverty—but after you examine the business's records (if necessary, the court will issue a subpoena forcing the spouse to turn them over), which are also shown to investors and banks who lend money to the business—you're likely to find a healthy balance of assets.

Even while you're negotiating the terms of your eventual divorce, you can do a lot to make compliance with the agreement more likely.

- Don't insist on an unreasonable, punitive disposition of property or vengefully high continuing payments. Not only will your spouse be less willing to comply, but the court will be less willing to approve or enforce an arrangement like that.
- Don't make visitation unduly difficult. Not only does it punish the children by denying a relationship with the noncustodial parent, but it makes it much less likely that the parent who is shut out will keep on writing checks to support the children he or she hardly ever sees.
- Concentrate on increasing the property settlement, if necessary by agreeing to smaller continuing payments (maintenance, child support). That way, you'll have assets (which can be sold or used as loan collateral, if you have to), plus funds to invest.
- Get an injunction (restraining order) preventing your spouse from transferring assets at all until the divorce is final—and for less than their fair market value after the divorce. This prevents your spouse from "selling" valuable assets to friends for a few dollars, then claiming that he or she lacks the money to make payments. The classic— and probably apocryphal—instance of this is the newspaper ad offering a brand-new sports car for $100. The first lucky caller is told that the offer is both legal and perfectly legitimate: "My husband ran

away with his secretary, and he told me to sell his car and send him the money."

• Ask your lawyer to review your state's procedures for enforcing separation agreements and divorce decrees. Before you need them, get the addresses and phone numbers of courts and government agencies that can help you collect overdue amounts.

Choosing a Lawyer

You need a divorce lawyer with plenty of training and experience—not just in your state's divorce law, but in taxes and financial planning. I think you're better off with a polite, even conciliatory lawyer than with one who aims at steamrollering the opponent (and the opponent's lawyer). The more screaming (or deadly politeness), the longer the whole process takes, and the more ill feelings linger.

The best alternative is for each spouse to have a lawyer throughout the whole process of negotiation and litigation. This costs more than if they share a lawyer—but avoids a host of possible problems. There are ethical problems for a lawyer who tries to represent clients whose interests differ. Should the lawyer try to safeguard the richer spouse's assets, or try to get as much money as possible for the poorer client? (The lawyers' ethical code makes it clear that a lawyer is allowed to represent both spouses *only* if the divorce is uncontested and the spouses are in substantial agreement about the major issues.)

It's often a good idea to involve an accountant in the divorce process in addition to the lawyers. This is especially true if you have a complex tax situation, or if one spouse is trying to find out if the other is concealing income or assets.

Divorce Mediation

A divorce mediator is another professional who can help expedite a fair financial settlement. Divorce mediation started because many people feel that the legal system itself creates problems. The court system is an "adversary" system, whose aim is to designate a winner and a loser—not to find out the objective facts. In this analysis, the adversary system causes delays and involves lawyers who are more interested in complete destruction of the other party than in a quick, fair settlement. (Not incidentally, a drawn-out, hostile procedure generates more legal fees than a fast, amicable one.)

Although I'm a lawyer myself, I have to concede that there's some truth in these allegations. But I don't think that "do-it-yourself" divorce is a good alternative. It's true that you can buy divorce kits, complete with instructions, in most states. Even if you can't, you can get the official forms at the courthouse, and get more or less help from the court clerk in filling them out. In all probability, you can get yourself a divorce that will be legal and will allow you to remarry—but it's just as likely that you won't make the best financial and tax deal without professional help.

One way to cope is to use a divorce mediator to supplement the services of your lawyer. Some divorce mediators are lawyers; others are psychologists, social workers, or specialists in arbitration. Their job is to work with the spouses, find out what areas they agree on, and help them find an amicable solution to disagreements. The goal is to make an agreement that's fair to both sides, and this will be carried out by both sides.

Sometimes the mediator meets with each spouse in turn, "shuttling" between them; but usually both spouses join the mediator for the discussions. The risk is that either the mediator will dominate the discussion, imposing personal ideas of fairness, or that the spouse who dominated the marriage will continue to dominate the mediation sessions. Feminists caution that women may suffer in the mediation process, bargaining away their fair share of the couple's property or fair maintenance and child support.

So if you choose mediation, make sure your mediator won't take control of the discussions—and check his or her credentials and experience. There's no licensing process for divorce mediators, and anyone can hang out a shingle.

For an agreement reached through mediation to have legal effect, it must be written up as a separation agreement or placed in a court's decree. Usually, the lawyer(s) handle that; ideally, the mediator and the lawyers work together. Otherwise, if the couple and mediator are not sophisticated about financial and tax issues, they could arrive at an agreement that has bad tax consequence, or that leaves one spouse short of cash. And even if a lawyer points this out, the couple may be unwilling to go back to "square one" and renegotiate the agreement that was arrived at so painfully.

In short, divorce mediation is not a substitute for top-flight legal advice. But it *can* greatly reduce the hostility involved in a divorce. Anyway, it's a lot cheaper to do your negotiating with the help of one person paid $50 an hour than having two lawyers yell at each other at $100 an hour apiece.

Working with Your Lawyer

One of your lawyer's functions is to teach you about your state's divorce laws, and what you can expect.

• How long the process will take; if you must go to court for a hearing, and if so, what's involved (anything from standing in a courtroom with a bunch of other people who want divorces, raising your right hand, and being told you're all divorced—to a six-week jury trial with dozens of witnesses); how high you can expect the legal fees to be; how they're computed and paid (some lawyers charge a flat fee, others a fee per hour; the amount to be paid in advance and the billing practices also vary).

• The pros and cons of getting a fault divorce if your state has both fault and no-fault divorce. To sum up, if you charge a fault ground, you have to prove it—which can be difficult; the case will take longer to resolve. Depending on the state (and the fault ground), the "guilty" spouse may not be entitled to support payments; fault can also affect entitlement to equitable distribution. Filing for divorce on fault grounds can be a strategy: The hope is that the other spouse will be so embarrassed that he or she will offer a better settlement if you agree to change the case to a no-fault one.

•Whether a "conversion" divorce is a possibility. Some states (New York is an example) allow conversion divorces. That is, the couple can file for a legal separation, not a divorce. They negotiate a separation agreement, then abide by its terms. After they've been separated for the length of time specified by state law, they can "convert" the legal separation to a divorce by applying to the relevant court. This is an easy, comparatively nontraumatic and inexpensive procedure.

Separation Agreements

For most couples in the process of divorce, negotiating a separation agreement is the most important step. Depending on state law and the facts of the case, it may be impossible to get a divorce without a separation agreement (many no-fault laws are set up this way); or it may make the process much easier (if the court hearing the divorce case can adopt the separation agreement and turn it into an order of the court).

Divorce courts have the power to review separation agreements, and can strike out provisions that they feel are unfair or oppressive, substituting provisions that seem more appropriate to the judge. Usually, though, the court approves the agreement and issues a divorce decree ending the marriage.

The couple has two choices: The separation agreement can either "merge" in the court's decree or "survive" it. (The separation agreement is written either to say "This agreement merges into the decree of the court," or "This agreement will survive the decree of the court.") The choice between merger and survival is an important negotiating issue.

If the separation agreement "survives," then the agreement remains in force as a private contract. That means that neither spouse can have the other one penalized for contempt of court for failure to obey the separation agreement. But the trade-off is that neither spouse can go back to the divorce court and ask for a modification of the provisions of the separation agreement (such as a reduction in alimony payments). Both spouses must consent to any modifications—and it's unlikely that either spouse will do that without getting something in return.

If the agreement "merges," it becomes part of the official decree of the court. Violations can mean contempt penalties (fines, or even a jail term). A person who signs an agreement which merges can go back to court and ask that the decree be modified if circumstances change. This is often done when the paying spouse remarries. It's up to the court, and not the other spouse, to decide when modification is appropriate. So merger creates a benefit and a corresponding risk for both spouses:

tougher enforcement powers balanced against the risk that the court will later modify the decree at the request of the other spouse.

Equitable Distribution

Separation agreements are central to the process of divorce because all states either follow "community property" principles (that is, all marital property is deemed to belong to both spouses, and must be divided— either straight down the middle or in a way that is fair) or "equitable distribution" principles. Equitable distribution means that the contributions that both spouses made to the marriage (monetary and otherwise) must be considered in dividing property—so must their needs. In most states, fault is not considered in equitable distribution, but a few states limit or deny equitable distribution to a "guilty" spouse.

The spouses themselves can use the separation agreement to decide what division of property would be fair; if there's no separation agreement, or if the court won't approve the agreement, the court must make a division of property.

The first step (either for spouses negotiating an agreement or for the court) is to find out just what the couple owns, and which assets should be considered separate property of the individual spouse (for instance, assets they owned before the marriage and brought with them to the marriage), and which assets are marital property to be divided between the spouses.

Usually, property the spouses owned before marriage remains their separate property—unless the owner took steps to turn it into joint property (by giving a half-interest to the spouse, for instance), the separate property won't be subject to division. Similarly, any property accumulated during marriage is usually considered marital property subject to equitable distribution. States treat gifts and inheritances to one spouse during marriage, and income building up on separate property during the marriage, in various ways: Sometimes these will be separate property; sometimes they'll be treated as marital property.

Next, a value must be set for each asset—easy enough for 100 shares of an actively traded stock (just look in the newspaper—as long as you've decided which day's value will count!). It's a little tougher for a house (how much do comparable properties sell for—and which properties are comparable, anyhow?), and really tough for a small business or an art collection. Last but not least, it must be determined how the property will be divided—not just the percentage of the total each spouse will receive, but who will get specific assets. This makes a big difference for tax purposes.

Although there are variations from state to state, and from case to case, factors like these are used to decide what division of marital property is equitable.

- How long the marriage lasted
- Each spouse's age and health

• Each spouse's employability and earning capacity (taking child care responsibilities into account)
• The value of each spouse's separate property; the income he or she gets from it
• The amount of alimony or maintenance to be paid by the richer to the poorer spouse
• The tax effect of the division
• Marital misconduct (in some states), including "dissipation" of family assets—whether by a long-term pattern of gambling or excessive spending, or a predivorce credit-card binge or raid on the safe-deposit box

Advanced Degrees

One of the toughest points involves the treatment of one spouse's professional degree, obtained with the help of a spouse who worked to keep the student spouse in school—and who may have given up professional aspirations or postponed having children to do so. A few states simply say that the professional degree itself, or a license to practice a profession, is a marital asset which can be divided. A few states say that the degree isn't an asset at all, and the ability to earn more belongs entirely to the spouse with the degree and doesn't have to be shared. However, there are other approaches.

• The spouse who supported the other spouse can be given extra maintenance (but not an extra share of marital property) as a reward.
• A spouse who gave up professional opportunities can be granted rehabilitative alimony (short-term alimony to allow him or her to get professional training), or a larger share of property, to pay back the amount spent on the other spouse's education.
• Although the degree or license is treated as separate property, the value of the professional practice minus its assets (e.g., X-ray machine, lawbooks) can be treated as a marital asset.

Alimony

Alimony, which is also known as maintenance and spousal support, is different from equitable distribution. Equitable distribution is a one-time division of the couple's property. The theory is that each spouse takes the property he or she already owns. Alimony, however, is a payment or series of continuing payments made by the richer spouse to the poorer spouse, as a substitute for the support provided during the marriage.

It's easy to confuse lump-sum alimony payments with equitable distribution (and just as easy for the IRS to become equally confused)—so make sure the separation agreement and divorce decree make it clear how lump sums should be treated. A paying spouse who falls behind on alimony or child support is often ordered to make a lump-sum payment to catch up; here, too, the court should make it clear whether the lump sum is equitable distribution or a support payment because the tax consequences are very different. And if you're the paying spouse, and send a single check that covers several purposes (alimony, child support, and catching up on past payments), either indicate how the check should be divided, or use a separate check for each.

As explained on page 233, a spouse can get "temporary alimony" to support himself or herself for the period between the filing of a divorce case and the time it's heard. Once the case has been heard, "permanent alimony" may be ordered. But "permanent" in this case simply means that it isn't temporary and limited to the pretrial period: It doesn't last forever.

Some states forbid permanent alimony; others limit it to spouses who are not and cannot become self-supporting. Some state laws specify the maximum amount of time for which alimony can be ordered (two, four, or six years). It's common for "rehabilitative alimony" to be ordered: This is short-term alimony to rehabilitate a spouse by providing funds for education or professional training to increase earning capacity. Finally, in some states, alimony will be restricted or denied for spouses proved "guilty" of fault.

If you're going to be on the paying end, your job as a negotiator is to find reasons (whether practical or based on state law) why alimony should be denied or limited.

If you're going to be on the receiving end, your job is either to make sure you have a right to receive alimony that, combined with child support (if you're a custodial parent) and your salary and assets, will permit you to support yourself and your children—or to make sure that you get a large enough share under equitable distribution to take care of your needs.

It's very important to do this negotiating before you get to court. Very few spouses get large amounts of court-awarded alimony. Many judges feel that *anybody* can get a well-paid job (regardless of background, work history, or child-care obligations) and, therefore, are reluctant to order large amounts of alimony. And even if the divorce decree says that you're entitled to a certain level of alimony and child support, that doesn't mean you'll be able to collect it!

Whichever side you're on, take a careful look at the tax consequences of alimony. In general, the person who pays alimony gets a tax deduction (especially helpful for a person in the highest tax bracket)— and the person who gets alimony has to pay taxes on it.

Child Support and Custody

However, child support does not have tax consequences—if you pay it, you don't get a tax deduction; if you receive it, you don't have to pay taxes on it.

One of the most important functions of a separation agreement or divorce decree is to decide the custody of any children born of the marriage. Usually, one parent will have legal custody of all the children, and the other parent will have visitation rights as provided by the agreement or decree.

However, other arrangements are possible. "Split custody" means that one parent has legal custody of some of the children; the other has custody of the rest. "Shared custody" means that one spouse has legal custody during the school year, the other during vacations. "Joint custody" means that both parents are legal custodians of the children, with equal legal rights to—and responsibility for—making decisions about the children's future.

Joint custody is a controversial legal issue. Some states have a presumption in favor of joint custody; in these states, a good reason must be shown for one parent to get exclusive legal custody. Other states have a presumption *against* joint custody; if you want it, you have to prove that it's in the best interests of the children.

Joint custody makes it more likely that the parents will continue to have some sort of relationship after the divorce because they have to make plans for the children. This can be a real source of stress for the ex-spouses, but can result in a stronger relationship between parents and children. It's also been found that parents with joint custody tend to be more conscientious about making child-support payments. But joint custody is not a cure-all; postdivorce financial and emotional problems are still likely to occur.

Child custody also affects the disposition of the family home. Usually, both spouses agree that the children should not have to move (and disrupt their school life and other activities) unless it's absolutely necessary. So the parent with custody (or the parent with whom the children live most of the time) will probably continue to live in what used to be the family home. However, various legal arrangements can be made.

- As part of the equitable distribution process, the custodial parent can be awarded the family home outright, while the other parent gets other marital property.
- The noncustodial parent can get ownership of the family home, but the custodial parent continues to live in it—either permanently or until the youngest child grows up and leaves home. Sometimes the custodial parent pays rent for the home; sometimes he or she lives rent-free, and this factor is considered in setting alimony and child support levels.
- The spouses can own the family home jointly (again, the spouse who actually lives there may have to pay rent to the other spouse). Maybe they'll sell it when the last child leaves home, and split the proceeds.
- As a last resort, if money is very tight, the family home may be sold, and the sale proceeds divided between the spouses.

In real life, not every "family home" is a single-family house. If the family lives in an apartment, it's important for the separation agreement or divorce decree to straighten out which spouse has the right to stay in the apartment after the divorce, whether he or she is entitled to a new lease from the landlord when the current lease expires (this is a matter of local landlord-tenant law as well as negotiation between the spouses), and who has the right to buy the apartment if the apartment building is converted to co-op or condominium form. These "insider's rights" can be worth thousands of dollars, so they can't be neglected during the negotiations.

Modification of Decrees

Even the best-negotiated settlement and the best-argued court case can deal only with the facts that existed at a certain time. If the facts change later, what used to be a fair and workable arrangement can become intolerable. Therefore, courts have the power to modify divorce decrees (including separation agreements that are merged into the decree).

It's important to realize that even if the separation agreement survives the divorce decree, courts still have the power to modify the provisions dealing with custody and child support. The court's duty to protect the best interests of the children prevails over the parents' right to draft their own contract.

The general standard is that courts will modify divorce decrees if the person seeking the modification can prove a meaningful change in circumstances. It's common for paying spouses to ask for modification because their own income has decreased, or they've taken on new obligations by remarrying and having more children. The paying spouse may also want to limit or terminate the obligation because the receiving spouse has a "live-in" relationship. Receiving spouses also seek modifications—upward, this time—to cope with increases in the cost of living.

Modification is very much a matter of individual circumstances. Courts are not at all sympathetic to paying spouses who quit well-paid jobs, then claim they can't afford to pay alimony or child support. Surprisingly, courts also usually refuse to modify a maintenance order just because the receiving spouse is living with an unmarried partner. Unless the separation agreement or divorce decree specifically states that payments will end if the receiving spouse cohabits, the court will probably look at the economic, not the moral, aspects of the situation. Modification will probably be denied unless the live-in lover is supporting the ex-spouse, not just sharing expenses the way a roommate would.

Enforcement after the Divorce

Once the divorce has been granted, it's common for paying spouses to fall behind on their obligations. If you're the receiving spouse, the first step in effective enforcement is not to fly off the handle immediately. There's an understandable tendency to believe that unless the check arrives on or before the due date (preferably by special messenger), the ex-spouse has undertaken a dastardly plot to avoid all future payments. But often, the check really *is* in the mail, or there will be a slight delay but the full amount will arrive close to the scheduled date.

If that doesn't work, the next step is to see if informal means of enforcement can work. Maybe your ex-spouse has a temporary financial bind that will be cured as soon as a customer pays a bill, or after the business's busy season; maybe he or she can make up the difference by adding a few extra dollars to the next few checks.

If that fails, it will be necessary to use the legal system's methods of enforcement. Timing is important here. Courts won't be too sympathetic if you rush to sue when a $15 check is one day late—but they won't be any more sympathetic if you wait six years and then expect your ex-spouse to produce thousands of dollars at one time. In fact, it may become legally impossible to collect arrears (overdue payments) once a certain amount of time has elapsed. Discuss your state's laws with your lawyer *before* the divorce.

If your separation agreement has not merged, your remedy is to sue your ex-spouse for breach of contract. If the agreement has merged, your ex-spouse may be guilty of contempt of court. However, contempt of court means more than mere failure to pay: It requires that a person who had the resources to pay deliberately refused to abide by the court's order.

Depending on the facts and on state law, it may be possible to have your ex-spouse's property seized and sold to pay arrears. It may also be possible to get an "income execution order" (popularly called a "garnishee") directing your ex-spouse's employer to pay part of his or her salary to you. Labor law protects employees against being fired just because their income has been attached to pay debts—including debts to an ex-spouse.

Enforcement in Other States

It's tough enough to collect when your ex-spouse lives three miles away—it might seem impossible to collect when he or she lives 3,000 miles away. But you don't always have to sue in the courts of the state where your ex-spouse now lives. All the states have adopted a law called the Uniform Reciprocal Enforcement of Support Act (URESA), so ex-spouses can collect child support (but not alimony) from a separated or divorced spouse in another state—without spending money on a lawyer or private investigator.

A parent who has already been awarded child support can "register" the court's decree with the courts in the state where the other parent is now living. A parent who needs child support, but who hasn't been awarded it, can file a petition in the courts of his or her own state. The other parent will be summoned to court, given a chance to tell his or her side of the story, and in appropriate cases, that state's courts will order the noncustodial parent to pay child support (including unpaid back child support).

To put teeth into this process, the court in the "responding" state can order the noncustodial parent to make payments directly into court, instead of to the ex-spouse, require a cash deposit or other bond as security for the payments, and hold the paying spouse in contempt of court if he or she doesn't pay up as required.

The Child Support Enforcement Amendments of 1984 help in cases where URESA doesn't work. Each state is now required to have procedures for collecting child support—including deducting the payments from the parent's income, putting liens on real estate he or she owns, and intercepting tax refunds. States can also report nonpayment of child support to credit bureaus. A child support order can also require a parent to include children in his or her health insurance—a point to keep in mind if you're a custodial parent without health insurance for your children.

Divorce and Taxes

Not only must a couple planning divorce decide how to share their property, they must also find ways of making and collecting continuing payments; they'll also want to arrange their financial affairs to save taxes.

One thing you won't have to worry about: Transfers of property between spouses (whether related to a divorce or not) are never subject to gift tax and have no effect on income tax as long as the couple files a joint return.

A couple can file a joint return in any year in which they're separated, but if they're divorced on December 31, they're considered unmarried for the entire year. They must file either as single persons or as heads of household (unless they remarry during the year). This can be a major negotiating point for the spouse with less money, who's in a lower tax bracket. He or she simply refuses to sign a joint tax return unless the other spouse (who has more to lose by filing as a married person filing separately, at higher tax rates) provides some financial incentive.

Property transfers made under equitable distribution don't have immediate tax consequences—if your spouse transfers the family home, or 200 shares of General Motors stock to you, you won't have to pay income tax on the transfer.

The problem gets more complicated when the property transferred is "appreciated" property (property that has increased in value since the couple acquired it). Although there is no tax on the appreciation at the time of the transfer, the spouse who gets the property must pay income tax on the profit when he or she sells the property. Furthermore, the taxable profit is the difference between the sale price and the price at which the property was acquired in the first place. This can mean a big—and unexpected—tax bill; and it's especially painful because there are no more special, low tax rates for capital gains, and it's no longer possible to use income averaging to blunt the pain of unusually high taxes in one year.

How does this rule apply when the family home is transferred from one spouse to another, or transferred from joint ownership to ownership by one spouse? Neither spouse has a profit, so neither has to worry about the "rollover" rules or the one-time exclusion of home-sale profits for senior citizen taxpayers. (See page 175 for a discussion of these tax breaks for homeowners.) If the family home was jointly owned before the divorce, and the spouses sell it to someone else, both spouses are entitled to use the "rollover" provisions so they won't have to pay taxes on the profits.

Similarly, both of them qualify for the once-in-a-lifetime exclusion of home-sale profits earned by a taxpayer over the age of 55. But it really is a one-time tax break; if a divorced person remarries, he or she will not get a second senior-citizen exclusion to go with the new spouse.

Alimony, Child Support, and Taxes

Alimony is taxable income when it's received, and a tax deduction for the paying spouse when it's paid. This is true of catch-up payments for back alimony as well as current payments. Child support is neither deductible nor taxable.

If the separation agreement or divorce decree fails to separate out alimony from child support, the whole shooting match is taxed as alimony *unless* the amount is scheduled to change based on something to do with the children. Let's say the agreement calls for payments of $400 a month, dropping to $300 a month when the older child reaches 18, $200 a month when the younger child reaches 18. This is treated as $200 of alimony, $200 child support, for tax purposes.

However, if the paying spouse sends a check that isn't large enough to cover both the alimony and the child support obligation, for tax purposes the check is applied first to child support until all the child support is paid—the check isn't divided proportionately.

As a result of the new tax code, personal exemptions have increased. Therefore, claiming a child as a dependent has more tax impact than ever before. The general rule is that the custodial parent gets to take the dependency deduction—unless he or she has definitely given up the right to claim the child as a dependent. (The old rule depended on the percentage of support each parent provided.)

This is another important subject for negotiation. The spouse who has custody can make the decision to keep or give up the deduction on an annual basis (and the other spouse's promptness in making payments will be a motivating factor); he or she doesn't have to make a once-and-for-all surrender.

The new tax code also requires divorcing spouses to supply one another with their Social Security numbers—and to report the receiving spouse's number if an alimony deduction is taken. That makes it easier for the IRS to see if the receiving spouse paid income tax on the alimony.

Defining Alimony Just because a payment is alimony for practical purposes doesn't necessarily make it alimony for tax purposes. To count as alimony under the Internal Revenue Code, payments must be:

• In cash—emeralds, shares of stock, and sports cars are too reminiscent of equitable-distribution property settlements.
• Made under either a written separation agreement or court decree; informal payments don't count.
• Made at a time when the couple are living in separate households. The deduction is unavailable if they're living in the same home— even if they can't afford a second household, and even if they refuse to speak to each other.

Large sums of alimony have a further set of rules. If the payments are supposed to be over $10,000 a year, they will not count as alimony *unless* they are also supposed to be made for six years or more. Once again, the idea is to prevent a paying spouse from agreeing to a large property settlement in one year (or stretching over two or three years), then claiming an alimony deduction for the settlement. But this provision adds a few fascinating zingers to the already complex business of negotiating a divorce.

It's a real incentive for the receiving spouse to sign a separation agreement because it's very unlikely that a court will order alimony lasting more than six years to a spouse who is capable of being self-supporting. But if the paying spouse pushes too hard and cuts down on the number of years alimony must be paid, the alimony deduction can disappear—and the paying spouse is stuck footing the entire bill, with no help from Uncle Sam.

Once that's under your belt, you should be aware that the tax code also includes "recapture" provisions. If the so-called alimony in the first year after the divorce is more than $15,000 higher than the average of the payments in the second and third years (or the second-year payment "bulges" more than $15,000 over the third-year payment), then the paying spouse has to pay income taxes on the excess. The theory is that the paying spouse got an alimony deduction even though the payments weren't really alimony, and must pay back the excess deductions. The "recapture" rules apply whether both spouses agreed to the imbalance, or whether it occurred because the paying spouse fell behind on the payments.

However, recapture is not required if the payments stop because either the paying or receiving spouse dies, if the receiving spouse remarries, or if the payments go up and down because the receiving spouse is entitled to a share of the income of the paying spouse's business (which, naturally, fluctuates).

Summing Up

Now that you understand the basic financial principles behind divorce negotiations, you can use the following worksheet to estimate the amount that will be available for support payments. Remember, a divorce creates many additional living expenses (in addition to the costs of the divorce itself—lawyers, accountants, court costs, etc.).

WORKSHEET

1. Give the monthly income each spouse earns: H $_____ W $_____
2. Give the amount of income-producing property the couple owns (marital property only; not separate property): $ _____

3. Monthly income from this property: $ _____

4. How do you propose to divide this property?   H_____% W_____%

5. If you now live in an apartment, give the monthly rent: $ _____
6. If you now live in a house, co-op, or condo, give the monthly mortgage payment (plus maintenance fees): $ _____

7. Which spouse will stay in the family home?   H_____   W_____
8. Will the spouse who moves out have to contribute to the costs of the family

   home? No:_____Yes: $_____a month.
9. Will the spouse who remains in the family home have to pay rent to the other

   spouse? No:_____Yes: $_____a month.
10. For each spouse, estimate monthly expenses for the postdivorce period (when there will be two households). The custodial parent should include the expenses for the children:

	H	W
Rent/mortgage	$_____	_____
Food	$_____	_____
Clothing	$_____	_____
Taxes	$_____	_____
Work/business expenses	$_____	_____
Automobile expenses	$_____	_____
Utilities	$_____	_____
Loans, credit card payments	$_____	_____
Medical expenses/ health insurance	$_____	_____
Life insurance	$_____	_____
Tuition/ education expenses	$_____	_____

IRA/other
retirement plan $_____   _____

Entertainment $_____   _____

Other $_____   _____

Total $_____   _____

11. Take the salary figure from Item 1; add income from assets that are separate
    property, plus income from each spouse's share of the marital property, if
    divided as you propose.
TOTAL INCOME FOR EACH SPOUSE:

                   $_____ $_____

                            * * *

With any luck at all, each spouse's income will be higher than his
or her expenses. However, the usual result is that the custodial parent
will have a "shortfall": His or her expenses will exceed income. The best
result would be for the paying spouse's income to be high enough above
expenses to enable him or her to make up the difference. Again, the
usual result is that the paying spouse can't afford this. If this is your
situation, review the figures again, and see where you can cut down
expenses and perhaps increase income, to bring the paying spouse's
ability to pay closer to the receiving spouse's and children's needs.

57. REAL LIFE: GREG CLOW

Greg Clow doesn't think of himself as a part-time father. He loves both his
children, he worries about both of them, and he wants both of them to have the
best things in life—including the education to prepare them for successful careers.

But only one of Greg's children, his two-year-old daughter Marie, lives with
Greg and his wife Lisa. Greg's son, five-year-old Paul, lives with his mother,
Greg's ex-wife Janice. His weekends with Paul are great (but sometimes he
wishes that he had more time with Lisa and Marie). He and Lisa earn good
salaries. In fact, sometimes it surprises Greg that his family income is so high;
he never expected to earn so much. But he never expected that his expenses
would be so high, either. At the end of the year, there isn't all that much left for
vacations, home improvements, savings, investments—but Greg knows that he
can't neglect the investment program that will secure the children's future.

Greg knows that his income is crucial to two families, not just one. If anything
happens to him, well, both Janice and Lisa are working, and the children won't
starve. But the first thing to go will be their chance to go to a private college
instead of the state university; the next thing to go will be their chance to go to

the state university without working their way through. And there may be some months when a high utility bill means no new clothes, no new basketball shoes, no piano lessons.

To protect both his children and both his families, Greg is looking for security. He won't indulge in speculative investments that might mean big bucks (and, more likely, will mean a big hole in the bank account). Although he's far from a millionaire, he feels his tax burden is too high, so he wants to take advantage of whatever shelter opportunities exist after the Tax Code of 1986. Because his children are young, he has a long-term investment outlook; he wants safe growth, preferably with tax-shelter aspects.

The Numbers

Greg earns $42,000 a year as assistant personnel manager of a medium-sized metal casting company. Lisa earns $28,000 a year as a nurse practitioner. They also have investments worth about $50,000, which give them about $5,000 a year in interest and dividends. So they have $75,000 a year in income (and they can borrow against the value of their investments, if necessary).

Just before Marie was born, Greg and Lisa bought a house in a pleasant neighborhood where property values were on the rise. It proved to be a good investment: now they have $50,000 equity in the house (which can be tapped for a home equity loan or credit line, if they need it). But they paid only $750 a month for the apartment where they lived as newlyweds; now they pay about $15,000 a year for the mortgage, property tax, and insurance. (Insurance on the mortgage and property tax are tax-deductible.)

Even given these and other deductions, their income tax works out to almost $20,000 a year. To Lisa and Greg, this seems like a millionaire level of tax, and much too much for a working couple to pay. In fact, it's one of their largest expenses—larger than the mortgage; larger than their living costs ($14,500 a year pays for food, clothing, baby-sitters, commuter tickets, and other necessities of life); and much larger than the alimony and child support ($8,000 a year) which Greg has always been conscientious about paying. They also spend about $3,200 a year on an auto loan and life insurance. Their expenses total about $60,700. They're doing pretty well because their income is $75,000. That gives them $14,300 a year to enhance their standard of living, or to invest to meet future goals.

The Answers

Greg Clow needs a financial services professional to explain his needs to him. After drawing up a "capital needs assessment," the planner tells Greg that he is running short on life insurance, considering the fact that he is a member of two families. And Lisa Clow has no life insurance at all. Lisa needs a policy; Greg needs at least one policy to benefit Paul, one to benefit Lisa and Marie. (He may also need to provide for Janice, depending on his own wishes and the way financial arrangements for their divorce were structured.)

For the Clows, there are three choices: term insurance, whole-life (with a lower face value, but cash value and tax advantages), and investment-oriented variable- or universal-life coverages. The choice depends on which of the packages offered to them offers the best combination of price, return, financial and tax advantages. If they choose an investment-oriented product, they'll need a smaller investment portfolio.

They have a reasonable amount to invest each year: almost $14,000, less the cost of additional insurance. They don't really need additional income; they do need to know that funds will be available in the long term, for college expenses and their own retirement. Good choices include:

• Growth stocks where the Clows can think of themselves as investors for the long term; they should favor stocks to "buy and hold" over quick plunges in and out of the market.
• Bonds with maturity dates calibrated to retirement and college entrance dates.
• Tax-exempt municipal bonds (but if tax-free income is the goal, they must be careful to pick tax-exempt bonds, not the new taxable "munis").
• If they don't want to monitor individual investments, they should think about long-term growth funds, well-managed bond funds, or unit trusts (see page 107 for the difference), or growth and income funds. They should probably avoid "junk bond" funds (because they don't really need more income, and definitely don't need high risks) and "aggressive growth" funds and "over the counter" funds (again, too risky).

For tax shelter, they might consider shifting some of their existing investments to the tax-exempt sector, and they should look at investments that are likely to increase in value instead of those that pay immediate dividends or interest because the increase in value is not taxed until the asset is disposed of. Real estate might fit this profile—but the choice of properties, or syndications, REITs, or REMICS (see page 126 for a discussion) should not be made without independent professional advice from someone who is savvy about both the real estate market and taxes.

The more assets they accumulate, and the more their assets appreciate in value, the more likely it is that Greg and Lisa will have taxable estates. So they'll need estate-planning advice for the best way to set up their wills, trusts, and giving programs (see page 286). Creating a trust for the benefit of each child might be a good practical and estate-planning move (because it assures that assets and income will be ready when tuition bills come due, and because assets are removed from the creator's estate). However, until the children reach age 14, there will be no "income-splitting" advantage because their investment income is generally taxed at the parents' rates (see page 252 for an explanation of the "kiddie tax").

58. Coping with Tax Problems

There are three situations in which you may have to deal with the federal income tax system: filing a tax return and paying your taxes, long-range planning to reduce taxes in the future, and dealing with the IRS when you're audited or when the IRS claims you've underpaid your taxes.

The Tax Code of 1986 (TC '86) makes enormous changes in America's tax system. Some of these changes are helpful: Many low-income people are now exempt from federal income taxes. Some middle- and high-income people will be paying lower taxes because there are fewer tax brackets (only three; the old system had fourteen) and the maximum tax rate is lower (33%, instead of 50%).

However, only some taxpayers will pay less tax because the new tax system also eliminates many of the deductions that people used to reduce their tax bills. Sales taxes are no longer deductible; it's harder to qualify for a deduction for medical expenses, casualty and theft losses, and miscellaneous deductions (because you don't get a deduction unless the amount you want to deduct is higher than a certain percentage of your income).

You used to get a significant tax break if you had profits from selling investments, rather than interest income or ordinary salary income. Under the new system, "capital gains" are treated almost exactly like "ordinary income." (See page 139, covering the tax treatment of investments, for more on this subject.)

In short, theoretically you'll pay lower tax rates under the new system—but you'll be taxed on more of your income.

Withholding

You fill out a W-4 form at work, telling your employer how many "withholding allowances" you claim (see page 41). With this as a basis, your employer withholds money from each paycheck (and sends it to the federal government) to pay your income and Social Security taxes. Every year, your employer sends you a W-2 form summarizing your earnings and the amount withheld.

The employer is supposed to send out the W-2 form by January 31. Make a fuss if you don't get it by mid-February: Not only do you need the information to pay your taxes, you have to attach the W-2 form to your tax return.

Most people are "over-withheld." That is, the amount taken out of their paychecks is larger than the amount of federal tax they must pay, and they are entitled to a tax refund after all their deductions are taken into account. Most people who get tax refunds welcome them—but in fact, if you get a tax refund, it means that you let the government use *your* money without paying interest on it.

It usually makes more sense to increase the number of withholding allowance you claim, to reduce or eliminate your tax refund. (But make sure you still pay most or all of your tax obligation, otherwise, you'll have to make up the difference with your tax return, and pay a penalty for underpayment.) When does it make sense to be over-withheld? If you find it difficult to save, you might let Uncle Sam set up a "forced savings" plan for you—then use your tax refund to fund your IRA or reduce your credit card balance or invest.

Estimated Taxes

Some taxpayers find themselves in the opposite situation: Withholding doesn't even come close to covering their tax obligations. This could happen if the taxpayers have a lot of income that is not subject to withholding (if they're free-lancers, not regular employees; if they have a lot of investment income; if they earned a lot of profits by selling a home or stocks or bonds). They have two choices: Either they can pay a heavy tax penalty each year for underpayment of taxes, or they can make estimated tax payments four times a year (in January, April, June, and September) to make up the difference between the amount withheld and the full amount of tax they owe.

If you find yourself in this situation, what you want is Form 1040-ES, a short, simple form (it's about the size of a business envelope). You give your name, Social Security number, the amount of estimated tax you think you'll owe for the full year, and the amount you're paying in this installment; you enclose a check for the amount of the installment (put your Social Security number on the check) and mail the 1040-ES and your check to the IRS Service Center for the area in which you live. You can start making estimated tax payments in April, June, or September (instead of January) if you have a sudden rush of extra income during the year.

You can get the 1040-ES from any IRS office, most banks, and some libraries; the instruction sheet will tell you which service center should get the form (and your check). Don't worry—once the IRS starts to think of you as an estimated taxpayer, you'll get a package of estimated tax forms (with neat little preaddressed envelopes) every year.

Filing an Annual Tax Return

Speaking of every year, you must file a tax return every year, as long as you have more than a few thousand dollars' worth of income. (The amount varies depending on your "filing" status—whether you're single, married, or a head of household, and on whether you're elderly or blind.) You must file a tax return even if you have paid all your taxes through withholding (and you'll want to file a tax return so that you can collect your refund, if the government owes you money).

Anyone who can be claimed as a dependent on another taxpayer's return, and who has more than $500 in "unearned" income (that is, investment income such as interest or dividends), *must* file a tax return. This requirement is imposed to prevent families from "shifting income" from a high-bracket parent to a low-bracket child by giving income-producing assets to the child. This used to be a good tax-planning idea before TC '86 changed the rules and imposed a "kiddie tax."

The purpose of the new "kiddie tax" rules is to tax the unearned income of children under the age of 14 at the parent's "highest" tax rate. (However, the first $1,000 of unearned income is exempt from this rule.) Children over 14 who have unearned income will be taxed at rates based on their total earned and unearned income—that is, they'll probably be in the lowest tax bracket. These rules have two practical effects. First, it probably doesn't make sense to transfer assets to children under 14 because you won't gain any tax benefit; there probably will be a tax benefit if you transfer assets to a child over 14, but the size of the benefit depends on the amount involved—you won't gain much if you transfer property that earns an annual income of $632.

Second, filling out a tax return for a child is even more complicated than filling one out for an adult because the rules for the standard deduction (amount of deduction you can claim without having receipts or other evidence to prove what you spent) and personal exemption (an amount that can be deducted from income, to take into account the fact that taxpayers have families of different sizes) are more complex for children. You *will* need to get a Social Security number for each child older than five (another new tax code requirement)—and you may need professional help in completing tax returns for your children if they have to file.

Many (Un)Happy Returns

If you have to file a tax return, you have to use one of the three forms in the "1040 series." Any taxpayer is allowed to use the "long form," Form 1040. Some taxpayers have to use the long form; others have a choice between the 1040 (which is longer and harder to fill out, but makes it possible to use a wide variety of deductions and credits to reduce their tax bills) and the shorter, simpler 1040EZ and 1040A.

Form 1040EZ is less than a page long; to use this form, you must:

• Be single
• Have no dependents
• Have a total taxable income under $50,000
• Get all your income from salary, tips, and interest—and if you have interest, it must not be more than $400; if it is, you must use the long form
• Not itemize your deductions

Form 1040A is two pages long; to use it, you must:

• Have less than $50,000 in total taxable income
• Get all your income from salaries, tips, dividends, and/or unemployment compensation
• Not itemize your deductions

If you are entitled to substantial itemized deductions (for instance, for large charitable contributions, medical expenses, casualty losses), you'll want to file Form 1040 so that you can use these deductions to reduce your tax bill. You *have* to file the long form, whether you want to or not, if:

• Your taxable income is over $50,000
• You're married, file a separate return, and your spouse itemizes deductions—if one spouse itemizes, both have to
• You have any income from self-employment

•You earned any profits (or took any losses) selling investments such as stocks, bonds, mutual fund shares, or investment real estate
•You're a landlord, and you have to pay taxes on the rent your tenants paid (but you can claim deductions for expenses of being a landlord)
•You sold your house, and have home-sale profits to report (even if you don't have to pay tax on them because of the "rollover" provision described on page 175, or the "over-55 exclusion" described on page 175)

If you're in a complicated tax situation, ask your tax advisor about the tax form(s) you'll need to file.

How to Get Tax Forms

Once you're a veteran taxpayer, the IRS will mail you a package of forms each year—based on the ones you used in the preceding year. However, if you're a brand-new taxpayer (welcome to the club!), or if your tax situation has changed, you'll need additional or different forms. You can:

•Get the forms from your tax preparer, if someone else prepares your taxes.
•Go to the nearest IRS office for the forms.
•Mail-order the forms you need directly from the IRS (allow plenty of time). The forms are free—so are helpful publications explaining various tax situations. If you live in the western states, the address is "Forms Distribution Center, P.O. Box 12626, Fresno, CA 93778"; in the midwest, it's "P.O. Box 9903, Bloomington, IL 61799"; in the east and south, write to "P.O. Box 25866, Richmond, VA, 23260."
•Get the forms from a bank, post office, or government office (for example, Social Security offices frequently carry the forms between January and April).
•See if your public library has a looseleaf book with official IRS forms; if it does, you can photocopy the forms you need—the IRS will accept the copies. Just be sure you get the current year's form instead of an obsolete one!

Your Filing Status

There are four filing status possibilities:

•Single—for people who were not married on December 31 of the year in question. (See below for the treatment of widows and widowers.) Single taxpayers pay the highest rates.
•Married and filing a joint return with your spouse. If you're married on December 31, you can file as a married person for the whole year; you don't have to divide the year into times when you were single and times when you were married. The rates for joint returns are the lowest, and you qualify for various tax breaks.

• Married, but filing a separate return from your spouse. There are only two good reasons to file a separate return: Either you have advice from a qualified professional that you are one of the rare taxpayers who can benefit from this strategy, or your spouse refuses to sign a joint return (usually because you're in the middle of an acrimonious divorce case).

• Head of household—you are single, and pay at least half the costs of maintaining a home for your child or for a parent who can be claimed as a dependent. Head-of-household tax rates are lower than rates for single people or married people filing separately, but higher than rates for married people filing jointly.

Tips for Preparing Tax Returns

• Collect all your information. (You'll need it even if a tax pro prepares your return.) You'll need W-2 forms from your employer(s), which show your salary and the amount of income and Social Security tax already withheld. Not only is this information important, but you'll have to attach a copy of each W-2 form to your tax return. Form 1099 is an "information return," telling you (and the IRS—it gets copies of all 1099s) how much income you earned from self-employment, interest, dividends, and other forms of income that are not subject to tax withholding. If you haven't gotten your W-2 and 1099 forms by early February, contact the organizations that paid you the income, and make a fuss until you do get the forms.

You'll also need a total of your charitable contributions, business expenses, child-care expenses, and other potential deductions. You can keep track of them throughout the year, as part of the budgeting process—or use the following worksheet:

WORKSHEET

1. Check off each form as you get it, and include the amount:

   ☐ W-2 form(s) $_____

   ☐ 1099 from_____Bank $_____

   ☐ 1099 from_____Bank $_____

   ☐ 1099 from your broker showing profit (loss) on the sale of_____

   ☐ 1099 from _____ Corp., showing dividends of $ _____

   ☐ 1099 from _____ Corp., showing dividends of $ _____

   ☐ Other 1099s (explain):_____

   _____

2. Other income: Your state tax refund from last year:

   $_____ Income from self-employment or moonligh-

   ting:_____

   $_____Rentals paid by tenants: $_____

   Other (explain): $_____

   _____

3. Medical expenses: Cost of transportation to get medical treatment, health insurance premiums paid, and the cost of eyeglasses, dentures, and hearing aids:

   Date   Description   Amount   Check #   Amt. Paid by Insurance

   ____   _____   _____   _____   _____

   ____   _____   _____   _____   _____

4. Charitable contributions: Property donated to charities (e.g., clothes donated to rummage sale)

   Date   Description   Charity   Check #   Amt./Value

   ____   _____   _____   _____   _____

   ____   _____   _____   _____   _____

5. Investment expenses: Seminars, investment publications, brokerage fees encountered in order to earn a profit on investments:

   Date   Description   Check #   Amount

   ____   _____   _____   _____

   ____   _____   _____   _____

6. Business expenses: Automobile mileage, business entertaining, air fare and hotel bills for business trips, etc.

Date   Description   Paid To   Check #   Amount   Am't Reimbursed

——   ————   ————   ————   ————   ——————————

——   ————   ————   ————   ————   ——————————

7. Child care expenses: If you are a single parent, or if both spouses work, give

the amount paid for child care so that you could work: $————————

8. IRA contributions: Date——————Amount $—————Contributed

to:——————————————Your Age:——————————————

9. IRA withdrawals: Date——————Amount $—————Withdrawn

from:——————————————Your Age:—————————

10. Alimony paid: $————————————————————————

Alimony received: $————————————————————————

* * *

•Start early. The earlier you file your tax return, the earlier you'll get your refund. And even if you owe tax, it makes a lot of sense to compile all your information and fill out the forms early—then sign and date them, write the check (don't forget to put your Social Security number on the check), and mail your return close to the due date. That way, you won't sit down on the evening of April 14—only to find out that you don't have all the forms you need, or that you don't have all the facts and figures required to fill out your return.

•The official package of forms from the IRS gives you two copies of each form—theoretically, one for scratchwork, one to file. But your nerves will be in much better shape if you get extra copies of the forms, or photocopy the ones in the package, so that you'll have plenty of extras if your computations result in a frantic mess of chicken-scratchings. If you do calculations on a separate sheet, label everything so that you can check your work—and you won't have to puzzle about from where a particular set of figures came.

•Pick up a copy of Form 4868 every year, "just in case." This form entitles you to a four-month automatic extension of time to file your tax return—so if you don't have the information you need, or if you throw in the towel and get a professional to do the return instead of doing it yourself, at least you won't have to pay penalties for late filing. However, this is not an extension of your time to pay. In other words, do this if you know you're entitled to a refund, but can't figure out how much—or send the IRS a generous amount of money, and straighten out the whole thing later. There are many situations in which you have a right to file an amended return on Form 1040X— and correct past tax mistakes, either paying the amount you owe or claiming a refund.

Tax Help from the IRS

Our tax system is complex, and not everyone can afford to hire a lawyer or accountant. For free advice, you can turn to the IRS.

- You can go to the nearest IRS office, or call, for advice. But watch out—if you follow advice from an IRS staffer, and the advice is wrong, you are subject to whatever interest and penalties would have been charged as if you'd made the mistake all by yourself. The IRS doesn't stand by the advice its personnel provide.
- IRS offices are busy places, especially during tax season (the first three and a half months of the year). To cut down on the congestion, IRS has a "Tele-Tax" service. You can dial a toll-free number, and listen to prerecorded tapes about 150 important tax topics (for instance, IRS services, steps in choosing a tax preparer, your rights if you're audited, bad debt deductions, and the appropriate forms to file). If you still haven't gotten your refund ten weeks after you file your return, you can also call "Automated Refund Information" and find out what happened.
- Many helpful—and free—IRS publications can be ordered from your forms distribution center. For instance, Publication 502 explains the tax treatment of medical and dental expenses, 504 gives tax help to divorced and separated taxpayers, and 526 explains when charitable contributions are deductible.

However, there are times when you won't be able to handle your tax problems all by yourself—even with help from the IRS. You could have a very complex tax situation: You might have to make decisions about business income and expenses; you might have moved from another state partway through the year, and have to file tax returns in two states; you might have to make decisions about tax accounting (for instance, whether certain expenses are deductible this year, or should be spread out over several years).

Then again, you might want advice on just how far you can go without breaking the law. As you can imagine, the IRS will interpret every controversial provision of tax law in the way that yields the highest tax bill! In either of these cases, you'll want professional help.

Tax Advisers

- *Tax preparers* (H&R Block is the best known) fill out tax returns; the price depends on the number of returns you need (federal only? federal and state? short form? long form with several forms and schedules attached?) and the complexity of your tax situation. Tax preparers don't give advice about tax strategies to follow in the future. The advantage of tax preparers is that you can get returns done quickly, conveniently (during tax season, there's probably an office near your home or place of business), and relatively inexpensively. The disadvantage is that the personnel may have only a limited amount of training, and won't be able to cope with complex tax problems; they may not know about recent developments, or subtle interpretations of the tax laws that entitle you to legitimate deductions.

•The *certified public accountant* (CPA) is the best tax adviser for most taxpayers. CPAs are trained to do tax planning as well as filling out forms. CPAs do most of their work during tax season—so don't expect a leisurely consultation if you drop by the office on a breezy day in April! In fact, it makes much more sense to shop for a CPA during the fall, for the following year's tax return. That way, you can talk to several, compare their fees, find one who'll be easy to work with, and get some advice about tax planning and record keeping.

•*Lawyers* are trained to interpret the tax code, IRS regulations, and court cases dealing with taxes. Lawyers who get an LL.M (master's degree) in taxation are especially well trained in the deepest subtleties of tax law. You might turn to a tax lawyer for sophisticated tax planning (for example, a strategy for dealing with a large estate), or if you're involved in a serious hassle with the IRS, and may have to go to court.

Tax Planning

The Tax Code of 1986 has made tax planning much more difficult—but much less important. It's more difficult because many deductions have been abolished, and well-established strategies (like transferring property to relatives in a lower tax bracket) won't work any more. It's much less important because there are fewer tax brackets and lower rates. It would make a tremendous difference if you could get income taxed at 11% instead of 70%; it doesn't make as much difference if income is taxed at 15%, not 33%.

However there are still some worthwhile tax-planning steps you can take.

•It's worthwhile to delay paying taxes, even if you'll have to pay them eventually. So consider adding some growth stocks to your portfolio—you won't have to pay taxes on the appreciation (increase in value) until you sell the stocks. And think seriously about getting or adding to an IRA. You may qualify for a tax deduction (see page 34)—you'll surely accumulate a valuable investment fund without paying taxes on appreciation until you retire and start drawing funds from the account. Similarly, 401(k) plans (see page 29) give you a chance to defer taxes and build a fund for secure retirement.

•You won't make meaningful tax savings by giving income-producing property (e.g., stocks with high dividends or bonds) to children under the age of 14 because of the "kiddie tax" explained on page 252. However, you may be able to save taxes by transferring property to older adolescents.

• See how tax-exempt bonds, bond funds, and money market funds compare to their taxable counterparts. In many cases, you'll earn more from these tax-free investments than you would from comparable taxable investments, after taxes.

• As explained on page 245, it makes a big difference to your tax bill *how* you divide assets during a divorce, who gets the appreciated assets, and whether payments from the richer to the poorer spouse are called alimony or child support. So get tax advice as part of the legal advice if you're getting a divorce—and negotiate hard for arrangements that meet your tax planning needs.

• The deduction for "consumer interest" (interest on obligations that is not mortgage interest, and is not business- or investment-related) is being phased out. For 1987, 65% of consumer interest remains tax-deductible; the percentage is only 40% for 1988, 20% for 1989, a mere 10% for 1990, and none after that. However, "qualified residence interest" (basically, interest on home equity loans—see page 189 for details) remains deductible, so it can make sense to substitute home equity loans for other forms of credit.

• Sometimes you can speed up or slow down expenses to fit your tax needs. For instance, if you have almost enough medical expenses to qualify for a deduction (only expenses above 7.5% of your adjusted gross income are deductible), you can have routine medical needs such as checkups and dental cleanings done right away, so your expenses for the year will be greater, and the deduction will be available. (Adjusted gross income, or AGI, is your total income, adjusted by deducting certain amounts, such as alimony you paid and IRA contributions, that qualify for favorable tax treatment.)

Well, maybe it's all for the best. If you have nothing to gain by fancy tax planning and elaborate transactions that are meaningless without tax benefits, then you won't bother with them—and you can spend more time on budgeting and looking for productive investments.

Audits—and Other Really Big Tax Problems

There's method to their madness: IRS computers are programmed to "recognize" returns that look funny. That is, the numbers may not add up, required forms may be missing, the taxpayer may have failed (or refused) to report income that the IRS knows about from the person or organization paying the income, or the taxpayer may have claimed deductions much higher than the average for taxpayers with comparable income and number of dependents.

So your return may be "flagged" because it seems out of the ordinary. This doesn't necessarily mean that you are a tax cheat, or even that you made a mistake—it could just mean that you had unusually high deductible expenses; and by proving this to the IRS (by submitting copies of bills and cancelled checks), you can solve the whole problem.

How does the IRS know what's normal? By conducting "TCMP audits." The TCMP is the Taxpayer Compliance Measurement Project. The IRS selects an unfortunate few taxpayers—unfortunate because they have to document every single figure on their tax returns. The IRS uses the results of TCMP to set average ranges for tax deductions.

Audits.   The simplest audit is the "correspondence audit": the IRS requests verification of a simple matter of record. If you can supply proof, you're out of the woods. (If not, the IRS will send you a deficiency notice—in effect, a bill—and you'll either have to pay up or go through the IRS appeals process.)

For more complex matters, where the dispute is not so much about facts and figures as about interpretation of tax law, there will be either an "office audit" (at the IRS office) or a "field audit" (at the taxpayer's home or place of business). If you're asked to participate in an office audit, but you think the glitch can be solved through correspondence, send the IRS copies of the relevant documents (hang on to the originals—you may need them!) and ask to have the matter treated as a correspondence audit. The worst that can happen is that the IRS will refuse—and you're no worse off than you were before.

You can go to the audit yourself, and bring any witnesses you want. If you're married and file a joint return, either spouse can go to the audit. Or, you can bring a tax adviser—or send him or her in your place. You can be represented by a lawyer, a CPA, or an "enrolled agent." An enrolled agent is a person who has passed a tough IRS exam on the technicalities of tax law. Many enrolled agents are former IRS personnel, so they're familiar with the way the IRS looks at things, and know the procedure thoroughly.

The advantage of sending a representative is that he or she probably won't start screaming at the IRS staffer—and probably won't blurt out a confession of tax misdeeds of the past. However, professional fees can be high, and the representative won't be as familiar with your records and your budget as you are. You could go yourself, then "buy time" by asking for another appointment (this time with a professional adviser) if you can't cope with the audit by yourself. Or, you could pay for an hour or two of advice from a professional, then go to the audit on your own.

In a way, an audit is a kind of negotiation. The IRS staffer has a large caseload, and is rewarded for disposing of cases quickly (while still recovering a reasonable amount of money for the treasury). If you can show that you had a reasonable basis for the tax positions you took, you may convince the auditor to agree with you—or at least, to reduce the amount the IRS is asking. It's always in the back of the IRS staffer's mind that there are plenty of other cases to cope with—so accepting a reasonable compromise for a fast solution helps both the taxpayer and the bureaucrat.

The negotiation process swings into high gear when the IRS auditor draws up the "proposed adjustments" to the tax return that was audited. You can accept the IRS conclusion, and pay the resulting tax bill or try to get the proposed adjustments made a little more favorable. If you agree to a compromise, you get ten days either to pay in full or work out an arrangement for paying in installments. That's the end of the line—you can't change your mind and appeal.

If you want to keep on fighting, you can use the IRS's internal appeal system and/or use the federal courts to litigate. It depends on how much money is involved, and how angry you are: Very few people would devote three years and thousands of dollars' worth of legal fees over a $227 dispute.

To make it easier (and less expensive) for taxpayers to go to court, the federal tax court has a simplified procedure for tax cases involving $10,000 or less; the taxpayer doesn't even need an attorney. However, if you choose to use this procedure, you can't appeal the court's decision.

Penalties.   You can be hit with some very stiff penalties for falling afoul of the tax laws.

• There is an "underpayment" penalty for failing to pay at least 90% of your income tax, or an amount equal to 100% of the previous year's tax, through withholding and/or estimated tax. The penalty depends on the interest rates the IRS charges at the time of the underpayment; the IRS sets interest rates twice a year based on market rates. There's a special IRS form (2210) for determining if you can escape the penalty (for instance, because your income fluctuated throughout the year)—and for computing the penalty, if you can't.
• The IRS also charges interest on the "deficiencies" determined by audits, until the taxpayer ponies up.
• The penalty for late filing (unless you have an extension) equals 5% of the tax due per month or fraction of a month—up to a maximum of 25%. If you're sixty days or more late, there's a minimum penalty: the smaller of $100 or the amount owed.
• The "negligence" penalty is 5% of an underpayment detected by an audit, plus 50% of the interest on the underpayment. The negligence penalty is a punishment—it's imposed only when a taxpayer is careless or disregards IRS rules or an outright warning from the IRS. It won't be imposed if the taxpayer makes an honest mistake, or misunderstands the application of a tax rule.
• The "civil fraud" penalty of 50% of the underpayment, plus 50% of the interest, is imposed when the IRS believes there is proof of fraud, but a criminal prosecution is not justified. Negligence penalties and civil fraud penalties can't be applied for the same misconduct—the IRS has to choose one.

What If You Can't Pay?

The IRS has a lot of enforcement power: It can seize your property, garnish your salary, or padlock your business. You'll certainly want to pay the IRS whatever amount it's finally determined that you owe—but what if you don't have the money? In that case, negotiate with the IRS. By filing Form 433 (Statement of Financial Condition), you can show that you really can't afford to pay the full amount—or that you can pay, if the IRS will consent to a reasonable plan of installment payments. IRS Form 656 is used to submit "offers of compromise." You can also try to get penalties compromised, even if the underlying debt must be paid in full.

Summing Up

It's been estimated that about four months' worth of salary for the average taxpayer goes to various taxing authorities. If one-third of your dollars go to taxes, you'd better believe that collecting tax information, getting authoritative tax advice, filing tax returns, and coping with IRS examinations are important topics. But be of good cheer—the budgeting process described in Part Two will give you most of the information you need to prepare a tax form and prepare a tax plan.

59. Preparing for a Secure Retirement

If you think of retirees as feeble old codgers tottering into the sunset, you'd better change your mind. Today's retirees are often healthy, vigorous, and deeply involved in life. They're not old fogeys; many of them aren't even old. People can retire in their sixties, with at least a decade or two of life expectancy. Some people accept a succulent early retirement package, retiring at 55 when their company wants to cut down on staff. There are even entrepreneurs who start a business, take it public when it becomes successful, and "retire" in their thirties.

When Can You Retire?

Now more than ever, retirement is an individual and personal decision. Maybe the best choice for you is an early retirement; maybe you should keep working past 65 (especially if your spouse is younger and remains in the work force).

If you don't want to retire, and you can still do your job, federal law protects you from being forced out. Employers with twenty or more employees are not permitted to impose compulsory retirement at *any* age. There are exceptions to this rule—such as some tenured college professors, top-level executives entitled to very large pensions, and workers whose jobs affect the public safety (police officers, firefighters, airline pilots).

If you do want to retire, you'll have to decide when. If you hate your job, you may want to retire, or move on to a more enjoyable second career; if you love your job, you'll want to stay on as long as possible. The age at which you retire will also affect the size of your pension and Social Security benefits.

When Do Your Pension Benefits Begin?

The documents setting up a pension plan include a definition of "normal retirement date"—the date on which an employee can retire without permission from the employer, and still receive full benefits. This is usually the first day of the first month after the worker's sixty-fifth birthday. Traditionally, this is also the first date on which full Social Security benefits would be available, but the Social Security retirement age will be gradually increased. Pension plans are also allowed to set a special retirement date—ten years from the beginning of plan participation—for workers who are hired after age 55.

Early Retirement

Pension plans also include an "early retirement date" (usually five to ten years before the normal date). You can retire on the early retirement date, with your employer's consent, and receive a pension—but the pension will be reduced because you will receive it for more years than if you retired on the normal date. If you retire without the employer's consent, you receive the vested part of the pension, but forfeit the nonvested part. Therefore, for older employees who are not yet fully vested, waiting a year or two to retire can make a big difference in the eventual pension.

Federal law requires that those who retire early get reduced pensions—but doesn't require that those who retire late get extra-large pensions. Many plans do not provide for higher pensions for late retirees; in fact, some don't even give the employee "service credit" (more years of employment taken into account in computing the pension) for work after the normal retirement date.

Is that fair? There are two sides to the question. One side is that the employee should get a larger pension because, by deferring retirement, he or she also defers the employer's obligation to pay a pension. The other side is that the employee, after all, is still collecting a salary—which is almost guaranteed to be higher than the pension.

Financial Planning for Retirement

Many of the financial planning problems remain the same after retirement as before. Couples who marry (or remarry) late in life may find that their children's college expenses peak around the time they were thinking of retiring. So they may postpone retirement so that extra income will be available; or, they may use IRA, annuity, or pension plan funds to pay tuition. There's no penalty on IRA withdrawals after age 59½ even if the money is used for purposes more typical of younger people. Many older couples have paid off the mortgage on their homes, so home equity loans are a real possibility for this (or any other) financial need.

This highlights one of the major differences between pre- and post-retirement planning. A couple (or older single person) who owns a fully paid-off house doesn't have to worry about fluctuations in interest rates. They don't have to meet the mortgage payment every month, although utility costs and real estate taxes may be a worry.

If you're in this situation, check with the local office for senior citizens' concerns. You may be entitled to property tax relief, relief from increases in utility rates, or special help with winterizing your home to cut heating bills. Older apartment renters may also be entitled to protection from eviction if their apartment building is converted to co-op or condo ownership when they're unwilling or unable to buy the apartment (or co-op shares).

If you're like most people, most of your income during your working lifetime comes from salary. If you have a good savings plan and make realistic investment choices, you can supplement your salary with investment income and profits from selling investments that have increased in value. During retirement, financial security rests on the "three-legged stool": the combination of Social Security payments, employer-paid pension, and your own investments (including your IRA). The third one is the only one that's really in your control.

This section will explain what your options are with regard to the employer's pension plan, how to estimate Social Security benefits, how to deal with IRA accounts once you retire or reach age 59½, and how retirement income is taxed (if you have a high income, part of your Social Security benefit may be taxable income—and this may affect your investment choices).

Social Security: Who Qualifies?

The formal name for Social Security is OASDI (Old Age, Survivors, and Disability Insurance). Not only does this system provide the familiar retirement benefits, but it also provides benefits to disabled workers and their families, and to the surviving spouses (and sometimes, the children) of deceased insured workers. If the marriage lasted long enough, benefits may also be available to the ex-spouses of workers.

"Insured workers" are those who have participated in the Social Security system by paying Social Security taxes and having their employers pay matching taxes. Social Security (Federal Insurance Contributions Act, or FICA) taxes are calculated very differently from income taxes.

Income taxes are known as "graduated" or "progressive" taxes because the tax rate increases as income increases. Furthermore, part of a person's income is not taxed: A personal exemption and standard deduction reduce the amount of taxable income. A person with very low income may not have to pay income tax at all.

The FICA tax is charged at a flat rate. For 1987, employer and employee each pay 7.15% of the employee's compensation; self-employed persons pay 12.3% of their earnings. But this tax rate only applies up to a "ceiling" ($43,800 for 1987, meaning a maximum tax of $3,131.70 for employees, $5,387.40 for the self-employed)—no more FICA tax is charged after tax is paid on the maximum amount. In effect, that means that people who earn a lot pay a *lower* FICA rate than those who earn less because part of the highly paid person's salary is not subject to Social Security tax.

In a sense, then, lower-paid workers pay more for Social Security than the higher-paid. But in a sense, they get more from the system: lower-paid workers have a higher "replacement ratio" (percentage of their salary replaced by Social Security) than those with bigger salaries.

One way to look at it is that Social Security isn't a very good bargain for high-paid employees, and that they must look to pensions and investments for most of their retirement income. The other viewpoint is that FICA taxes are so high that they prevent low-income workers from saving (because their take-home pay is reduced)—but they don't put much of a crimp in a senior executive's investment plans.

What Will Your Benefits Be?

The general rule is that you're "fully insured" and qualified to collect a full benefit at retirement age once you have participated in the Social Security system for forty quarters. Retirement and disability benefits for a fully insured worker, and benefits for his or her spouse and survivors, are based on the insured worker's Primary Insurance Amount (PIA).

It would be very easy to calculate your PIA if it were a percentage of your salary when you retired—25%, for instance. But that wouldn't be fair—your salary probably increases over time, and your final salary is not a fair representation of your average salary throughout your career. It wouldn't be too hard to calculate your PIA if all you had to do was find out your salary for every year you worked, and take a percentage of each year's salary.

Well, that's not the way it works. As you've already seen, there's a maximum amount on which FICA tax is charged. Today, the amount is high, so most employees pay FICA tax on their entire salaries. But the amount used to be much lower, so most employees used to earn some money that was not subject to FICA tax. The tax rate has also increased frequently, so computing a person's PIA involves many adjustments because of the change in tax rates.

As a rough estimate, though, Table 9 shows what you can expect if you retire in various years—at age 62 or age 65. (Those who retire at 62 get a reduced benefit.) The table shows monthly benefits for those who earned a low income (under $7,000 a year), average income (about

$17,000 a year), or high income (about $40,000 a year or more) during an average year.

However, the younger you are, the harder it is to make predictions. *Anything* could happen to the Social Security system in the meantime; tax rates and maximum salaries subjected to FICA tax are bound to keep changing; and you could change your career, and end up with a much higher (or lower) salary than you now earn.

When Can You Start to Collect Benefits?

Under current law, you can retire and start collecting Social Security retirement benefits at age 62. However, your benefits will be reduced to compensate for the fact that they will be paid longer than if you had retired at the "normal" retirement age. The current normal retirement age for the Social Security system is 65; however, the normal age is being moved up gradually, until it reaches 67 in 2016. Retirement benefits are increased if you stay at work and defer retirement until age 72. (No more increases after 72, though; and the increase won't raise the benefits payable to your dependents or survivors.)

This is probably the least of your problems, but if you're entitled to a pension in the mid- or high-five figures, and retire before the normal Social Security retirement age, the Internal Revenue Code requires your pension to be reduced to compensate for the longer period of pension payments. Just thought you'd like something to which you could aspire.

Marriage and Social Security

If a couple have both reached retirement age, they are both entitled to Social Security benefits. However, a person can draw Social Security benefits either as a retired worker (based on his or her own earnings) or as a retired worker's spouse (the spouse's benefit equals half the retired worker's benefit). Social Security law sets a maximum in benefits any family can receive, based on the higher earner's Primary Insurance Amount.

In effect, this means that married women who have jobs outside the home are making a charitable contribution of the Social Security taxes

TABLE 9.   ESTIMATED SOCIAL SECURITY BENEFITS

	Low Income		Average Income		High Income	
	62	65	62	65	62	65
1988	$350	$434	$ 530	$ 659	$ 702	$ 882
1989	$371	$467	$ 563	$ 711	$ 750	$ 955
1990	$392	$482	$ 597	$ 736	$ 799	$ 994
1991	$416	$502	$ 634	$ 767	$ 853	$1,041
1992	$437	$527	$ 670	$ 806	$ 908	$1,100
1995	$510	$618	$ 788	$ 952	$1,095	$1,320
2000	$653	$799	$1,030	$1,248	$1,487	$1,797

on their income; they don't collect any more Social Security benefits than if they had never worked for a salary.

Working after Retirement

Retirement doesn't suit everybody. Some people get stir-crazy without the stimulus of work and the social contacts made there. Some people discover that their retirement income is disappointingly slim, or their expenses surprisingly high. So they get a second, postretirement job, or consider doing so.

If you're in this situation, be aware of the effects of working once Social Security benefits have begun. Income taxes don't stop when you retire, and any earnings will be subject to Social Security taxes. Depending on the way your new employer's pension plan is written, you may or may not be entitled to pension credits based on your work; and you probably won't stay there long enough to vest in the new employer's plan. (These problems are less likely to occur if you can be rehired by your original employer.)

Your Social Security benefits will also be reduced if you earn more than a specified amount between the time you start collecting benefits and age 70. For 1987, the most you can earn without penalty is $8,160—only $6,000, if you retired early. In 1987, 1988, and 1989, each dollar of excess earnings cuts your Social Security benefit by 50¢. Starting in 1990, benefits will be cut only 33¢ per dollar of excess earnings.

The harshness of these rules is tempered a little for your first year of retirement. It's treated as a "grace year," and a separate computation is made for each month.

Taxes on Social Security Benefits

Until 1983, Social Security benefits were tax-free income. But since that time, 8% to 10% of Social Security recipients have had to pay income tax on part of their Social Security benefits. These taxpayers must compute "modified adjusted gross income," which means adjusted gross income (a basis figure used in calculating taxable income) plus items that receive favorable tax treatment. The most common item that receives favorable tax treatment is interest on tax-free investments such as tax-exempt mutual bonds. Social Security recipients must then either pay income tax on half the Social Security benefit, or on modified adjusted gross income plus half the Social Security benefit, minus a "base amount." The base amount is $25,000 for a single person or a married person separated from the spouse, and $32,000 for a married person filing a joint tax return. The effect of the base amount is to exempt low-income Social Security recipients from the tax. But the base amount is zero for married persons who file separate income tax returns, so taxability of Social Security benefits is much more likely in this situation. (In general, filing a separate return carries a high tax bill; the system is designed to encourage married couples to file joint returns.)

Summing Up

For many retirees, Social Security benefits are a major source of income—or even the *only* source of income. These benefits will be helpful to you once you retire (and you certainly paid enough throughout your working life to get them). But Social Security benefits probably aren't large enough to maintain your standard of living. The best situation is one where you supplement Social Security with a pension from your employer, your own retirement savings (such as IRAs and annuities), and a healthy investment portfolio that will continue to yield income and profits after retirement.

60. Benefits from Your Employer

As discussed on pages 25 to 31, ERISA and other federal laws do not force your employer to offer any kind of pension plan, but they do place limits on the way the plan can be administered. The employer must follow rules about contributions, eligibility for plan participation, and vesting. Rules are also set down for the choices which can—and the choices which must—be offered to plan participants when they retire and receive their pensions.

There are two major methods of paying pensions: in a lump sum and as an annuity (series of regular payments). If you're given a choice between the two, there are two important factors to considers: taxes and your investment skills and priorities. Once your employer hands you a lump sum, you become responsible for using and investing the sum wisely.

Lump Sums

You could use a lump sum to:

- Pay off your mortgage.
- If you're an apartment-dweller, buy a home.
- Purchase a unit in a retirement or life-care community (life-care communities are more medically oriented, and promise lifetime health care in return for payment. Usually you make a very large payment when you enter; you may also have to make continuing "rent" payments to the retirement or life-care community).
- Invest the lump sum to produce the retirement income you'll need.
- Keep the lump sum undisturbed (and untaxed) for a while by rolling it over to an IRA; you won't have to start withdrawals (and tax payments) until you reach age 70½.

Annuities

Not everyone feels confident enough to make major investment decisions regarding lump-sum payments. One way to cope is to take the lump sum and buy an annuity from an insurance company. If the lump sum is large enough, you can hire a portfolio manager or investment adviser to make the decisions.

Many retirees receive a regular monthly pension—either because their plan doesn't offer a lump-sum payment, or because they prefer to leave the investment decisions up to the employer. In effect, they're buying an annuity from the employer.

Whether or not this is a wise decision depends both on the investment market in general (when stock prices are booming, things look pretty good for everyone) and the pension fund's investment performance compared to the market.

Alternatives

As a result of the federal Retirement Equity Act (REA), the normal option for married retirees is the "joint and survivor annuity": payments that continue through the lifetime of both the employee and his or her spouse, whichever dies later. For the pension to be paid in any other form, both spouses must give their consent in writing; the employee spouse can't make the decision alone.

The other possible choices include payments for a certain number of years (e.g., ten or twenty) and payments for the employee's life alone, ending at his or her death, without continuing payments to the surviving spouse. The normal trade-offs apply: The longer the time over which payments must be made, the smaller each payment will be.

If you choose payments for a certain number of years, and live longer, you'll either have to do without the pension income, or find some way of replacing the payments after they stop. But if you choose lifetime payments, or joint and survivor payments, the longer your life expectancy (or the combined life expectancies of you and your spouse), the greater the risk that your monthly payment will be too small to meet your needs.

If you choose payments over your lifetime only, make sure that your spouse's own pension plus Social Security survivor's benefits, plus your insurance coverage and whatever you leave to your spouse, will provide enough resources for a comfortable life. And watch out—although there are more elderly widows than widowers, you can't assume that all wives outlive their husbands. Any financial plan must take into account the possibility that the husband will be the survivor.

Pensions and Taxes

Before the Tax Code of 1986, the financial planning cliché was that pensions (and investments paying off postretirement) were especially valuable. Not only were taxes deferred, but the retiree would be in a much lower tax bracket than before retirement, so the taxes to be paid would be smaller than if the same income had been received before retirement. That's not necessarily true after the tax reform act.

Another big change is that lump-sum distributions used to get favorable treatment. Although the usual tax rule is that all income must be taxed in the year it's received (and at that year's tax rates), the law before TC '86 allowed "ten-year forward averaging" on lump sums from pension plans. No, the taxpayer wasn't allowed to spread out the tax payment over ten years, but he or she paid in a single year ten times the tax on one-tenth the lump sum. This was a tax break because tax rates were a lot lower on small amounts than on large ones.

Current law only allows five-year averaging. The lump sum is taxed in the year it's received, but at the rate of five times the tax on one-fifth of the lump sum. But even this less-generous tax break is limited. It's a one-time deal, and you must be over 59½ to use it.

If you were over 50 on January 1, 1986, you get a special exception. You can continue to use capital gains treatment for lump-sum distributions (described in the next paragraph), and you can use ten-year averaging for lump sums. You don't have to wait until the age of 59½, and you can use ten-year, not five-year, averaging.

If part of your lump-sum distribution comes from work done before 1974 (the effective date of ERISA), you may be able to treat some of the pre-1974 funds as capital gains. But this is a difficult, technical matter—check with your employee relations counselor or tax planner to see if you qualify, and if so, whether this cuts your taxes.

And if you get more than $112,500 a year from your pension plan (this amount will be adjusted upward to cope with inflation) or get a lump sum of $562,500 or more, you may have to pay a 15% penalty tax for "excess distributions from a retirement plan." Just thought you'd like to know.

61. Tapping Your IRA

Before TC '86, IRA taxation was pretty straightforward. IRA owners made contributions (but not more than the maximum allowable amount; if they did, a penalty tax was assessed). The purpose of the IRA was to make money available for retirement at an age falling somewhere in the normal range. Therefore, withdrawals before age 59½ were subject to penalty tax; so were failures to at least start withdrawal by age 70½. Tardy withdrawals were penalized because the IRA was supposed to be used for retirement planning, not left intact and left to the taxpayer's heirs.

The Tax Code of 1986 adds an additional layer of complexity. Now you can make IRA contributions that are nondeductible—so you have a major accounting problem. Tax policy says that income is supposed to be taxed once, not twice: So, if you've already paid income tax on the money (because nondeductible IRA contributions are made with after-tax dollars), you shouldn't have to pay tax again when you withdraw money from your IRA.

Those who retire in the future will have to allocate their IRA accounts between the amounts that come from deductible IRA contributions (which haven't been taxed yet and, therefore, must be taxed after retirement), and those that come from already-taxed, nondeductible contributions. The IRS hasn't announced how to do this yet (after all, no one has already retired after making nondeductible contributions)—the calculation process will be a tough one.

IRA Penalties

There's a 10% penalty tax (now double the 5% penalty under former law) for premature withdrawals from an IRA account. A premature withdrawal is one that takes place before the IRA owner reaches 59½, unless:

- He or she is disabled.
- He or she has died, and the beneficiary is withdrawing funds from the IRA.
- The withdrawal is made in a series of payments (annual or more frequent) that stretches over the life expectancy of the IRA owner. This exception can also be used if the payments are made over the "joint lifetimes" of the IRA owner and his or her beneficiary. (That is, if you have a life expectancy of eighteen years, your spouse has a life expectancy of twenty-six years, the payments can be made over a twenty-six-year term because that's the "joint life expectancy" of the two of you.) Or, the regular payments can be in the form of an annuity for a fixed number of years.

IRA Withdrawals—Without Penalties

Once you reach the magic age of 59½, you can withdraw as much from the IRA as you like, without tax penalty. Whatever you withdraw is taxed as ordinary income. (Things will be different once people start retiring with IRAs that include nondeductible contributions.) You can take out the entire amount in the account and spend or invest it; or you

TABLE 10.   IRA WITHDRAWAL

Amt. in IRA	7%			8%		
	10 yrs.	15 yrs.	20 yrs.	10 yrs.	15 yrs.	20 yrs.
$ 24,672	$ 286	$ 222	$ 191	$ 299	$ 245	$ 202
$ 49,344	$ 573	$ 443	$ 383	$ 599	$ 456	$ 403
$ 78,954	$ 917	$ 710	$ 612	$ 958	$ 730	$ 648
$ 98,844	$1,148	$ 888	$ 766	$1,199	$ 914	$ 811
$126,004	$1,463	$1,133	$ 977	$1,529	$1,165	$1,034
$216,362	$2,512	$2,214	$1,677	$2,625	$2,001	$1,775

can set up a regular program of withdrawals. Table 10 shows the monthly withdrawals you can make, based on various amounts in your IRA (these weird-looking numbers come from the table on page 35 showing how your IRA grows at various interest rates), how long the monthly withdrawals continue (ten years, fifteen years, twenty years), and the amount the IRA continues to earn as you make withdrawals (7% and 8% figures have been used because these are realistic figures; you may even be able to do better—and make larger monthly withdrawals).

After age 59½, then, there's no such thing as an excessive withdrawal as far as the tax code is concerned. But there is such a thing as an "insufficient withdrawal"—and unless you withdraw at least as much as the tax law requires, you'll have to pay a stiff tax penalty: 50% of the difference between the minimum required withdrawal and the amount you actually did withdraw. The penalty is imposed because IRAs are supposed to give you a tax break to save for retirement—not to accumulate money to leave to your heirs.

You can keep all the money in your IRA without penalty until April 1 of the year after the year in which you reach age 70½. After that, you must either take all the money out of the IRA (and pay income tax on the whole shebang) or make the required withdrawal. The required withdrawal usually equals the amount in the account divided by the remaining years in your life expectancy. That is, if you have $100,000 in your account, and a life expectancy of ten years, you'll have to withdraw at least $10,000 to escape the penalty; if you only withdraw $7,000, the penalty will be $1,500 (half of $3,000).

However, if you really want to preserve the IRA for your heirs, tax law allows you to make withdrawals over "joint life expectancy." You can even decide who will be the one whose life expectancy is used. You could choose your spouse—or someone much younger than you, such as your daughter or even your grandson. If that person has a thirty-year life expectancy, you won't be penalized if you stretch out withdrawals over thirty years.

Standard Deduction for Senior Citizens

You are entitled to some income tax relief as a senior citizen, even if you don't have an IRA. The Tax Code of 1986 greatly increases the standard deduction (from $3,670 to $5,000 for married taxpayers filing jointly and for surviving spouses, and from $2,480 to $3,000 for single people). It also allows an extra $600 standard deduction for those married persons, widows, and widowers who reach age 65 during the taxable year ($1,200 if they are both elderly and legally blind); the additional standard deduction for a single person is $750 (or $1,500 if the person is both elderly and legally blind.)

However, this tax relief is less generous than what the earlier law allowed. Elderly people used to get a tax credit; and tax credits, which reduce the amount of tax due, are more useful than tax deductions, which only cut down the amount of potentially taxable income.

62. Investments for Senior Citizens

Older investors typically are less interested in risk, more interested in assuring a steady, predictable income (or, if they think inflation will increase and/or interest rates rise, an income that fluctuates with interest rates and keeps them ahead of inflation.) The fruits of a lifetime of saving and earning are available to them, ready to be harvested through the retirement period.

Tax-free municipal bonds can be very attractive to older investors (especially if they're in a high tax bracket), but they must be aware that this income may affect the taxability of Social Security benefits.

Other possible choices include taxable municipal bonds (if the return is high enough to make up for the tax), corporate bonds (either lower-yielding but safer investment-grade bonds, or riskier, high-yield "junk bonds"), money market funds (especially if the interest rates start climbing again), high-dividend stocks (the classic choice is utility stock), income-oriented mutual funds, Ginnie Maes and Ginnie Mae funds (see page 129), and other real estate securities. If you want to invest a lump sum from a pension or an IRA, consider the immediate annuity (described below).

This is not to say that if you're an older investor, you *can't* do well with a portfolio of high-tech companies, gold mine stocks, and "vulture funds" (mutual funds that invest in possible turnarounds of bankrupt companies and failed real estate projects). There are no hard and fast rules; but most older investors are more conservative, and do think more about income than long-term growth.

Annuities as Investments

Insurance companies sell annuities. In the simplest form, the annuity buyer gives the insurer a chunk of capital (or makes an initial deposit and adds to it later). During the "accumulation period" (from the purchase of the annuity to the time payouts start), the insurance company invests the capital. When the "distribution period" comes, the insurance company either gives the investor a lump sum (consisting of the additional capital plus appreciation) or makes regular payments—for a certain number of years, for the investor's lifetime, or for joint lifetimes. You can also arrange for a beneficiary you choose to get a refund if you die before your entire annuity investment has been paid out.

This will probably remind you of the IRA and pension rules; and the tax consequences are similar. Annuities are discussed in this section because there's a 10% penalty for withdrawing money from an annuity before you reach 59½ (unless you're disabled, or unless you get the series of regular payments described on page 272). Unlike an IRA, you can contribute as much to an annuity as you want; also unlike an IRA, you can never get a tax deduction for annuity contributions. However, if you can't deduct IRA contributions anyway, because of your income level, you might prefer an annuity to an IRA. You still get to defer tax on the appreciation until retirement—and you have more flexibility in the amount you contribute.

Payments under an "immediate annuity" begin right away. You might make this choice if you have a lump sum to invest and are ready to retire. Payments under a deferred annuity begin after a specified amount of time. You might make this choice if you are some distance away from retirement, but want to make sure that you'll have a certain amount of monthly income after you retire.

You can choose between fixed annuities (which guarantee a certain rate of interest for a limited amount of time—then interest rates fluctuate) and variable annuities. If you prefer a variable annuity, the insurer lets you decide how your investment will be apportioned among the portfolios maintained by the insurer.

Estate Planning for Retirees

Although death can occur at any age, it's natural for older investors to think seriously about what will become of their property after death. There are two opposed strategies that can work well; professional advice is needed to choose the best one in a particular case.

- It can be a good idea for investments (e.g., securities, bank accounts) to be held jointly by a married couple, especially if each spouse's estate is too small to be subject to federal estate tax. That way, whichever spouse dies first, the other will automatically become the owner of the property, with no need to wait for a will to be probated. But this won't work if the couple wants the investments to be left to a child, friend, or other beneficiary instead of to the surviving spouse.
- "Estate splitting" can be a good idea if there's a good chance that estate tax will be due. In this strategy, property is transferred between spouses (the spouse who owns a particular asset makes a gift of the asset to the other spouse, or changes its ownership from himself or herself to the couple as joint owners) so that each spouse has an estate of approximately equal size. That way, no matter which spouse dies first, maximum advantage can be taken of the exemptions from federal estate tax.

Dealing with Possible Incapacity

Another consideration that is more powerful for older than for younger investors is the possibility of "incompetence" (loss of legal power to manage business and personal affairs) caused by physical or mental illness.

If a person becomes incapacitated (perhaps as a result of a stroke or Alzheimer's disease), the usual legal response is to have a conservator or guardian appointed. The difference between the two is that a guardian has much wider powers and is appointed when a person is judged legally incompetent and loses many of his or her civil rights. But this response isn't very satisfactory to the impaired older person or the family. The appointment process takes time and costs money; in the meantime, the impaired older person may be losing or squandering assets, or failing to pay bills because he or she is confused or ill.

Furthermore, although family members can take on these roles without getting a fee, it's common for lawyers to be appointed as conservators or guardians—with the right to receive generous fees from the impaired person's property. (These appointments are often used as political plums, to reward party loyalty.) There's also a risk that the conservator or guardian will steal from the "conservatee" or "ward."

Fortunately, there are alternatives to conservatorship and guardianship. A durable power of attorney is a legal document that is drafted while the person granting the power has the legal capacity to make contracts and enter into other transactions. (This is called "competency" or "capacity" in legal parlance.) The power of attorney gives someone else (typically, the spouse, a child, or a lawyer or other trusted counselor) the right to make decisions for the person granting the power, under specified circumstances.

The "attorney-in-fact" (the person allowed to make the decisions) could have the right to collect payments due to the person who granted the power, and pay his or her bills. Depending on state law, the attorney-in-fact may also be allowed to make health care decisions for the disabled person: to transfer him or her to a nursing home, to consent to an experimental treatment, or to terminate life support systems, for example.

The power of attorney is called "durable" because it remains legally effective even after the person who created it becomes legally incompetent. In fact, some states allow what is called a "springing" power of attorney: It doesn't spring into action until the grantor becomes incompetent. Until then, he or she can make decisions and manage business affairs personally.

Powers of attorney must be used carefully. Unfortunately, sometimes the attorney-in-fact takes advantage of the position to loot the disabled person's assets. It's also possible that the attorney-in-fact will become disabled; for instance, if a married couple each name the spouse as attorney-in-fact, either or both could develop incapacitating health problems.

The "living trust" (a trust created by a contract, not as part of a will) is another possible answer. A trust is an arrangement under which the owner of property transfers the property to someone else, who will take care of the property (making investment decisions, for instance), pay the income, and distribute the trust property according to the instructions the property owner provides in the document creating the trust.

The trust will be professionally managed, and the needs of the property owner and his or her family can be taken care of by the trustee (the person or institution managing the trust)—even if the original property owner is unwilling or unable to make investment and legal decisions. Not all courts agree, but some courts have ruled that it is not necessary to appoint a guardian or conservator for a person who already has a living trust. Even if the trust grantor becomes disabled, the trustee will handle financial matters as well as could a conservator or guardian.

Living trusts used to be helpful for older people who wanted to protect their property against Medicaid asset limitations (discussed in the section on meeting health care costs). However, a 1985 law called the Comprehensive Omnibus Budget Reconciliation Act (COBRA), taking effect in 1986, limits the usefulness of trusts for this purpose.

Summing Up

In some ways, this is a frightening section. There *are*, after all, old people living in poverty, or impoverished by crushing medical costs. But the outlook is far from hopeless.

One outcome of a good career plan is a healthy pension, or income high enough to invest for retirement security. You can choose investments to fit your own risk profile, and to provide the level of income you select. The combination of Social Security, pensions, IRA withdrawals, and investment income, tailored to fit the possible need for a Medicaid application, should provide the funds you need.

You can get an estimate of your Social Security benefits from the nearest Social Security office and an estimate of your pension benefits from your employer's pension and benefits coordinator or your union representative.

Although no one can predict the future, you can make some projections about your postretirement lifestyle. You can anticipate when your mortgage will be fully paid off, and how that will affect your housing costs. Don't forget, retirement will cut some of your expenses: commuting and maintaining a business wardrobe, for instance. You'll probably want to spend more on travel and leisure—and you may be forced to spend more on medical care.

Depending on whether you had children, or the age at which you had them, you may retire just as the youngest starts college—or long after the children have left the nest and established themselves financially. This will affect whether you're helping them financially after you retire, or vice versa. It will also affect your need for insurance, and your estate plan: You may find it more important to secure your spouse's financial future than to leave money to your children or grandchildren. Or, your spouse could have adequate funds (especially in light of your insurance), but your children may need to be provided for.

Today, retirement can last more than a decade (even more than two decades). It can be an enjoyable, productive, prosperous stage of life—if you plan for it.

63. REAL LIFE: JOHN VENTURA/MAGGIE HINES

Maggie Hines had just realized it. She looked through the family album. Of course there was a picture of the family coming out of church every Easter. And of course there was Mom, in *that* hat. It was lavender straw, or started out lavender anyway, bleaching out over time. It had straw flowers around the crown. It made its first appearance every year at Easter, and then to church every Sunday until Labor Day, when it blessedly retired to be replaced by an equally ugly but more subdued number in black felt with a pheasant feather. When they were growing up, she and John had laughed at that hat, sometimes openly but more often behind Mom's back. How could she wear that thing? What mysterious power did it exert to make her fall in love with it?

But now she realized the truth. In each of those Easter pictures there was a new suit for little John, a new hat (and often a new spring coat) for little Maggie. As long as the children were still growing, still clamoring for roller skates and movie tickets and presents for sweet-sixteen parties, then that old hat was pressed into service for another season. (And Dad, behind the camera? Maggie couldn't even remember what he wore on those occasions, how often he could stand in front of a three-way mirror, as the tailor pinned the alterations in a brand-new suit.)

Their parents never hesitated, when it was time to buy something for John and Maggie. Now she and John realized that it was time to think about ways they could help their parents. Robert and Anita Ventura would never ask for help; it would violate their ethical code. So John and Maggie would just have to make sure that money was available; they could tactfully pay an overdue bill or slip a few dollars to the building superintendent to make sure repairs were done promptly.

The Numbers

It sure wouldn't be easy. Maggie's husband, Larry Hines, was an auto mechanic; she herself worked part-time in a gift shop. John Ventura was an appliance salesman, with his income fluctuating depending on the commissions to be earned on washer-dryers and self-defrosting freezers. His wife Julie also worked part-time; like Maggie, she had three active children to take care of. She did some free-lance artwork for a greeting-card company. Everyone worked hard, but the income for the two families added up to about $60,000 a year. It was tough to pay all the bills, meet the needs of their children, think about retirement— and also find some money to help their parents.

Well, they had some assets to work with. Between the two families, they managed to save about $5,000 a year, and they had investments (mostly savings bonds; some stock) totalling about $20,000.

The Answers

The task is to balance their own needs and the needs of their children against their parents' needs. As much as they'd like to help their parents, they can't short-change their own families. (And things are so much more expensive than they were when John and Maggie were growing up!)

Just thinking about aging and its disabilities made both John and Maggie aware of the risks of ill-health. So John and Maggie's husband Larry took out disability income policies so that their families will still get regular checks even if they are unable to work.

John and Maggie also took out variable life insurance policies on their own lives. The insurance portion provides protection for their spouses and children; the variable feature allows them to choose investments that can make the cash value appreciate rapidly. Then the cash value will be available for policy loans that can be used to help the older generation of Venturas.

Although the usual arrangement is for the buyer of an annuity also to be the annuitant (the one who receives annuity payments), it's okay for one person to fund the annuity and another to receive the payments. So John and Maggie bought an annuity for their parents. They began with an initial payment, and will make annual payments for five more years, at which time their parents (or the survivor, if only one is alive) will start to receive regular monthly checks. The checks will continue for ten years—by then, their father will be 78 and their mother 75. If they don't survive that long, the annuity payments will be made to John and Maggie—who will then be able to use the funds for personal needs.

64. Coping with the Cost of Medical Care

The miracles of modern medicine are seldom inexpensive. Many people, during their working lives, depend on health insurance provided by their employers to cover the major costs of health care. (Many of the insurance plans provided by the employer do not cover routine health care such as checkups. If your employer's plan is one of these, don't skimp—you could save a lot of money, as well as a lot of pain and anxiety, by having routine checkups—and following the doctor's advice for healthful behavior.)

If you have adequate health insurance provided by your employer, this system works pretty well for you. Sometimes, the employer has you pay a fairly small amount to pay part of the premium (say, $20 to $30 a month). Usually, the employer pays the entire premium, so your health insurance doesn't cost you any cash. I say that it doesn't cost you "any cash" if the employer pays the whole premium because, of course, it has an effect on your salary—the more the employer has to pay for health insurance premiums, the less likely you are to get a large raise.

This system doesn't always work well for employers, who have to spend a lot of money to provide health insurance. So they're looking for alternatives—requiring employees to pay a larger part of the premium; providing incentives for employees to quit smoking, exercise regularly, and otherwise stay healthy; researching or adopting HMO's, PPO's, and other measures designed to cut costs (see page 20).

The system certainly doesn't work well for the 37 million Americans who don't have health insurance. About two-thirds of that figure include full-time employees and their families; the rest are unemployed or retired from companies that don't continue their health-care coverage. (See page 22 for more about continuation coverage.) If you aren't currently covered by health insurance, you can:

- Change jobs—to an employer who does provide adequate health insurance.
- Buy your own health insurance. You can always contact health insurance companies, such as the local Blue Cross/Blue Shield system, and buy insurance as an individual. However, this is the most expensive way to buy insurance; group rates are always lower. Find out if any of the organizations to which you belong, or could join, offer group health insurance. For instance, if you're an engineer, there might be an engineering professional society that offers attractive group rates.
- If you're retired and over 65, then Medicare will take care of some of your medical costs. However, as explained below, if you expect Medicare to cover *all* of them, you'll be very disappointed and possibly broke. Think seriously about buying a "Medi-Gap" policy.

The problems of paying for health care are especially severe for older people. It's a sad fact of life that bodies wear out, and a person often needs the most—and the most expensive—health care after he or she has retired, and income has declined from its peak during the working years. These problems are severe for our society as a whole, as well as for the individual. Many politicians have proposed changes in the way we administer and pay for health care; so by the time you read this, there could have been a change in the way we pay for the "catastrophic illnesses" (illnesses requiring long stays in the hospital and intensive medical treatment) of people over 65.

Continuation Coverage for Retirees

Some companies continue to provide health insurance for retired employees. According to a 1986 Department of Labor survey, employers' group health plans pay about 50% of the cost of health insurance premiums for retirees who receive continued coverage, and about a quarter of their total health expenses.

Another 1986 survey of medium and large companies showed that about 38% of these firms did not provide any continuation health coverage for retirees; but about half gave retired workers the same health coverage as current employees. The other 12% provided a lower level of benefits for retirees. More than half the plans acted as "Medi-Gap" plans, supplementing the amounts that Medicare does not pay. However, other plans required employees to take care of the Medicare deductibles and copayments (amounts a Medicare recipient must pay for his or her own care).

You can find out how your employer handles continuation coverage by studying your group insurance policy and the explanatory materials your employer distributes about your employee benefits. If your company has an employee benefits coordinator, discuss it with him or her, or ask the personnel department.

Loss of health insurance can be tragic for a retiree who faces higher medical costs just at a time when income declines. The problem is especially acute for those who choose early retirement, or who are offered early retirement when the company is reducing its workforce. They may be left without health insurance from the employer, and when they're too young to qualify for Medicare.

One way to cope is for spouses to "stagger" retirement: for the younger spouse, or the one with more generous health benefits, to delay retirement so that employee coverage will continue. Another way is for retired or soon-to-be-retired employees to form their own "group" and buy a group policy from a health insurance company.

The Medicare Program

The Medicare program was created in 1965 to free senior citizens from the threat of impoverishment caused by illness. Ironically, many senior citizens covered by Medicare now pay a higher percentage of their income for medical expenses than their counterparts before Medicare existed—while the federal government spends billions of dollars for Medicare.

Medicare is far from being a complete system of health care for senior citizens. It covers acute illnesses only (e.g., heart attacks, amputation of a diabetic's gangrenous leg), not chronic care (for instance, residence in a nursing home for a bedridden diabetic amputee who can't live alone in an ordinary apartment).

Furthermore, Medicare doesn't cover the whole cost even of the kinds of treatment it covers. The senior citizen must pay a "deductible" before any Medicare benefits are available. Currently, this amount is $520. When a hospital stay is lengthy, the senior citizen must pay "coinsurance": $130 a day for the sixty-first to ninetieth day of hospitalization, and $65 a day for the twenty-first through the one hundredth day the senior citizen spends recuperating in a nursing home after being hospitalized.

How Medicare Works

The Medicare system is divided into Part A, which pays hospital bills (and some nursing home bills, if the patient is getting ready to go home after a hospital stay), and Part B, which pays doctors' bills. Most people are eligible for Medicare starting on the day before their sixty-fifth birthdays.

If you get Social Security benefits, you also get automatic coverage under Medicare Part A, without making a separate application. Part A is funded by Social Security taxes: Part of the FICA taxes paid by employers and withheld from employees' salaries go to Medicare.

If you are over 65 and do not yet receive Social Security benefits (for instance, if you haven't retired) you have to apply for Medicare. If you're covered both by Medicare and your employer's health plan, you will usually have to look to your employer's plan, not to Medicare, to pay your medical bills while you're still working. However, you have the right to give up benefits under your employer's plan and choose Medicare coverage instead.

Medicare Part B is optional, and senior citizens who want it have to pay a monthly premium. If you get a Social Security check, the Part B premium will be deducted (and if you pay income tax on part of your Social Security benefit, you must include the Part B premium in the income computation, even though you never get to spend this amount). If you don't get a Social Security check, but are eligible for and choose to participate in Part B, you'll be billed for Part B premiums. For 1987, the premium is $17.90 a month.

What Medicare Covers

Part A pays for hospitalization, nursing (but not private-duty nurses), and medications used in the hospital. Medicare coverage of hospital stays is subject to a complicated series of rules dealing with "spells of illness." Medicare pays the full hospital bill for up to ninety days of hospitalization in each "spell of illness"; then the Medicare patient must make a coinsurance payment of $130 a day. However, Medicare patients get a "lifetime reserve" of sixty days; they can draw on these "reserve days" to avoid making copayments.

Medicare won't pay for hospitalization unless at least sixty days elapse between "spells of illness." This rule is imposed to keep chronically ill patients from collecting the costs of long-term care from Medicare; but it's a terrible burden on older people who suffer a series of health problems requiring hospitalization.

In 1983, Medicare changed its method of paying hospitals to the controversial DRG (Diagnosis Related Group) method. The federal government pays a flat fee for Medicare patients, based on their diagnosis; hospitals don't get paid extra if the patient is in worse physical condition than others with the same diagnosis, or if the patient must stay in the hospital longer than anticipated because of complications. (The system does make limited exceptions for "outliers"—cases that "lie outside" the usual rules because they are unusually expensive to treat.)

The system was changed to encourage hospitals to cut costs. If they're paid by the day, they might keep patients longer than strictly necessary. However, critics of DRG say that the new system encourages hospitals to refuse treatment to the sickest (and least profitable) patients, and to discharge patients "quicker and sicker" so that the beds can be filled by non-Medicare patients or by Medicare patients in a more profitable DRG.

Medicare Part B pays doctor bills—anyway, some of them and part of them. It pays physicians' fees whether or not the patient was in the hospital when the doctor was consulted. Part B pays 80% of what Medicare calls the "reasonable charge" for a particular service; many doctors charge a lot more than these amounts. Medicare patients must pay a $75 deductible each year before collecting Part B benefits, and they must pay the difference between the actual bill and 80% of the so-called reasonable charge.

Medicare patients are allowed to pick their own doctors; they're not restricted to a particular group of doctors. However, it makes a big difference in convenience and cost if they select a "participating physician." A participating physician is one who agrees to bill the Medicare system directly—and not to charge more than the reasonable fee. A patient who goes to a nonparticipating physician must pay the doctor directly, then collect the allowable reimbursement from Medicare.

Even if they didn't belong to one during their working years, senior citizens can join Health Maintenance Organizations (HMOs), and the Medicare system will pay the HMO premium instead of paying doctors' bills under Part B.

What Medicare Doesn't Cover

Medicare doesn't cover any of these costs, even though they can be significant expenses for senior citizens.

- Custodial care—that is, care for senior citizens who do not need medical treatment or skilled nursing, but who do need help with activities of everyday life.
- Routine medical checkups.
- Eye exams, eyeglasses, contact lenses.
- Hearing tests, hearing aids.
- Orthopedic shoes.
- Routine care from podiatrists.
- Routine dental care or dentures.
- Medicines that patients take themselves at home (for instance, medication for high blood pressure). However, some states have special programs that pay for senior citizens' prescription drugs—check with your local Office for the Aging to see if your area does.

Medi-Gap Insurance

Because Medicare fails to foot all the bills, it makes sense for Medicare beneficiaries to get private insurance to fill in the gaps. In fact, about two-thirds of beneficiaries have these "Medi-Gap" policies. The policies vary in their coverage: Some insulate policyholders against all costs that Medicare doesn't pay, while others have very limited coverage.

Plenty of con artists try to cheat senior citizens, and the field of "Medi-Gap" insurance is no exception. Fortunately, there's an easy way to avoid rip-off policies in favor of reputable ones that provide good value. The Health Care Finance Administration (the federal agency that runs Medicare and Medicaid) has a voluntary certification program. Policies that meet the standards set down by the National Association of Insurance Commissions, that meet the standards of state regulators, and that pay out most of the premiums in benefits, can carry a special seal.

Look for the seal before you buy a policy! Theoretically, an excellent policy could refuse to carry the seal as a matter of principle, but in practice the best policies do have the seal.

New York State's Department of Insurance publishes a booklet each year comparing all the Medi-Gap policies available in that state; check to see if your state has a similar publication.

Medicaid, and Its Effect on Financial Planning

The Medicare system is far from living up to its original promise of freeing senior citizens from worries about health care costs. Deductibles and coinsurance can strain a senior citizen's budget severely, and although Medi-Gap insurance is available, it can be too expensive for a hard-pressed older person or couple.

The problem of chronic care (long-term home health care, or nursing home life) is even worse. Medicare does not pay for "custodial care"—help with daily activities such as cooking, shopping, bathing, dressing, getting around the house and around town. If you or someone in your family needs custodial care, there are three possibilities.

•Family members get together to meet the older person's needs.
•The older person or his or her family pays the very high cost of chronic care ($20,000 a year is average; it could cost as much as $60,000 a year).
•Medicaid could pay these costs.

In most health-care situations, health insurance provides at least part of the necessary funds. Although some insurance companies have recently begun to sell policies covering nursing homes and other long-term chronic care, few of today's senior citizens own these policies—and the policies are expensive, so they can't be a universal solution.

Medicaid

Medicaid is a program run by the federal government and the individual states. However, it's a Welfare program: to qualify, you must either be receiving public assistance, or have spent just about all your income and assets on medical care. Some people are deterred from applying for Medicaid because they're ashamed: After a lifetime of work, they feel embarrassed to collect benefits designed for the penniless. Others would be happy to make the system work for them—but they can't fit into the income and asset limitations.

A person who qualifies for Medicaid gets a Medicaid card, which can be used like a credit card to pay health care costs. Medicaid recipients are expected to spend just about *all* their income over the Medicaid limit (except for a few dollars a month for personal needs) on medical care. You are not allowed to save money, or use your income to pay the normal living expenses of your family. This is a very harsh result for people who must sacrifice the results of a lifetime of work, saving, and good judgment just because they get sick.

However, there are ways to use the system for your own benefit. Policy loans taken against the cash value of life insurance are not considered income, neither are amounts from a "reverse annuity mortgage" (a type of home equity loan under which the bank makes regular payments to a senior citizen homeowner, relying on getting the borrowed amount back when the house is sold after the homeowner's death).

Medicaid and Assets

No matter how low your income is, your Medicaid application may be denied if your assets exceed the qualification level set by the state in which you live. However, some assets are "exempt," and don't count in determining Medicaid eligibility.

The family home is the most important asset in this category. You should think long and hard about selling a house and moving into an apartment after retirement because you will lose an exempt asset; the money you get from the home sale will be counted against you if you must apply for Medicaid. If your house is too large, or unsuitable for a person with limited mobility, it might be a better idea to sell the house and buy a co-op or condo unit that *is* suitable.

Furniture is an exempt asset, so is an automobile. Stocks, bonds, and income-producing real estate are definitely *not* exempt assets. Neither is life insurance, but the value of a life insurance policy for Medicaid purposes depends on its cash value. So term insurance can be a good choice if you're concerned about Medicaid eligibility; so are policy loans against cash-value policies.

Property Transfers and Medicaid

Sometimes transferring assets can be a good tax- or estate-planning strategy. However, if you transfer property (unless you sell it for its fair market value), then apply for Medicaid within two years of the transfer, you might be treated as if you still owned the property, and your application might be denied. To avoid this, you must be able to prove that the transfer had some good reason other than qualifying for Medicaid—such as paying debts, or helping out other family members in financial trouble.

The Other Spouse

It often happens that one person in a married couple needs nursing home care; the other doesn't. If the sick spouse applies for Medicaid, the other spouse's income may be treated as if it belonged to the sick spouse. This means that the sick spouse won't qualify for Medicaid until all the family income has been spent on medical care. That leaves the "community spouse" (the one who is not in the nursing home) desperately short of money. Fortunately, the "deeming"—treating income as if it belonged to the sick spouse—usually stops a few months after he or she enters a nursing home.

Couples face another Medicaid problem. Medicaid authorities have the right to sue the community spouse to make him or her pay for the other spouse's medical care; spouses have a duty to support each other "in sickness and in health." But this cuts both ways: the community spouse can also sue the sick spouse for nonsupport, so at least some of the family income can go to the community spouse. Judges tend to be sympathetic to the latter argument.

How to Protect Yourself and Your Family

If you're a senior citizen yourself, or a "junior citizen" worried about aging parents, here are some strategic tips.

• Not everyone will need chronic care—but everyone should be prepared for the possibility.

• Talk to a lawyer or accountant who really understands Medicaid as soon as possible. Discuss whether transferring assets, setting up a trust, selling assets and leasing them back, or other financial planning strategies would be wise.

• If you want to help aging parents, tailor your assistance to Medicaid requirements. For instance, if you give them cash, the cash could make them ineligible for Medicaid—but if you pay their medical bills, the payment won't affect their eligibility.

• Explore the availability and use of reverse-annuity mortgages and policy loans (sources of funds that don't count for Medicaid purposes).

Let's hope that soon this section will become only a historical curiosity—that people will be able to look at retirement as a time of leisure, not a terrifying period where illness or disability could impoverish a whole family.

65. Estate Planning

Estate planning, a specialized part of financial planning, has two aspects. The first (especially important for the young family) centers on the need to make sure that lost earnings will be replaced, and homemaking chores carried out, if a spouse or parent dies. The investments and insurance that are part of the overall financial plan provide assets and income for the surviving family; Social Security and private payments (such as death benefits from employers) also provide income.

The second aspect of estate planning centers on the person or family with more financial security (and, perhaps, fewer financial needs). If both spouses have substantial assets, and the children have grown up and reached financial independence, then each spouse would be able to survive financially after the other's death. The priority here is not keeping the wolf from the door—it's making sure that the fruits of a lifetime of hard work and intelligent planning will be transmitted with as little fuss (and as little taxation) as possible.

As just explained, life insurance works in both situations. So do wills (everybody should have one), intelligent use of joint property (for married couples), and durable powers of attorney (explained on page 276). Estate planning is a complex, but not incomprehensible, process. It involves many people: family members, lawyers, accountants, insurance professionals, and financial planners. This discussion focuses on the basic elements of estate planning that everybody needs.

The assumption is that you will not have to worry about estate tax, either because your estate is too small (an estate of $600,000 or less is not subject to federal estate tax) or because you have used techniques such as insurance planning and bequests to your spouse to eliminate estate tax. If your estate is very large, or if you have special planning needs, consult expert estate planners; don't just rely on the simple techniques explained here.

This final section is an appropriate place to sum up the techniques explored throughout this book. Estate planning uses and amplifies the techniques of financial planning as a whole. To make an estate plan, you must:

- Understand what you own
- Keep current and complete records in a form that can be understood by an outsider after your death
- Review your property, and see if any of it should be sold or exchanged in light of your current financial goals; decide if assets that are now owned separately by one spouse should be transferred to the other, or transferred to joint ownership (or vice versa)
- Communicate honestly with your spouse and family members about needs and plans
- Work with skilled professionals
- Review your plan as conditions change (if your brother dies before you do, decide who should get the money and property you planned to leave to him in your will; your estate plan for a daughter will be different when she's a doctor than when she was a toddler) and as you add new resources (Congratulations! You now own a beautiful second home!) and develop new goals (you used to devote two hours a day to financial planning; now you'd rather play golf—or vice versa)
- Set up your estate plan so that it can be administered easily and inexpensively

Your Will

The legal requirements for a will are minimal. It must be a written document; the testator (person making the will) must sign it, and there must be witnesses. The function of the witnesses is to testify about the circumstances under which the will was signed, in case it's challenged.

The will must dispose of the testator's property (but not property that can't pass by will—see this page) and must appoint an executor to administer the distribution of the estate.

Within these modest rules, millions of different wills can be written. The estate planning team's task is to find the will that is best for the testator's personal situation (including tax factors). So beware of a lawyer who'll prepare a will for a small fee—but restricts his or her efforts to filling in the blanks in a preprinted will form or computer software. You need (and deserve) an individualized plan that aims at creative solutions—not the same old will rewritten for every client who walks through the door.

In addition to the elements that are legally required (such as the signatures of the testator and the witnesses), a basic will includes:

- Identification of the testator.
- "Dispositive provisions" disposing of property. The testator can catalog and dispose of each item separately. The risk here is that the item (let's say, a pair of gold-and-ruby cuff links) won't be in the estate when the testator dies. The general rule is that the intended beneficiary is out of luck, and gets nothing—unless the testator provided for a substitute item.

   Or, the testator can leave people certain amounts of money or specified percentages of the estate ("and to my daughter Barbara, I leave the sum of $25,000" or "to my son Frederick, I leave 25% of my estate, as measured after my just debts have been paid"). The risk here is that the estate will be too small to pay all the cash bequests. Most states have rules for parcelling out the available funds.
- A "residuary clause" disposing of everything that forms part of the probate estate (property that can be transmitted by will) and that is not otherwise disposed of in the will.
- Provisions dealing with things that *might* happen. A beneficiary might die before the testator does, or at the same time as the testator, so someone must be named as an alternate beneficiary.

   A guardian must be named in case the testator dies while his or her children are still minors and the other spouse has already died, or dies later without appointing a guardian.

   If there will be (or might be) federal or state estate taxes, provisions should be made for their payment—do all the heirs pay part, or do some of them get their bequests free of tax?
- "Rules of the road" for executors—their duties and powers. State laws provide a basic list of powers for executors, so it isn't necessary to spell them out. But it may be a good idea to give an executor additional powers that are not available without special authorization.

Who Gets What?

Even if you die without a will, the law of your state creates an estate plan. It's called "intestate succession": inheritance without a will. Each state has a set of rules for apportioning the property of people who die without valid wills. For instance, your state's rules might provide that if you die leaving a spouse but no children, your spouse inherits your entire estate; if you leave a spouse and children, the spouse gets one-third of the estate and the children share the rest; if you leave no spouse and no children, your surviving parent or parents divide your estate; if no parents, your brothers and sisters inherit, and so forth.

Should you bother to have a will, if the state's intestate scheme fits your needs? Yes, because most people want to make at least a few small personal or charitable bequests ("$500 and my gold watch to my nephew Evan; my set of the *Encyclopaedia Britannica* to the town library"). And yes, because without a will, disappointed would-be heirs could slow down the process of settling your estate by demanding a search for the "lost" will they're sure must be around somewhere (and must be very generous to them).

Joint property is sometimes nicknamed "the poor man's will." This is because when property is held jointly by two or more people, the surviving joint tenant(s) automatically inherit the share of the first joint tenant to die. The first one to die *can't* dispose of the property in his or her will.

However, joint property has its disadvantages. Banks sometimes "freeze" joint accounts after the death of an account holder, until they get evidence that the estate's executor or administrator has received an official appointment from the probate court. (If there's a will, the estate has an executor; if it doesn't, it has an administrator.) Banks do this because the deceased's debts must be paid out of the estate's assets—and this process could be frustrated or made impossible if the other joint account holder could clean out the account.

Therefore, if you're married and keep most of your money in a joint account, make sure each spouse has a separate account that can take care of the immediate cash needs until insurance proceeds can be paid, and the estate settled. Don't forget that both spouses need a separate account—there's no way to tell which will die first. A common estate planning mistake is to set up an elaborate plan that assumes that the husband will die first, which is not always the case.

The simplest possible will just names an executor and leaves your entire estate to one person. (You can even make your sole heir your executor; or you can name your spouse as your executor, even if you have a more complex will.) But the simplest way isn't always the best way.

If you leave your entire estate to your spouse, you won't have to worry about federal estate tax. There's an "unlimited marital deduction." That is, no estate tax is charged on any amount left to a surviving spouse. To qualify for the estate tax deduction, the money and property can be left to the spouse outright, put in a trust, or be a "life estate" (right to use the property during his or her lifetime, when it passes to whomever is named in the testator's will) or other "Q-TIP" (qualified terminable interest property) as allowed by tax law.

You'd think, then, that the best tactic would be to accumulate millions of dollars, leave the whole thing to your surviving spouse, and die happy, knowing that the IRS won't get a nickel. But, given the high divorce rate, many people die without a spouse to leave property—or make a will when they're married to one person, and die married to someone else.

The laws of most states provide that a divorce revokes any provision of a will that refers to the testator's ex-husband or ex-wife. That part of the property passes as if the ex-spouse had died before the testator. If you're in the process of divorce, you should know that most states also provide that separation does not revoke any part of a will. So if you die leaving a will that provides for an estranged or separated spouse, the spouse does inherit. The lesson? If you decide to separate, get a new estate plan and a new will immediately—and do the same if you re-marry after a divorce.

There's also an estate planning problem if the testator is survived by a husband or wife who does not remarry. The second spouse to die could have a very large, taxable estate, and the IRS would then collect more tax than it would have gotten if the family's assets had been divided into two estates of approximately equal sizes. (Why? The estate tax is a "progressive" tax—that is, rates get higher as the estate gets bigger. The estate tax on a $2 million estate is more than twice the tax on two $1 million estates.)

For example, if you think your estate will be large enough to be subject to federal estate tax, you can use *irrevocable trusts* (trusts whose terms can't be changed once they go into operation) to make gifts to your family. If you follow the rules, under the Internal Revenue Code, the money put into the trust will not count as part of your estate. If you contribute enough to the trust, you can escape estate tax entirely by reducing your taxable estate. It may also be possible to do this without paying gift tax, and even to save income taxes.

Remember, though, if your estate is less than $600,000, there's no federal estate tax. Below this level, you must worry about practical problems: your family's needs and ease of administration—not federal estate taxes.

Sample Estate Plans

Listed here are basic estate plans; they may not suit your needs. Get personal advice, and, of course, update your plan regularly.

• For a single person: Divide your estate among family members, friends, and charities. (Charitable bequests, like bequests to a surviving spouse, are not subject to federal estate tax.) If you're affluent enough to face estate tax, consider a "giving program" during your lifetime—systematically give away enough assets to reduce your estate below the taxable level.

• For a married person with young children: Leave most or all of your estate to your surviving spouse. Make sure your will mentions your children, and indicates that you are leaving them little or nothing because your spouse will take care of their needs. (This prevents the children from challenging the will, claiming that you forgot them, and demanding a larger share of your estate.) Make sure you designate a guardian for the children.

This plan doesn't suit all families. Maybe your spouse has significant separate assets, and doesn't need your estate. Maybe he or she is a second spouse, and you're more concerned with your children. In that case, you might establish trusts for your children, and leave most of the estate to them. But be careful: State law usually gives a surviving spouse a *right of election*—(the right to challenge a will and receive a stated percentage of the estate if the will made a smaller provision for him or her).

To avoid this, you and your spouse can sign an antenuptial (premarital) contract giving up your right to a share in the other's estate. You can sign contracts agreeing not to exercise the right of election—or you can simply refrain from exercising the right.

• For a married person with older children: Your primary emphasis will probably be on providing for your spouse, but you might want to make bequests to your children, either outright or in the form of trusts. It depends on their ages and financial needs. In addition to trusts (see this page), the Uniform Gifts to Minors Act (UGMA) and "powers in trust" can be used to leave money and property to minors. UGMA gifts and powers in trust are popular because they're easy to use and don't involve high legal fees to create or administer.

The UGMA allows you to name an adult as custodian for a minor. Then, lifetime or testamentary gifts for the minor can be made to the custodian, who will hold the money or property and turn it over to the child at age 18 or 21. A power in trust is a simpler way of handling small dispositions; for instance, you could leave your valuable stamp collection to your brother or sister, to be held for a niece or nephew, until the young beneficiary grows up.

You might want to "balance" bequests to your children, based on amounts you've already given them. If you paid one child's college and graduate-school tuition, while the other went into the military and then started a business, you might consider leaving more to the second child because the first has already gotten a larger share of family assets. Or, you might leave more to a child with chronic money troubles than to one who is extremely prosperous.

• For a divorced parent: If you're the custodial parent, you'll need to leave enough assets to take care of your children; and you must designate a guardian.

If you're the noncustodial parent, check your separation agreement or divorce decree. You may have agreed to maintain insurance for your children's benefit, or to make provisions for them in your will. Even if you haven't, be sure to balance the needs of your children against those of a second family (if you've remarried), blood relatives, and friends.

Trusts

A trust is a legal arrangement under which a person (called the grantor, settlor, or trustor) transfers property to a responsible person or organization called the trustee. This can be done either while the grantor is still alive, or as part of his or her will.

The trustee manages the property, invests it, and takes care of it during the trust term chosen by the grantor. The trustee follows the instructions in the trust instrument, and either distributes the income the trust earns each year, or every three months, to the "income beneficiaries" named in the trust instrument, or saves it up. The trustee also follows instructions about turning over the remaining property when the trust ends.

Trusts can also be classified as "revocable" or "irrevocable." If the trust is revocable, the person who sets it up reserves the right to change the trust's terms, or even take the trust assets back. These trusts can provide a great deal of convenience and flexibility, and can provide an alternative to probate (because the trust assets are distributed according to the terms of the trust, with no need to wait for the probate process to be completed, and without entering the public records). However, they don't remove assets from the estate of the person who sets up the trust.

If reducing your taxable estate is one of your financial planning objectives, consider an irrevocable trust. Properly drafted, this trust removes assets from your taxable estate. The trade-off is that you may have to pay gift and income taxes—and you definitely can't change your mind about the way the trust should be run, or who should get trust income and principal.

Trusts can serve a lot of different purposes. They can provide professional management for the trust property. If the grantor wants to help a minor, or a person who is or could be disabled by age, then the trustee can manage the incapacitated person's property and provide income when necessary. Trusts also have some tax advantages—but far fewer than before the Tax Code of 1986.

If any of these objectives seem worthwhile to you, ask your estate planning team about the role trusts should play in your estate plan.

Personal Property

A lot of the problems in estate planning come from the various items of personal property, of varying degrees of financial and sentimental value, that a person accumulates over a lifetime. The simplest way is just to leave the whole mess to the surviving spouse. This could create lingering ill feelings in the family if everyone expects to inherit the family heirlooms (Aunt Martha's silver candlesticks or your souvenir plate collection).

You can make sure that choice items are disposed of in your will. (Survivors will feel more kindly toward your memory if you provide substitute items for those that are no longer in your estate at the time of your death.) Or, you can shift the problem to your executor, and tell the executor to divide your personal property into four equal shares, and give one each to Michael, Edna, Lucille, and Stephen. Or, you can tell the executor to let Sandra, Jack, and Patricia take turns selecting items of personal property from your estate. Or, you could throw in the towel and tell your executor to sell the personal property and split the proceeds equally between Tom and Robert.

Administering an Estate

This brings us to the question of how your executors will administer your estate—or what you'll have to do if you serve as the executor of someone else's estate.

The executor is basically a traffic cop. His or her job (or its job, if the executor is a bank, trust company, or law firm) is to figure out what the estate consists of, discover and pay the deceased's debts, collect the proceeds of the deceased's life insurance, find the will and get it probated (declared a valid will by the appropriate court), and carry out the provisions of the will.

Whether the executor's job is difficult is determined by emotional factors (a bank can be more nonchalant about probating an estate than the testator's widow or widower—but the surviving spouse will care much more about it and won't charge the estate a fee) and on the condition of the testator's financial records. A really conscientious testator will ask before naming someone as executor (it's a lot of work), and will name a "successor executor" in the will in case the first executor named can't or won't take on the job, or can't finish it.

To be a really well-organized testator, keep these records up to date, and keep them in a safe, fireproof place where the executor can find them.

- The original of your will.
- Insurance policies; the addresses and phone numbers of insurance agents so that the executor can collect the proceeds.
- The name and address of your stockbroker; portfolio records that indicate if the securities are your sole property or are jointly owned.
- Mutual fund records.
- Bankbooks, checkbooks, and other records of banking activities.
- The deed to your house, showing whether you are the sole owner or whether it's joint property; the mortgage.
- Title and registration for your car.
- Keys to your safe-deposit box. State law usually prevents safe-deposit boxes from being opened until the executor has an official certificate of appointment from the probate court. It may also be required that someone from the state tax authorities be present when the box is opened—safe-deposit boxes are a popular resting place for undeclared (and untaxed) cash.
- A family tree, with the most up-to-date address you have for each

family member (or a date of death). This is important because your will can't be probated until all "distributees" (people who would receive anything under your state's "intestate distribution" scheme) have been notified and given a chance to challenge the will. If Cousin Clara can be located easily, it won't be necessary to take time (and spend money from the estate) to find her.

• Loan agreements, family budgets, credit card bills, and other records that indicate former debts that have been paid in full, and current accounts that may have to be paid from the estate.

• Summary Plan Descriptions, benefit statements, elections, and other documents showing your estate's right to receive a death benefit from your employer, a preretirement survivor annuity, or pension payments continuing after your death. (More about pensions on page 25, and the taxation of pensions on page 270.)

• Documents showing any money owed to you: records of loans you made, business accounts receivable, payments from a small business, and so on.

The executor has a lot of things to worry about (keeping the property secure until it can be distributed, getting the will probated, assessing claims for validity and paying the valid ones)—it's a substantial responsibility.

Summing Up

It's a lot more fun to think about what would happen if you were rich than about what will happen after you die. One of them is certain—the other is unlikely. But you can take good care of the money you do have, and watch it increase as you save and invest. And you can take good care of your family, and make sure their needs will be met after your death, by leaving a well-drafted will, adequate assets, and the right kind and amount of insurance.

AFTERWORD

We've come a long way together. We've covered everything from seeing a family member into this world to seeing one out. In between, we've considered ways to spend money sensibly, plan for the large expenses you can count on (home buying, college tuition) and those you may be faced with (the cost of a long illness).

But it's not all gloom and doom. We've also looked at ways to get more money, and enjoy the income and assets you build. A career is a way to collect a paycheck, a way to keep the electricity switched on and the rent paid—but it's also a way to learn and develop. We've learned about the ways in which a career enhances your own and your family's financial well-being in many ways: through employee benefits and as a source of retirement income.

We've done this together, because every book is a voyage of discovery for its author. For a book like this, the goal of the journey is to learn what its readers have to know, and then explain it to them in a way that's really useful to them. The readers carry on the journey, by using the book as a resource—a kind of map, or guidebook.

Without a map, financial planning can be a howling, hostile wilderness. With a map, you can see the territory for what it is: a pleasant place, with friendly natives (such as financial planners and knowledgeable brokers) and a few hostile ones (such as the con artists who prey on people who have some money and whose greed outpaces their common sense). You can enter this territory for a brief vacation (by undertaking your minimum planning responsibilities, and setting up a simple will and getting the bare minimum of insurance you need to meet your own and your family's needs). Or, you can "emigrate": learn more about the fascinating processes of budgeting and investing, and work actively to make your assets more productive.

To learn about a country, you must understand its history, its geography, its economic system, and what kind of people live there. To understand financial planning, you need to know about economics, sociology, history, mathematics, and law. It's a tall order . . . but not more than you can handle.

Now that you've read this book, are you all set to get rich quick? Hell, no. Have you learned The Four Rules That Are Guaranteed to Make You a Millionaire? No, because there aren't any rules like that. Can you now fire your accountant, your lawyer, your broker, and your auto mechanic because now you know everything they ever knew or ever will know? Well, by now you know what I'm driving at. There's always more to learn and more to do when it comes to financial planning. Economic conditions change, your attitude changes, your needs change, the legal rules change. But with basic knowledge (courtesy of this book, a close reading of pension and benefit materials, tax forms, insurance policies, and other documents), with the willingness to do a little work (and even make a few mistakes), you'll never be helpless. You'll always be able to understand where your money comes from; where it goes (and how to increase one and cut back on the other); and what your plans are for the future—plus your fall-back plans.

Please extinguish all smoking materials and put your seat in the full upright position. Enjoy your stay in the Personal Financial Planning Area. It was a pleasant journey—see you around.

INDEX